A DECADE OF
NEW COMEDY

A DECADE OF
NEW COMEDY

Plays from the Humana Festival
Volume Two

Edited by
Michael Bigelow Dixon
and
Michele Volansky

Foreword by Jon Jory
Introduction by Wendy Wasserstein

HEINEMANN
Portsmouth, NH

HEINEMANN
A division of Reed Elsevier Inc.
361 Hanover Street
Portsmouth, NH 03801-3912
Offices and agents throughout the world

Library of Congress Cataloging-in-Publication Data on file at Library of Congress

Editor: Lisa A. Barnett
Production: J. B. Tranchemontagne
Manufacturing: Elizabeth Valway

Printed in the United States of America on acid-free paper
99 98 97 96   DA   1 2 3 4 5 6

Contents

Foreword

Why, pray tell, is comedy a pariah in the American theatre? I speak as someone who reads hundreds of new plays a year, runs a large, well-funded new play festival and is eternally looking for something with a few laughs and a little weight. Audiences long to laugh, actors like to get them and directors love to inspire them, and yet most of America's resident theatres with an eight-play season do one or maybe two a year.

Well, it could be we don't write them because we've lost our collective sense of humor, or we overslept, or we think television needs all the jokes or . . . hmmm . . . it just doesn't get any respect because in this particular culture it doesn't buy any intellectual cachet. Smart people, the unwritten law must go, don't deign to do yuks.

People who write comedy must smoke cigarettes, drink straight bourbon and are kept in back rooms like caged orangutans waiting for the call of disreputable middle-aged stand-up comedians who do feminazi jokes.

Maybe.

Anyway, thank God, there is a small cadre of the unreconstructed who are keeping this ancient trade alive in the serious (the *very* serious) theatre. And here are a bunch of them who did it superbly, and we'll sell it to you under the table in a plain brown paper wrapper!

These are plays bringing tears to your eyes (of laughter) by examining divorce, corporate entombment, white guilt, black pretension, the violence industry, crass materialism, Fidel Castro, death and other hilarious subjects for your delectation. This is great stuff for the serious laugher, and it's wildly contemporary in its skewed visions, social roles and direct-from-the-headlines concerns.

In the main these playwrights are from the "ouch, that hurts" school of funny with advanced degrees in gallows humor. In a theatre where comedy is dying, I suppose that more than figures.

So welcome to the arena, keep your back to the wall, your hand on your newly legal concealed weapon, and all your senses desperately alert. Comic playwrights are back, they're mean and it's entirely possible they are laughing at you.

—Jon Jory
Producing Director
Actors Theatre of Louisville

Acknowledgments

The editors wish to thank the following for their assistance in compiling this volume:
Lisa Barnett
William Craver
Liz Engelman
Peter Franklin
Robert Freedman
Linda Green
Mary Harden
Marilee Hebert-Slater
David Kuntz
Jeff Rodgers
John Santoianni
Jimmy Seacat
Val Smith
Wanda Snyder
Alexander Speer
David Styne
Jack Tantleff
Joanne Tranchemontagne
Corby Tushla
Jeffrey Ullom

Introduction

I've always wanted to sign up for a comedy class. One of those "If you can draw this rubber chicken or make one hundred self-deprecating one-liners in just three minutes, you can become an accredited comedy writer!" I've always wanted to learn the secrets of the real pros, like always getting a laugh with words that begin with the letter "k" (kitchen, kangaroo, and ketchup are apparently hilarious) and, of course, the golden rule that laugh lines come in triplets. Once I learned every trick in the book, I'd hire a wicked witch with a knockout sleeping potion and snooze for at least a year in a forest so I'd forget every word of it.

Great comedy, a "C" word not a "K" word, comes from character, another "C" word, and the enviable ability of great writers to puncture pretention and pain. Great comedy is unsentimental yet its spirit, even at its bleakest, is overwhelmingly hopeful. Great comedy questions a society's truths, basic identity, and social norms. The writer neither goes exclusively for laughs nor the jugular. There is no formula for great comedy except the keenly observant eye and voice of the playwright. As far as I'm concerned, nothing deserves more respect in theatre writing than comedy, and this outstanding collection of plays from Actors Theatre of Louisville absolutely confirms my opinion.

The characters in these plays range from Marsha Norman's sophisticated and wry novelist, Trudy Blue, to Jane Martin's Tiger, a woman wrestler having a problem with her broken ribs. The settings vary from a mental institution in Forrest Hills, Queens, to Cuba in the 1960s. The writing styles are sharp and farcical, as in Arthur Kopit's *Road to Nirvana,* and absurdist, in Regina Taylor's hilarious *Watermelon Rinds.* But they all share a common search for identity, an edge that refuses to accept conventional givens. These writers break all the comedic rules and therefore push the boundaries of their worlds to create a much sharper universe.

Each of these authors are serious playwrights and these are very serious plays. They explode myths of race, gender, class, history, and even Hollywood. These plays are smart, tough, sad, and yet each achieves that remarkable and unexplainable feat of making a room full of strangers laugh out loud. That laughter, which is so often taken for granted, is one of the greatest joys of working in the theatre. Just ask any playwright standing in the back of a theatre who's heard an audience laughing.

I once overheard a theatregoer on the Long Island Railroad explain a recent experience at a matinee as, "I laughed, I cried, I loved it." While reading this collection, I laughed, I cried, and I wished I could see all of them. I would study comedy with every one of these very serious playwrights.

—Wendy Wasserstein
New York, 1995

Richard Strand

The Death of Zukasky

The Death of Zukasky was directed in 1991 by Nagle Jackson with the following cast:

THEODORE ZUKASKY .... Tom Lenoci*
BARRY MILLS .... Rod McLachlan
ANNE DESMOND .... Monica Merryman
A. C. TATTUMS........................ William McNulty
HENRY MARLINO .... Ray Fry

Stage Manager............................. Carey Upton
Assistant Stage Manager.................... Jay McManigal
Costume Design .... Michael Krass
Scene Design .... Paul Owen
Lighting Design............................ Karl Haas
Sound Design .... Darron West
Property Master.............................. Ron Riall
Casting—NYC .... Jay Binder
Dramaturg .... Michael Bigelow Dixon

---

*Member of the ATL Apprentice/Intern Company

CHARACTERS

Theodore Zukasky: A deceased executive.
Barry Mills: A corporate salesman.
A. C. Tattums: Another corporate salesman.
Anne Desmond: Yet another corporate salesman.
Henry Marlino: Their superior.

PLACE:

On the 22nd floor of a Chicago corporate headquarters.

The Death of Zukasky

SCENE 1

The office of Theodore Zukasky, Director of Sales for Hellas, Inc. The office is on the twenty-second floor of a glass tower in the Chicago loop. Zukasky's desk is large and expensive. There are large windows on the back wall overlooking the south side. Three chairs have been arranged in front of the desk for a meeting to be held at 8 A.M. this morning. It is nearly that now.

There is no light in the office yet, except for the light coming in the window. Gradually the light grows brighter as the sun rises stage left. As the room grows brighter we can see that Zukasky is sitting in a high-backed chair, feet up on his desk, apparently asleep, but actually he is dead. He died last night of unknown cause, shortly before quitting time. His body has not yet been discovered.

As the day grows brighter, we can hear some city noises from the street below. Also, outside the window in Zukasky's door, we can see that the hallway lights have been turned on. Indistinguishable voices can be heard and occasionally a shadow passes by. Outside the window overlooking the south side, our view of the sky is temporarily blocked as a window washer raises her scaffold and floats past the office on her way to forty-four.

The first discernable voice we hear is Barry Mills'. He is, in the vernacular of this corporation, a Level Four employee. He aspires to be Level Five. Zukasky was Level Five. He aspired to be Level Six. Then he died.

Barry is standing so that we can see his silhouette in Zukasky's door.

BARRY: Did anybody make coffee? *(No one answers.)* Anybody make coffee yet? *(No one answers.)* We gotta have coffee for the meeting. *(No one answers.)* So, does anybody know? Is there coffee? *(Barry is finally answered by Anne Desmond. Anne is also Level Four, aspiring to Five. She is annoyed with Barry for asking a question he knows the answer to.)*

ANNE: *(Off.)* Are you standing next to the coffee machine?

BARRY: Yes.

ANNE: *(Off.)* And is there any coffee made?

BARRY: No.

ANNE: *(Off.)* Well, there's your answer, isn't it? *(We can hear Anne slam the door of her office.)*

BARRY: So what's the deal? Is somebody going to make coffee? *(No one answers.)* We're going to need coffee for the meeting. *(No one answers.)* Shouldn't somebody be making coffee? *(Anne can be heard opening her door and stomping toward Barry. We see both now, silhouetted in the pane.)*

ANNE: Barry, what is the damn problem?

BARRY: We're out of coffee.

ANNE: We are not out of coffee. *(She picks up a packet and holds it in front of Barry's face.)* This is coffee. *(She picks up another packet.)* This is coffee too. We've got lots of coffee. Lots. It's almost like Little Colombia here.

BARRY: There's none made.

ANNE: No, that's true. Do you know what you could do if you really felt it was important to have coffee?

BARRY: I just thought . . . you know . . . before the meeting . . . somebody ought to . . .

ANNE: Don't make me point out the obvious. You want coffee; see if you can figure out how to get some.

BARRY: *(After a pause.)* So, anybody know how to make coffee? *(No one answers.)* Who knows how to work the coffee machine? *(No one answers.)* Hey A. C., you know how to make coffee?

A. C.: *(Also Level Four.)* Yes.

BARRY: Great. We need coffee for the meeting this morning. *(Barry's silhouette disappears. A. C.'s silhouette replaces Barry's.)*

A. C.: Well, I'm not making it. *(Anne enters Zukasky's office. She is thirty-five or so, wearing a print dress with penguins on it. She is carrying four identically bound folders each of which has the Hellas, Inc. logo on the cover. She also has a cup of coffee from Seven-Eleven. She turns on the light and notices Zukasky for the first time.)*

ANNE: Excuse me. *(Anne takes the Seven-Eleven coffee, pours it into a ceramic mug and then throws the cardboard cup away. She then sets the folders down, one by each chair and one by Zukasky. Barry comes into the office behind her.)*

BARRY: Is the coffee made yet?

ANNE: Shh! *(She points at Zukasky.)*

BARRY: *(Sotto voce.)* Is he asleep? *(Anne does not answer what she considers an obvious question.)* Shouldn't somebody wake him up? *(No answer.)* Are you going to wake him up? *(No answer.)* Somebody ought to wake him up!

ANNE: Wake him up! Wake him up! You wanna wake him up? Wake him up!

BARRY: I don't know how. *(Barry exits. We can hear him shouting in the hall.)* Anybody know how to wake up Zukasky? *(A. C. enters, Barry on his tail. A. C. has a cup of coffee from Seven-Eleven also.)* Do you know how to wake up Zukasky? *(A. C., ignoring both Barry and Zukasky, sits in one of the chairs and begins leafing through one of the folders.)* I mean, don't you think we ought to wake him up? *(A. C. takes a long moment to look up and stare at Barry. Then he returns to his folder.)*

ANNE: Hey, Barry, do that thing you do: Shut up.

BARRY: But we got a meeting and look at this guy: he's asleep.

ANNE: If it's important, he'll wake up. *(Anne seats herself next to A. C. and begins looking through her folder.)*

BARRY: But, Anne, somebody's got to take the initiative and. . . . You know what's going to happen? He's going to wake up halfway through the meeting and *then* somebody's going to get yelled at. If we just wake him up now, carefully, so he doesn't even know that we know he was asleep.

ANNE: Barry, don't start again. I am not about to . . . Barry, hey! Hey! Hey!! *Hey!!* HEY!!! Barry, God damn it, if you want to wake him up . . . WAKE HIM UP!

A. C.: Barry, be cool. *(Barry and A. C. stare at each other. Then Barry paces around the office, looking for a discreet way of waking Zukasky. With a pretentious display of casualness, he paces over to Zukasky and knocks on the desk near Zukasky's ear. Then, like a little boy ringing a doorbell and running away, Barry takes three large steps away from Zukasky. Zukasky, of course, does not move. Barry leaves the office and, a short time later, the phone next to Zukasky's head rings. Barry appears in the doorway, a phone receiver in his hand, checking to see if the ringing has waked Zukasky. It hasn't. A. C. and Anne have started to become aware that this could be a deeper sleep than they had first considered. Barry enters with a string of firecrackers. He places them in the ashtray on Zukasky's desk. A. C. and Anne make no effort to stop him. They have arisen from their chairs and are slowly moving behind Zukasky's desk to see if their suspicion is correct. Barry lights the firecrackers and runs out of the office. They go off; Zukasky does not move. Barry pokes his head in the door and begins to suspect the same thing A. C. and Anne suspect. To Anne.)* Do you have a mirror? *(Anne hands him her compact. Barry moves in closer to see what's going on. A. C. holds the mirror under Zukasky's nose. As soon as it becomes apparent that Zukasky is dead, Anne backs away suddenly, accidently pulling Zukasky's chair away from the desk which causes Zukasky to slide forward, out of the chair, onto the floor under his desk, his feet now sticking out the front—he looks much like a garage mechanic working under a car.)*

BARRY: He's dead. He's dead. We've been sitting in the same room with a dead guy. This is bad. This is a bad thing. We're all getting fired. I'm going to catch the blame for this.

ANNE: Uh-oh. Uh-oh. Whoops. I knocked him over. Oh my. Oh my. We have to pick him up. We can't leave him on the floor. Oh my. Oh my. I'm going to have to touch him.

BARRY: *(Screaming.)* CALM DOWN! CALM DOWN! *(There is a pause. A. C. and Anne are staring at Barry.)* You know, we should stay calm.

ANNE: I think, relatively speaking, we are calm.

BARRY: Right. Okay. Now here's what we do. We need a plan. We have to get our stories straight. First of all, we need to make it look like an accident.

ANNE: You idiot, it was an accident.

BARRY: What?

ANNE: We didn't kill him. We just found his body.

BARRY: Right. That's right. That's in our favor.

ANNE: In our fa . . . ? *(To A. C.)* Can you keep him busy while I figure out what to do? *(Pause.)*

A. C.: *(His mind is elsewhere.)* Hmm.

ANNE: One thing for sure: We can't leave him on the floor. *(A moment passes while A. C. and Barry look expectantly at Anne.)* Okay. We'll leave him on the floor.

BARRY: Maybe we should reenact our movements from the moment we came into work this morning.

ANNE: Barry, stop thinking. I'll call the police. They gotta be called, right? I mean, I've never done this before. Do we call a coroner? Is that how it's done?

BARRY: *(Both Anne and A. C. are ignoring him.)* Oh yes. Absolutely. As soon as we settle on a story. *(Barry empties the ashtray of firecrackers.)* Right. Don't disturb any of the evidence. They're going to want to see the room just like we found it. These firecrackers weren't here, were they? *(Wiping up fingerprints with his handkerchief.)* I'll just tidy up a little. Zukasky wouldn't want the police to find a messy office.

A. C.: Beats me.

ANNE: Okay, we call the police. Then we let the police handle it. And, of course, someone needs to inform Mr. Marlino. I'll do that. I'll go upstairs and talk to Marlino while you call the police.

A. C.: Right. *(Anne starts to exit.)*

A. C.: You know, this really changes the whole corporate infrastructure. *(Anne and Barry are both regarding A. C. oddly.)* Sorry.

Just an observation. *(A. C. exits. Anne follows him. Barry, for the first time, notices the coffee mug Anne left behind.)*

BARRY: Hey. Where'd this coffee come from? Did somebody make coffee? *(Seeing he is alone now, Barry shouts down the hallway.)* So what's the story? Are we having a meeting or what?

SCENE 2

It is the next morning. Someone, A. C. in fact, is lying on the floor underneath the desk. We know this because his feet stick out the way Zukasky's did when Anne knocked him out of his chair.

Anne enters. There are giraffes on her dress today. She has brought a framed abstract picture—circles and triangles, mostly—which she hangs on the wall. She moves without making a sound. She turns to leave and, for the first time, notices the feet sticking out from under the desk. She screams.

ANNE: Aaaaaaaaa!

A. C.: Aaaaaaaaa!

ANNE: Aaaaaaaaa!

A. C.: *(Still from under the desk.)* You scared the hell out of me.

ANNE: Me? I did?

A. C.: *(He comes out from under the desk.)* Don't you knock before entering a man's office?

ANNE: This is not your office.

A. C.: Well, that's a good point. That's a darn good point. On the other hand, this isn't your office either. Although I notice you're doing a little decorating. Expecting a promotion?

ANNE: I am here for today's meeting, which is due to start in about fifteen minutes. What are you doing here?

A. C.: I knew you'd be here, setting up for today's meeting, which is due to start in about fifteen minutes, and I figured it was time you and I got to know each other better. You know, Annie, I've been here a year and three months, I see you every day and yet we never talk. Does that seem right to you? No, of course not. So tell me, Annie, how the hell are you? What are your career ambitions? Are you married? Do you have kids? Is there something in your past that makes it hard for you to answer questions? Do you have a lot of close friends? Do you think you could learn to like me? *(Pause.)* Would it make it easier for you if I asked these questions one at a time?

ANNE: I asked you first.

A. C.: Another good point! So you did. What was it you asked me?

ANNE: What are you doing here?

A. C.: It worries you, doesn't it? You're afraid I just might have a reason. *(Pause.)* But I don't. You thought maybe they gave me Zukasky's job, didn't you? But they didn't.

ANNE: That doesn't surprise me.

A. C.: No, I don't suppose it would. It surprised me a little. But there's no reason it should surprise you. You know what might surprise you? *(Whispering loudly.)* They didn't give it to you either.

ANNE: You don't know that.

A. C.: You're right. I'm just guessing.

ANNE: What are you doing here?

A. C.: Whoa! Wait a minute! You're not playing fair. I answered your question; answer mine. Doesn't matter which one, actually. Pick one you like.

ANNE: You have no business being here.

A. C.: Where? Here? Sure I do. I work here.

ANNE: You have no business being in Mr. Zukasky's office. Under Mr. Zukasky's desk.

A. C.: Look, yesterday this was Zukasky's desk. Tomorrow it'll be Barry Mills' desk. But today it is Switzerland. I don't figure this is Barry's desk until Barry gets his butt in here and sticks a picture of his old lady on it. On the desk, that is. Not on his butt.

ANNE: Why do you keep saying Barry? No one has announced a replacement yet.

A. C.: Trust me. It's going to be Barry.

ANNE: Oh, be serious. Barry Mills . . .

A. C.: . . . is an idiot with tofu for brains, and the thought that you and I might be working for him is pretty scary, isn't it? But that's what's going to happen. *(With mock solemnity.)* I felt you should know.

ANNE: Any one of the three of us—even you—

A. C.: I'm sorry. This was a crummy way for you to find out. You still thought you were in the running, didn't you? Sorry. I'm sorry you didn't get the job and I'm sorry it was me who had to tell you. But it's going to be Barry. Before quitting time today, you and I are going to be working for Barry Mills. Gives you the willies, doesn't it? *(Anne is not sure how to take this.)* Look, I'll let you get back to work . . . *(Starting to exit.)*

ANNE: What were you doing under the desk?

A. C.: *(He seats himself in Zukasky's old chair and puts his feet up on the desk.)* I planted a bomb. It's set to go off at eleven thirty. If I were you I'd take an early lunch.

ANNE: What were you doing under the desk?

A. C.: I was looking for the access number of an illegal foreign account. Sometimes people tape them to the bottom of their drawers.

ANNE: What were you doing under the desk?

A. C.: I gave it a lube job and changed all the spark plugs. The drawer was sticking and that makes 'em hard to handle on the turns. *(A. C. leans to one side and makes car noises.)*

ANNE: Get out of this office.

A. C.: Look, Annie, you gotta believe me: I am on your side. You thought you were up for a promotion. That's a damn bummer. I feel for you. Really. You had my vote, not that anyone gave me a vote.

ANNE: You're making this up. You don't know any more than I do who is going to replace Zukasky. I don't believe a decision has even been made yet.

A. C.: You got me there. You're right. I'm just talking out my boo-hole. Talk to me later; we'll see how lucky I guessed.

ANNE: I just talked to Marlino ten minutes ago. He said no decision had been reached. I have no reason to doubt him.

A. C.: Did he mention they were going to make you Barry's private secretary?

ANNE: *(That really is a scary thought.)* You're lying!

A. C.: Of course I'm lying. They can't make you a secretary. You're Level Four.

ANNE: Yeah. No kidding.

A. C.: So they won't use the word secretary. They'll give you some nonpejorative sounding double speak title. "Assisting Partner." Or, "Co-manager." Or, "Director of Sales, Jr." But it won't make any difference because you will still be a secretary.

ANNE: You're making this up. How could you know this?

A. C.: I couldn't. I'm just guessing. Come to me tomorrow and tell me what you're doing that a secretary doesn't do.

ANNE: I am a Level Four manager. Same as you. Same as Barry.

A. C.: It'd be easier to believe that if you didn't have giraffes on your dress.

ANNE: The way I dress . . .

A. C.: . . . is way over on the juvenile side. If you want to get promoted, you oughta wear pinstripes instead of endangered species. That's just friendly advice.

ANNE: Are you deliberately trying to make me mad?

A. C.: No! No! Exactly the opposite. I want you to like me. I want you to trust me. I want you to believe that I am on your side. I am trying to gain your confidence. That is why I am saying all these things that I wouldn't otherwise say. I am talking to you as a friend.

ANNE: I just think you're an asshole.

A. C.: Well, building a friendship takes time.

ANNE: Billions of years, sometimes.

A. C.: I'm serious about this now. You and I need to be friends. You and I need to have a private, serious, mano-a-womano talk. We need to have the single most important discussion of your career. And we need to do it soon.

ANNE: Go away.

A. C.: Yes ma'am. Maybe another time. (*A. C. starts to leave.*)

ANNE: Wait a minute! Stop!

A. C.: Now, for example. Now is good for me.

ANNE: How did you get in here?

A. C.: Oh, uh, I just walked in.

ANNE: The door was locked. I just unlocked it. Do you have a key?

A. C.: I was here yesterday afternoon talking to the cops. It got late so I spent the night.

ANNE: Because no one other than Mr. Marlino and myself . . .

A. C.: *(Emptying his pockets.)* Some change, keys to my apartment and my car, a pack of matches . . .

ANNE: . . . Mr. Marlino and myself—we are the only two . . .

A. C.: You know, that's funny about the matches because I don't smoke.

ANNE: We are the only two allowed to have a key to this room. That's policy.

A. C.: And a damn fine policy it is. Let out too many keys and there's no telling who will spend the night in your office. Maybe some dead guy.

ANNE: How did you get in here?

A. C.: The truth is—and this *is* the truth—I came in the window.

ANNE: A twenty-second floor window?

A. C.: I just rappelled down from twenty-three. It's not that hard.

ANNE: I demand to know how you got in here.

A. C.: Oh my. You demand to know. Aren't you pompous? Even for a Level Four manager, but especially for a soon-to-be-personal-assistant-slash-co-operations-manager. But Annie, I already told you: I came in through the window.

ANNE: You also told me you spent the night.

A. C.: Well, you're right. I did say that. And that was a lie. I'm sorry. How can I expect you to trust me when I lie to you? I could kick myself around the block for that. The truth is— and this is really the truth now—I came in through the window. *(He crosses his heart and gives a boy scout pledge.)* Anything else you want to know?

ANNE: No, Mr. Tattums. I think I will let Mr. Marlino decide how to handle this. Good-bye.

A. C.: That's a bad plan, Ms. Desmond. I know you don't believe me because I lied to you and, God knows, I deserve only your contempt, but being up front with Mr. Marlino is, believe me, the world's worst idea. I want you to trust me and I know that the only way that can happen is to start right now by telling you the truth and so I'm telling you the truth: no way is it a good idea to tell Mr. Marlino that you found me in this office.

ANNE: Thank you for that advice. Good-bye.

A. C.: One more tidbit. This is just to build my credibility. If I keep telling you the truth, eventually you will believe me, right? *(Anne does not respond.)* Well, why don't I just continue under that premise, anyway. This is the truth: The only way you are going to move up in this company is by getting rid of Barry Mills. Because—and this is the Great Overriding Truth—as long as you work for Barry Mills, you will be a secretary. That is an immutable law: "I work for Barry Mills ergo I am a secretary." *(Anne does not respond. She is staring dumbly at A. C.)* Psst. Hey, Annie. You know what I think?

ANNE: No. What do you think?

A. C.: I think you're starting to believe me. *(And maybe she is.)* I have to get ready. We gotta do meeting in about a minute, right? *(A. C. exits. Anne, left alone now, stops for a moment to think. Then she lies on her back and pulls herself under the desk so that her feet stick out just as A. C.'s did earlier. A. C. silently pokes his head back in the door, sees Anne under the desk, smiles and exits. Anne is still for a moment. Henry Marlino, a Level Five in his fifties, enters the room. He stares at the feet under Zukasky's desk.)*

MARLINO: Excuse me?

ANNE: Aaaaaaaaa!

MARLINO: Anne? What are you doing?

ANNE: *(Scrambling, she crawls out from under the desk and comes to attention. She is holding a sheet of paper in her hand.)* Sorry . . . I was . . . setting up. For the meeting.

MARLINO: Are we meeting under the desk?

ANNE: No! No!

MARLINO: You know, I gotta wonder what were you doing under there.

ANNE: Well, uh, . . . Mr. Tattums—well, A. C.—you know A. C., of course.

MARLINO: Yes. He's a good man.

ANNE: I agree! He's a good man.

MARLINO: Why do you bring up A. C.?

ANNE: Well, uh . . . he was here. He . . . uh . . . he told me this drawer was stuck. And it was. And I loosened it for you. It works fine now. See? *(She pulls the door out of its tracks.)* Couldn't be any smoother than that. *(Replacing the drawer.)*

You might want to take it easy when you open and close. . . . Well, it works now. Anything else you need fixed?

MARLINO: I'll let you know. *(Barry and A. C. enter and sit in front of the desk. Marlino sits in Zukasky's old chair. Anne is still standing, shell-shocked. All eyes fall on Anne, waiting for her to sit so they can start the meeting.)* Ms. Desmond?

ANNE: Sorry. *(She runs for a chair.)*

MARLINO: Thank you. *(Everyone is silent and reverent for awhile. Marlino picks up Zukasky's name plate and gazes at it fondly.)* I'm going to miss this guy. *(Marlino throws the name plate in the wastebasket.)* You know, last night I went to see the Chinese Acrobats. I was particularly struck by this one act they did. There was a platform, maybe four feet high, and one of the Chinamen is standing on that platform. Then another Chinaman brings him a chair and four champagne bottles. So he takes the chair, puts it on top of the champagne bottles and then he does a handstand on top of the chair which is on top of the bottles which is on top of the platform. A handstand! *(Everyone tries to murmur "impressed" sounds.)* So okay, it doesn't sound like much so far. I couldn't do it, but still, I shelled out twenty-two fifty and I need to see a little better than that. But this little Chinaguy is just getting started. Because they bring him a second chair. And he sets that second chair on top of the first chair—upside down, you understand, so the legs are pointing up at the ceiling—and pulls himself up into a handstand again. Are you picturing this?

BARRY: Uh . . .

MARLINO: He's doing a handstand on top of a chair which is on top of a chair which is on top of four champagne bottles which are on top of a platform which is already four feet off the ground. And I think, pretty good. I don't know that it's worth twenty-two fifty, but it's pretty damn good anyway. I figured that was it. And then they bring him *another* chair. Three chairs. They got three chairs stacked on top of each other—balanced on champagne bottles—and on the top they got a Chinaman doing a handstand. Now that's amazing. That's goddamned amazing, don't you think?

BARRY: Uh . . .

MARLINO: But then they bring him *another* chair. And I'm thinking, it's impossible. No way is this guy making four chairs. But he keeps going. He makes four chairs. And five chairs. Five chairs! *(Barry whistles.)* He's almost touching the ceiling. They can't reach him from the ground anymore—they're handing him chairs on the ends of poles. And this crazy Chinaman ends up stacking *six goddamned chairs on top of four champagne bottles on top of a four-foot platform and he's on the top doing a handstand!* I can't figure how he's doing it. Looks like he ought to fall, but he doesn't. And then—*then*—he takes the top chair and tips it on an angle so that only the back two legs are touching the seat of the chair beneath it and *then* he kicks up into a handstand again. *Then he goes up on one hand!*

BARRY: One hand!

MARLINO: *Every time I think he's done as much as he can do, he does something more! (Marlino pauses and makes sure everyone is listening, which they are. Then he repeats, quietly, but with emphasis . . .)* Every time I think he's done as much as he can do, he does something more.

ANNE: Yes sir. I see your point.

MARLINO: What?

ANNE: I said, I see your point.

MARLINO: You see my point?

ANNE: You were making a comparison, weren't you?

MARLINO: A comparison. Hell, I was just talking about the crazy Chinaman. That's what he did.

ANNE: Oh. I thought you were making a comparison.

MARLINO: Between what two things?

ANNE: Well, Mr. Zukasky and the acrobat.

MARLINO: *(Pause.)* I don't get it.

ANNE: Never mind.

MARLINO: Zukasky wasn't a Chinaman.

ANNE: I was reading in.

MARLINO: And he sure as hell wasn't an acrobat.

ANNE: I'm sorry. I was looking too deeply.

MARLINO: I worry about you sometimes, Anne.

ANNE: Sorry.

MARLINO: Of course. *(Pause.)* Anyway, the fact is that Zukasky's dead and someone's going to have to fill his slot. One of you three guys, in fact. *(To Anne.)* You with me?

ANNE: Mr. Zukasky is dead and one of us three guys is going to have to take over his job.

MARLINO: That's good. *(Addressing the whole group again.)* One of you three guys. A terrific collection of talent. I mean that. *(To A. C.)* Mr. Tattums, you've only been with the company a short while, but already we are seeing very promising results. You learn fast. That's a good thing. You don't say much. Maybe that's a good thing. Maybe not. Depends on what you're thinking. But for a man of your age, you have done very well. You should be proud.

A. C.: Thank you, sir.

MARLINO: Are you proud?

A. C.: Uh, yes, sir.

MARLINO: That's good. You should be.

A. C.: Yes, sir.

MARLINO: And Barry, . . .

BARRY: Yes, sir?

MARLINO: *(As if he is speaking to his favorite son.)* Barry. Popular and easy to get along with. But you're hard too; tough as a pit bull terrier. That's what it's all about, Barry. You have been with this company, what, five years? Entered at Level Three; worked your way to Level Four. And you've brought in three major contracts—most notably, of course, the Conklin Industries contract—not to mention promising leads on two others. That's a remarkable achievement, Barry.

BARRY: I'm proud, sir.

MARLINO: Well, that's good. That's real good. Be proud. Excellent. *(Barry is grinning from ear to ear.)* And Ms. Desmond, . . .

ANNE: Sir?

MARLINO: How long have you been with us?

ANNE: Ten years, sir.

MARLINO: *(A little surprised.)* That long? My.

ANNE: Uh, . . . thank you, . . . sir.

MARLINO: And of course, Anne, you're a woman.

ANNE: Well, uh, yes . . .

MARLINO: Remarkable achievement.

ANNE: I've always been a woman.

MARLINO: Yes. Remarkable. And you should be proud. Are you?

ANNE: Well, yes . . .

MARLINO: Say it like you mean it.

ANNE: I'm proud, sir.

MARLINO: *(Coaching her.)* I'm *proud,* sir!

ANNE: I'm *proud,* sir!

MARLINO: *(She didn't quite get it.)* I'm *proud,* sir!

ANNE: I'm *proud,* sir!

MARLINO: *(As if it is the first time he heard her say it.)* Well, good. That's just great. You should be proud. *(Suddenly aware, Marlino stares at Anne's dress.)* What are those things on your dress?

ANNE: They're giraffes, sir.

MARLINO: Giraffes?

ANNE: Yes, sir.

MARLINO: Do you own a suit?

ANNE: Uh . . .

MARLINO: *(Abruptly, to A. C.)* A. C., do you think a woman could handle Zukasky's job?

A. C.: Well, uh . . .

MARLINO: I do.

BARRY: So do I, sir.

MARLINO: Do you? Do you think a woman could sit behind this desk?

BARRY: Yes, sir.

MARLINO: Well, I happen to agree with you, Barry. No reason at all that a woman couldn't handle a job like this. I want you to know that, Anne. If you don't get the job, that won't be the reason.

ANNE: That's reassuring, sir.

MARLINO: Barry, you're my man. *(To Anne.)* You with me?

ANNE: Barry, he's your man.

MARLINO: Right. But not because you're a woman. And Anne, you will be Barry's co-director. You follow?

ANNE: *(Her eyes are fixed on A. C.)* Barry's a director. I'm a co-director.

MARLINO: Exactly. A. C., I want you to try to take up some of the slack by covering Barry's old job until we can find a replacement for him.

A. C.: Sir, what was Barry's old job?

MARLINO: Sales.

A. C.: I'm already a salesman.

MARLINO: Well, good. You should understand the process then.

A. C.: Sounds like a challenge, sir.

MARLINO: Right. *(A moment passes. Anne is staring at A. C.)* You know, those acrobats . . . one of the things they did was to come out with a dozen bamboo poles stuck straight up into a couple sawhorses. And then what the guy would do is stick a soup bowl on top of one of the poles and spin it. After he got three or four of them going, the first one would start to fall and, just in the nick of time, he'd run over and jiggle the pole a little bit and the bowl would start spinning again. It always looked like one of the bowls was just about to fall, but he always got to it before it fell. And, slowly, one by one, he got all twelve bowls spinning on all twelve bamboo poles and he never let a one of them drop. *(To Anne.)* Do you understand?

ANNE: Yes, sir. They had twelve poles mounted vertically and the Chinese gentleman managed to get a bowl spinning on top of each of them.

MARLINO: No. That's not what I meant. Do you know what I mean, A. C.?

A. C.: Well, uh . . .

BARRY: I know, sir.

MARLINO: Okay then, Barry, what did I mean?

BARRY: That even though Zukasky died, we still need to keep our bowls spinning.

MARLINO: Exactly, Barry. That's exactly what I meant.

SCENE 3

It is only a little later in the day. A. C. is, once again, alone in the office. He has one of the chairs stacked, upside down, on top of another chair and he is standing atop the two, reaching for an overhead lighting fixture. Anne enters in a rage.

ANNE: *What are you doing in here? (She pushes him off the chairs, grabs one of them and, like a lion tamer, backs A. C. up against the desk.)* How did you know? What, do you listen at keyholes? Are you tapping into E-mail? *(Suddenly aware.) And what are you doing now?!* Are you crazy? How do you get in here? What are you doing to the furniture? What are you doing in this office? Are you for real or were you sent by the gods to torment me?

A. C.: You know, you're taking this better than I thought you would.

ANNE: I'm taking it piss-poor. I've worked here for ten years and that Marlino thinks I'm a Kelly girl. What does he see in Barry Mills? "Popular"? "Easy to get along with"? Do you know anybody that actually likes Barry Mills? And, ". . . tough as a pit bull . . ."!? That drip isn't even as smart as a pit bull. How could they give him my job?

A. C.: Things don't always work out like you think they're going to.

ANNE: *(Focused back on A. C. again.)* Yeah. But they worked out like *you* thought they were going to.

A. C.: Well, . . .

ANNE: How come? How come things worked out like you thought they were going to? *Exactly* like you thought they were going to? How did you know they were giving my job to Richie Cunningham? Are you planting microphones under upper management desks? Is that what you were doing under there earlier? *(Anne drops to the floor and pulls herself under the desk again, this time in search of microphones. She does not, however, stop talking.)* And why did you tell me everything before the meeting? What do you want out of me? *Are you trying to humiliate me? (Back out from under the desk.)* I've had it with you, buddy. I'm serious. I earned this stupid job. I was the only logical choice! How could you know they were going to give it to Barry Mills! How did you know? How did you know? *How did you know?!*

A. C.: You know, it's hard to talk to you when you're like this. Why don't you calm down—

ANNE: *(Raising the chair again.) Don't mess with me anymore!* I am really serious about this. I want to know how you knew.

A. C.: Put the chair down.

ANNE: Tell me.

A. C.: Put the chair down.

ANNE: *Tell me!*

A. C.: Put down the goddamned chair! This is not good sales technique! I can't talk under this kind of pressure. Just put the chair down so I can give this conversation my full attention!

ANNE: Tell me how you knew! I'm dangerous now. No telling what I might be capable of. I have reached my limit, buddy. I'm ready to kill somebody, it might as well be you. *(Anne puts the chair down slowly. Then she sits in it, facing A. C.)*

ANNE: All right. Tell me, A. C., how did you know that the job I've worked ten years to earn would be given to Barry Mills?

A. C.: I guessed. *(Anne is up immediately, brandishing her chair again.)* I guessed. I guessed. Don't hurt me. I make one lucky guess and you're trying to kill me? I am on your side. I think you should have gotten the promotion. You wanna hit somebody, *hit somebody on level five.*

ANNE: Hold still. I really want to hurt you now. Stop moving around. I'm not leaving until I bean somebody with a chair. Now hold still. *Hold still!* HOLD STILL, GOD DAMN IT! *(Anne thinks a while and then gives up. She lowers the chair and sits in it again. She is in the center of the office, near no other furniture, looking very lonesome.)*

ANNE: *(Very quietly.)* A. C.?

A. C.: Yes?

ANNE: Why won't you tell me how you knew?

A. C.: *(He kneels beside her as if he is about to propose.)* I did, Annie. I did. I swear to you, I just guessed.

ANNE: A. C.?

A. C.: Yes?

ANNE: I hate being called Annie.

A. C.: Sorry.

ANNE: You say you want me to believe you. You say you want me to trust you. But you won't even tell me how you knew they were going to give my job to that insufferable clown.

A. C.: Anne, you're just going to have to believe me on this one. It was a guess. That's all. Just a guess.

ANNE: You guessed that they were going to give the job to Barry Mills?

A. C.: Yes.

ANNE: You guessed that they were going to make me "co-director"?

A. C.: Yes.

ANNE: You guessed that Marlino was going to make fun of my giraffes?

A. C.: Yes.

ANNE: You're full of shit up to your eyebrows.

A. C.: The truth is, Anne, Barry was the logical choice.

ANNE: Oh stop.

A. C.: Barry has a gift, Anne. It may not be obvious to you, but he has a genuine gift. A precious and wonderful gift. Barry Mills knows how to make money. That is his talent and his reason for being. There are things that I won't do for money. There are things that you won't do for money. But if there are things that Barry Mills won't do for money, they haven't been discovered yet. Now it is true that Barry's an idiot, just like you said. But Barry knows the one thing he needs to know: he knows how to take money. You, on the other hand, would fuck up a free lunch. That is how I knew they were going to give this job to Barry. You wanna know how I knew? That is how I knew. That is how I knew. *(Pause.)* That is how I knew.

ANNE: What do you mean there are things I wouldn't do for money? What kinda crack is that?

A. C.: It's not a crack. I'm just saying you've got ethics. I'm saying you have a conscience.

ANNE: You're saying I'm a sap.

A. C.: In a nutshell.

ANNE: I resent this.

A. C.: In some places they admire ethics. I think it's charming. It just sort of makes it hard to take you seriously, you know?

ANNE: This is really sexist.

A. C.: Sexist?!

ANNE: The only reason you assume I have ethics is because I'm a woman. You've never actually seen me do something ethical.

A. C.: Okay. I'm sorry. You're not ethical.

ANNE: I take money as well as Barry does.

A. C.: No you don't.

ANNE: Yes I do.

A. C.: It's not the same thing. Look, let's say some guy sees you on the street and says, "Here, Anne. Here's some money. No strings attached. You didn't earn it; I just wanna give it to you." If somebody just wanted to give you money, you're telling me that you could take it?

ANNE: Oh, this is stupid.

A. C.: Well, Barry wouldn't think it was stupid. Barry would take the money.

ANNE: So would I.

A. C.: Of course you would. Who wouldn't? Free money? Who wouldn't take free money? If some guy wants to give you his money, why shouldn't you take it?

ANNE: What's your point?

A. C.: I don't believe you. That's my point. My point is I don't believe you.

ANNE: Well, it's going to be hard to prove, isn't it?

A. C.: Not really. *(He reaches into his wallet and takes out a dollar.)* Here. Here's a dollar. This is your lucky day. Take a dollar, no questions asked.

ANNE: Oh, get out of town.

A. C.: You don't want the dollar, huh?

ANNE: Uh, no. No, thank you.

A. C.: Okay, you hear yourself? You told me you would take the money, but when I tried to give you the money you say, "No, thank you." So my original premise is the right one: you would fuck up a free lunch. Now, you wanna know why you won't take the money?

ANNE: No, actually.

A. C.: Fortunately, I am willing to tell you anyway. It's because all I offered you was a crummy dollar. I mean, what can you do with a dollar? Pack of cigs is a buck seventy-five now. Dime paperbacks are four and a quarter. Maybe a candy bar and a newspaper. That's about the best you could do with a dollar. Do you want a candy bar and a newspaper?

ANNE: Uh, no.

A. C.: Exactly. You don't want a candy bar and a newspaper so what good is a dollar to you? And that's why you won't take it when I offer you a dollar, right?

ANNE: Uh, . . .

A. C.: Let me put it this way: If I had offered you twenty dollars instead of one dollar you probably would have taken the whole proposal more seriously and you probably would have taken the twenty, right?

ANNE: Probably.

A. C.: Probably. So here you go—here's twenty dollars—take it and be a happy lady. *(A. C. takes twenty from his wallet and sets it on Zukasky's desk, next to the one.)*

ANNE: For what?

A. C.: For nothing. For I want to give it to you. For here. Take it.

ANNE: What is it you want me to do?

A. C.: I want you to pick up the money and put it in your purse. Then it will be your money. It's gotta be the easiest twenty bucks you'll make today.

ANNE: Why are you doing this?

A. C.: What's the difference? Maybe I'm nuts. Maybe I'm generous. I just want to give you twenty dollars.

ANNE: No. No, thank you.

A. C.: Right. There it is again. "No, thank you." You won't take my dollar and you won't take my twenty dollars. Only, it's getting harder, isn't it? I'll bet if I offered you a hundred dollars you'd take it. Don't you think? What if I offered you a hundred dollars?

ANNE: *A hundred dollars?*

A. C.: Whoa! That struck a nerve. We like twenty dollars, sure. Twenty dollars is nice, fun to dance with, take it to the sock hop. But a hundred dollars! Whoopee! We're going to the prom! We love a hundred dollars, don't we?

ANNE: You're ridiculous.

A. C.: Yeah. I'm a ridiculous guy. But the question is, would you take a hundred dollars?

ANNE: Hypothetically, you mean?

A. C.: Of course.

ANNE: Well, buddy, if you're willing to set a hundred dollars out here, I'm willing to take it.

A. C.: Okay. So what have we learned? You won't take my one or my twenty but a hundred you'd take, is that it?

ANNE: You're not really offering, are you?

A. C.: No. Just asking.

ANNE: That's what I thought.

A. C.: But you would take it, right? That's what we decided, right? If I offered a hundred dollars, you'd take it.

ANNE: Yeah. Sure. I'd take a hundred dollars.

A. C.: *Great! Now I'm offering! (He takes a hundred dollars out of his wallet and sets it next to the twenty and the one.)* There you are! Hundred bucks; all yours. Pleasure doing business with you. All you gotta do now is pick it up.

ANNE: All right, stop it.

A. C.: You are not picking up your money.

ANNE: Look, I can't take money from you.

A. C.: You can't? Why is that?

ANNE: Just leave me alone.

A. C.: Okay. Okay. This goes against my better judgement, but . . . Suppose I make it five hundred. How do we feel about five hundred? Can we take five hundred dollars?

ANNE: I, uh . . .

A. C.: Think. Think. Think. Think what you could do with five hundred dollars. *(She does.)* Five hundred dollars. Five hundred dollars. Do we want to have five hundred dollars?

ANNE: Is this a hypothetical offer or a real offer?

A. C.: You mean, if it's hypothetical you'll accept it and if it's real you won't? *(He takes four more hundred dollar bills and counts them out onto the desk.)* So, what's the story? Do we want five hundred dollars?

ANNE: No, thank you.

A. C.: "No, thank you." You drive a hard bargain, lady.

ANNE: Look, I don't want your five hundred dollars.

A. C.: What about my seven hundred dollars? You want that? Or my nine hundred dollars. Let's just look into Mr. Wallet and see . . . *(He peers into his wallet and takes out a bill.)* Uh-oh, kids! Look who's here! It's . . . *(Pausing for effect.) William McKinley!*

(Beat.) Suppose I give you this five hundred dollar bill to go with the other five. That's a thousand dollars. Suppose I give you a thousand dollars. *(Beat.)* Notice, also, that I have not taken back either the twenty or the one so this is a total of one thousand and twenty-one dollars that you could take home today just for playing, "Pick Up the Money." So what do you say, Ms. Desmond from Chicago, Illinois? Do you want the money or not?

ANNE: No, thank you.

A. C.: "No, thank you." The epitaph of the woman destined to remain at Level Four. *(He gathers the money and puts it back in his wallet.)* You wanna know the truth? I ain't had much of a year so far. If you had taken my money, I couldn't have made rent. But I knew—I absolutely knew for a fact—that there was no possible way you were going to take my money. Pretty amazing, huh? It takes a special kind of person to take money—just take it. So, you wanna know how I knew? That is how I knew. *(Pause.)* That is how I knew.

ANNE: Why did you do this? *(Barry enters.)*

BARRY: Oh, A. C. Glad you're here. *(To Anne.)* What are you doing here?

ANNE: I, . . . uh . . .

A. C.: We were discussing business.

BARRY: Oh.

ANNE: I was just leaving.

A. C.: *(Quickly, before Anne leaves, and for her benefit.)* Say, Barry?

BARRY: Yes?

A. C.: *(Holding out a bill to him.)* Suppose I give you a dollar.

BARRY: *(Pocketing the bill.)* Sure. Thanks. *(Anne exits, slamming the door.)* What's biting her?

A. C.: Don't know. She's kind of unstable.

BARRY: She is?

A. C.: That's what Marlino says.

BARRY: No kidding.

A. C.: *(Indicating the office.)* Good stuff, Barry. The place suits you. Seriously. It looks good on you.

BARRY: It's a nice office, isn't it?

A. C.: It's beautiful. You got a window with a view of . . . *(He looks out the window.)* . . . the housing projects.

BARRY: I thought I had a lake view. Marlino said . . .

A. C.: Hey, I'm sure you do. If Marlino said lake view . . .

BARRY: Let me see. *(He rushes to his window.)*

A. C.: . . . then there's gotta be a lake out here . . .

BARRY: It's the projects. That's my view.

A. C.: . . . somewhere.

BARRY: I got a view of Robert Taylor Homes.

A. C.: *(His face is pressed against the window and he is looking along the outside wall of the building.)* There it is!

BARRY: *Where?*

A. C.: Press your face against the glass and look east. *(Barry does so.)*

BARRY: I don't see it.

A. C.: Press harder. *(A. C. applies gentle pressure to Barry's head.)* Look right along the side of the building.

BARRY: *(The words are muddled because his face is smushed.)* Next to the statue?

A. C.: East of the statue.

BARRY: Wait a minute! I can see it! I can see it!

A. C.: *(Loosening his grip on Barry's head.)* Told you.

BARRY: *(Pressing his face still harder against the glass.)* There's a sailboat! I can see a sailboat!

A. C.: Lake view, buddy. You got yourself a lake view.

BARRY: *(Coming back to his desk.)* It sailed behind the building.

A. C.: If Marlino says you got a lake view, you got a lake view.

BARRY: It's not really much of the lake . . .

A. C.: But it's something! That's the point. Most guys don't see any of the lake. At least you got some of it, and you should be darn proud.

BARRY: Well, sure . . .

A. C.: I mean, look at the size of this office.

BARRY: It's a big one, isn't it?

A. C.: What do you got here? Two hundred square feet?

BARRY: Two hundred forty.

A. C.: How much?

BARRY: Two hundred forty.

A. C.: Really? You think so?

BARRY: Marlino said it was . . .

A. C.: Then, hey, that's probably right. If he's saying two-forty then, some way or another, it must be two-forty.

BARRY: Uh-huh.

A. C.: Only, it looks smaller.

BARRY: He said . . .

A. C.: And I'm sure he's right. I'm not saying it *is* smaller. I'm just saying it *seems* smaller. But still big, you know? It seems like a big office. Just not quite that big.

BARRY: He promised me two-forty.

A. C.: There you are. That's good enough for me. If he says its two-forty, it's two-forty. I wouldn't even bother to measure it. Anyone asks me, I'll tell 'em it's every bit of two hundred and forty square feet.

BARRY: You think it's less?

A. C.: What do I know? Am I an interior decorator? It's a big office, okay? You should be proud.

BARRY: Well, sure.

A. C.: Big office, lake view, private secretary . . .

BARRY: I got a secretary?

A. C.: Sure. Anne Desmond.

BARRY: I thought she was co-directing something or other.

A. C.: Sure. That's nineties euphemism for secretary.

BARRY: Really?

A. C.: Sure. Janitors are building engineers and secretaries are co-directors. But they still do the same jobs they always did.

BARRY: Are you sure?

A. C.: Look, do you need help directing?

BARRY: No.

A. C.: I'm telling you bud: You got yourself a secretary.

BARRY: Wow.

A. C.: Sure. Wow. Secretary. That's good. That's a good thing. With, of course, the one obvious drawback.

BARRY: Sure. The drawback.

A. C.: So congratulations . . .

BARRY: *(Growing worried.)* The drawback.

A. C.: . . . I could not be happier for you . . .

BARRY: There's always a drawback.

A. C.: . . . I hope this thing works great for you.

BARRY: What is it?

A. C.: What is what?

BARRY: The drawback. The one obvious drawback. What is the
one obvious drawback?

A. C.: Well, you know, . . .

BARRY: Sure I do. It's uh . . .

A. C.: I mean, in this type of job . . .

BARRY: Sure. In a type of job like this . . .

A. C.: Needing support like you will . . .

BARRY: Sure. Needing support the way I'm going to need it . . .

A. C.: I mean, loyalty is going to be a very big thing . . .

BARRY: Sure. Loyalty.

A. C.: And the person you will need the most loyalty from is . . .

BARRY: Sure. I'm going to need the most loyalty from . . .

A. C.: Need I say more?

BARRY: *Yes! Say more!*

A. C.: Well, it just seems to me that you are going to have to rely
heavily on the loyalty of your support staff. And number one
on that support staff is Annie Desmond. So you are in a
position of needing a tremendous amount of loyalty from . . .
*(He can't lead him any more obviously than that, so he waits for
Barry to answer.)*

BARRY: *(Slowly.)* Anne Desmond.

A. C.: That's been bothering you too, huh?

BARRY: Sure. Sure, it bothers me. Why does that bother me?

A. C.: No reason. I'm probably imagining things. Sorry I mentioned it.

BARRY: Is there something bad about Anne Desmond?

A. C.: Hey! I'm not saying a word. Other people gossip; I don't
gossip.

BARRY: What? What do they say about Anne Desmond?

A. C.: Nothing! Least ways, you didn't hear it from me.

BARRY: She seems smart.

A. C.: Oh, she is. Very smart.

BARRY: Hard working.

A. C.: You bet. She's a hard worker.

BARRY: So what's the problem?

A. C.: If she goes around knifing people in the back, you didn't
hear it from me.

BARRY: She knifes people in the back?

A. C.: You didn't hear that from me!

BARRY: How do you know that?

A. C.: I don't. It's probably not true. It's probably just a very well-travelled rumor.

BARRY: My God.

A. C.: Look, you're worrying over nothing. What can she do to you? She's just a secretary.

BARRY: Sure. She's just a secretary.

A. C.: Maybe she's a little on the ambitious side.

BARRY: You're kidding. She's ambitious too?

A. C.: Well, aren't back stabbers usually ambitious?

BARRY: Oh God.

A. C.: The rumor is, if you turn your back on her she will steal the chair right out from under you.

BARRY: *(Embracing his chair.)* She will?

A. C.: How do I know? It's just a rumor.

BARRY: What do I do?

A. C.: Nothing. Quit making a big deal over this. Just be a little careful.

BARRY: Yeah. I'll be careful.

A. C.: Make sure she understands you're in charge.

BARRY: Well, I am in charge, you know.

A. C.: I know. Make sure she understands that.

BARRY: Oh.

A. C.: You're the boss, right?

BARRY: Well, yeah.

A. C.: And what is she?

BARRY: My secretary.

A. C.: Exactly.

BARRY: Anne Desmond is my secretary.

A. C.: That's good. Except for one thing.

BARRY: What's that?

A. C.: She likes to be called, "Annie."

AUTHOR'S NOTE: If an intermission is taken, it should be taken here.

SCENE 4

Barry is pacing the office, carefully placing one foot in front of the other, measuring from wall to wall. Each time he reaches a wall he says, "Damn."

Anne enters and watches Barry pace for a while. She is wearing a suit. Barry looks up momentarily and sees Anne.

BARRY: Oh. Hello, Annie. *(Anne noticeably twitches on being called, "Annie.")*

ANNE: Uh, is there something I can help you with?

BARRY: Shh. I'm measuring my office. *(He reaches another wall.)* Damn.

ANNE: Can I get you a tape measure?

BARRY: I don't need a tape measure. My feet are exactly twelve inches long.

ANNE: How convenient.

BARRY: *(Snapping.)* What?!

ANNE: I said, uh, how convenient. How nice. Uh, it must be nice to have feet that are twelve inches long. Exactly.

BARRY: It is, as a matter of fact.

ANNE: I would think so. *(Anne turns away from Barry and crosses her eyes.)*

BARRY: Of course, . . .

ANNE: Yes?

BARRY: They are new shoes.

ANNE: New shoes?

BARRY: New shoes. And they feel a little roomy. You know?

ANNE: Roomy.

BARRY: Could be throwing off the data, you know?

ANNE: Roomy shoes. Throwing data.

BARRY: If I had a . . . , you know . . .

ANNE: Tape measure?

BARRY: *Not a tape measure!*

ANNE: *Not a tape measure!*

BARRY: But a . . . *(Pause.)*

ANNE: *(Very timidly.)* Ruler?

BARRY: *A ruler! Yes!* If I had a ruler . . .

ANNE: I think there's one in the desk. *(Anne crosses to the desk and*

sits in the chair behind the desk in order to look in the front drawer.
Barry screams.)

BARRY: Aaaaa!

ANNE: *What?!*

BARRY: *What are you doing?*

ANNE: *I'm looking for a ruler!*

BARRY: *Get out! Get out!*

ANNE: *I'm out! (Anne leaps from the chair and clears the desk area.*
There is a silence during which the two stare at each other suspi-
ciously.)

BARRY: Were you able to find a ruler?

ANNE: Not yet.

BARRY: Maybe I better look.

ANNE: Good idea. *(Barry sits, maybe a little bit overly firmly, in his*
chair. He then opens the center drawer of his desk, removes a ruler
and measures one of his feet.)

BARRY: Twelve inches. Exactly. You know?

ANNE: Twelve inches.

BARRY: You son of a bitch.

ANNE: Who? Me?

BARRY: No. Not you. You're a woman. You can't be a son of a
bitch. You're just a . . . *(Pause.)* . . . woman. You know?

ANNE: Woman.

BARRY: Right.

ANNE: Do you need something, Barry? Or should I just go back
to work?

BARRY: Are you my secretary?

ANNE: What?

BARRY: Are you my secretary?

ANNE: I am a Level Four.

BARRY: I know. Are you my secretary?

ANNE: I am a co-director.

BARRY: Yeah. What I need to know is, what does that mean?

ANNE: I'm not exactly sure, but . . .

BARRY: What is your job?

ANNE: Well, to assist you.

BARRY: With what do I need assistance?

ANNE: I'm not sure. That would be up to you.

BARRY: So what's the story? Are you my secretary?

ANNE: I can do almost anything you need to have done.

BARRY: Right now I need to find out if you're my secretary.

ANNE: I can do most of the jobs that you would normally associate with a secretary.

BARRY: I don't need most of the jobs that I would normally associate with a secretary. I need a secretary. Are you my secretary?

ANNE: *(Beaten.)* Sure.

BARRY: Great. I need you to take a letter.

ANNE: What?

BARRY: Take a letter.

ANNE: You're kidding. *(No he isn't.)* Do you have a pad? *(Barry hands Anne a legal pad from his top drawer. Anne sits and prepares to "take a letter.")*

BARRY: Do you take shorthand?

ANNE: Barry, no one has taken shorthand since they invented dictaphones.

BARRY: I was hoping you took shorthand. Okay, forget it. Draw a square.

ANNE: Do what?

BARRY: Draw a square.

ANNE: Draw a square?

BARRY: Do you not know how to draw a square?

ANNE: No. I can draw a square.

BARRY: Then draw a square. *(Anne draws a square.)*

ANNE: I've drawn a square.

BARRY: Now, inside the square write, "Memo from Barry Mills."

ANNE: You want that inside the square?

BARRY: Yes. I like to have my name inside boxes.

ANNE: I see.

BARRY: I think it looks more professional.

ANNE: I see. *(Anne starts erasing the square.)*

BARRY: What are you doing?

ANNE: I need to make a bigger square.

BARRY: Oh. Go ahead. *(Anne makes a bigger square and writes in it.)*

ANNE: I've drawn a bigger square and written "Memo from Barry Mills," in it.

BARRY: Fine.

ANNE: It's actually more of a rectangle.

BARRY: A rectangle is fine. Now draw a floor plan of this office.

ANNE: How big? *(Barry makes a box with his fingers. Anne begins drawing. Barry speaks as she draws.)*

BARRY: Then draw an arrow pointing to this wall. *(Barry has his hand on one of the interior walls.)* And write this memo: "Dear Mr. Marlino: I am calling for bids to have the indicated wall, paren., see illustration, close paren., moved four feet south. That will increase the square footage of my office to two hundred forty square feet, the square footage I was promised when I accepted this job. Very truly yours," et cetera. You know?

ANNE: You're increasing the size of your office?

BARRY: Yes.

ANNE: By moving this wall?

BARRY: Yes.

ANNE: That means the office on the other side of this wall will be smaller.

BARRY: I suppose.

ANNE: That's my office.

BARRY: Is it?

ANNE: Yes. It is.

BARRY: Well, that's not the point.

ANNE: It's not?

BARRY: No. It's not. The point has more to do with what I need. I need a bigger office.

ANNE: And do I need a smaller office?

BARRY: I'm not doing this just to make your office smaller. I don't want you to think that.

ANNE: What do you want me to think?

BARRY: Send the memo first. Later we'll decide what you should think.

SCENE 5

It is a few days later. The wall Barry indicated has been mostly torn out. All that remains are the aluminum studs and some conduit which ties together various outlets. On the other side of the wall,

barely visible through the aluminum bars, is Anne Desmond's office.
A. C. enters on Barry's side and sees the havoc. He calls through the
wall to Anne.

A. C.: Hey Anne. Where's your wall? *(Anne crosses to the wall and*
peers at A. C. between two studs which she hangs on as if she were
in a prison movie.)

ANNE: I want you to kill him for me.

A. C.: This has been hard on you, huh?

ANNE: I want him dead. I want him to suffer and then I want
him to die.

A. C.: So what are we waiting for? We can get him, Anne. We
can get him gone if you'll just trust me.

ANNE: Oh, cut it out. He's got a job here for life. Marlino loves
him.

A. C.: You have to trust me on this. You have to. Look at me.
Look how sincere I'm looking. This is what I look like when
I'm being honest.

ANNE: You look about the same.

A. C.: I'm going to tell you this, Anne. I'm going to tell you this
thing because I trust you. Even if you don't trust me, I trust
you.

ANNE: Don't. Don't trust me.

A. C.: I do.

ANNE: *Don't!*

A. C.: There is a file, Anne.

ANNE: I don't want to hear this.

A. C.: There is a file, somewhere in this office, which could put
Barry Mills out of work. It might be a memo or a letter or a
child's scrawl on a scrap of legal paper. But it is in here
somewhere.

ANNE: Stop talking, A. C.

A. C.: This is why you keep finding me in this office, Anne. He
and Zukasky had a deal going. I know that for a fact. And if
we can find their file it will put Barry Mills a million miles
from Chicago. All we gotta do is find their file.

ANNE: You know, every time I think you're being honest you also
get real weird.

A. C.: It's in here somewhere. It has to be.

ANNE: Are you really serious?

A. C.: Only he's got it hidden. It could be rolled up and inserted into the hollowed out leg of a chair. It could be under the veneer of his desk top. It could be on microfilm, made to look like the design on his pencil holder.

ANNE: That's nice, Sybil. Can I talk to A. C. now?

A. C.: The only thing we know for sure is, it is not taped to the bottom of the top drawer of his desk. We already looked there.

ANNE: What do you mean "we"? I didn't look. You looked.

A. C.: You looked too. After me. I saw you.

ANNE: I was looking to see what you were looking for.

A. C.: Whatever. I appreciate the help.

ANNE: I was not helping you.

A. C.: Sure you were. And I appreciate it. But listen, Anne, if you find that file, call me. Okay? That's important. Don't you do anything with it because you'll screw it up. If you give the file to me, I promise you, I will have Barry Mills looking for work in northern Wisconsin before Friday.

ANNE: What does it look like?

A. C.: I don't know.

ANNE: Oh. Well, I'll keep an eye out.

A. C.: No, see, I got that figured. Here's what you do: Watch him through the wall. I am going to give him this very confidential document. *(He shows Anne a bright orange piece of paper.)* Notice that it is on bright orange paper so that you can keep an eye on it. Watch him. Covertly. Tell me where he hides it. With luck, he will put it with his other confidential documents. Then we got him.

ANNE: What's on the document?

A. C.: Nothing. It's crap. I made it up.

ANNE: Not that one. The one we're looking for.

A. C.: I'll tell you later.

ANNE: See, this is what makes me think I don't really trust you.

A. C.: Sure you do.

ANNE: A. C., I am not going to help you with this.

A. C.: Sure you are.

ANNE: Just because I don't like Barry does not mean I am going to spy on him.

A. C.: Sure it does.

ANNE: I'm not going to do it. Put it out of your tiny brain.

A. C.: Okay. Fine. It's forgotten. I'll be waiting.

ANNE: I don't like you any better than I like Barry, you know. What makes you think I'm going to help you?

A. C.: Because, although you do not like me, you believe me. You trust me.

ANNE: What have I ever done to make you believe that?

A. C.: You bought a new suit. Nice. I like it.

ANNE: Get real. I've had this suit for ten years. Don't even consider the idea that I bought it because you told me to.

A. C.: Funny, it looks brand new. Mind you, it looks ten years out of date, but this is the first time you had it out of the closet, right?

ANNE: I don't wear it often. But not because . . .

A. C.: Well it's nice. I mean that. Very nice.

ANNE: Thank you.

A. C.: You might want to go just a shade more conservative. The pattern screams a little.

ANNE: It's a pinstripe. What is more conservative than pinstripe? Pinstripe is quintessential conservative. Pinstripe means conservative.

A. C.: It's kind of a bright pinstripe. I'd look toward muting that when you replace this suit.

ANNE: Why would I be replacing this suit? I can get two years of wear out of it.

A. C.: I agree. Only those years were nineteen-eighty and nineteen-eighty-one.

ANNE: You are such an asshole.

A. C.: I am just trying to help. *(An afterthought.)* Oh, listen, I know you don't trust me, because you just told me you didn't, but there is one other thing I ought to warn you about: Make sure you hang on to your keys.

ANNE: What are you babbling about now?

A. C.: Your keys. You know, your keys. Hang on to your keys. You'll need them.

ANNE: My keys.

A. C.: Keys are important. Keys are a symbol. Keys are always a symbol. That's important. Hang on to your keys. That's crucial.

ANNE: Who's going to steal my keys?

A. C.: Maybe no one. But, just the same, I would keep an eye out for you know who.

ANNE: You think Barry wants my keys?

A. C.: How would I know? I got no way of knowing. I'm not saying that. This is what I'm saying: Hang on to your keys.

SCENE 6

It is the next day. A. C. is talking with Barry.

A. C.: Keys are important. Keys are a symbol. Keys are always a symbol. She loves to point out that she's got a key and I don't. That's a real big thing with her. It's kinda scary. I'd watch that.

BARRY: You think I ought to get back the key?

A. C.: I'm not saying that. Whatever you think is best. That's your decision. All I'm saying is that she has an unhealthy interest in keys.

BARRY: She's going to think I'm being pushy.

A. C.: There is a difference between being assertive and being pushy.

BARRY: You think asking for the key back is assertive?

A. C.: Absolutely. And if she insists on keeping the key—well, that would be, you know . . .

BARRY: Pushy, huh?

A. C.: I didn't say that. I'm saying this: Do you like that picture on your wall?

BARRY: It's okay.

A. C.: Who hung it there?

BARRY: I don't know.

A. C.: Annie Desmond. Annie Desmond is trying to push that thing into your life.

BARRY: Annie hung that there?

A. C.: Does it look like something a man would pick out?

BARRY: Maybe. It's just shapes.

A. C.: It's not just shapes. It's circles and triangles.

BARRY: So?

A. C.: Circles and triangles, Barry. Circles and triangles.

BARRY: Circles and—

A. C.: Think, Barry. Circles. What do circles remind you of? What do triangles remind you of? (*A. C. draws two circles in mid air at chest height and, below them, a triangle.*)

BARRY: (*Suddenly horrified.*) Oh my God!

A. C.: Annie Desmond came into your office—*your office!*—and hung circles and triangles on your wall. What is she doing in your office in the first place?

BARRY: Well, I don't . . .

A. C.: Is there some reason she should be in here when you're not here?

BARRY: No. No.

A. C.: Well, don't tell me. Tell her.

BARRY: Circles and triangles.

A. C.: A client comes in here, sees circles and triangles on your wall—he's going to laugh at you, pal.

BARRY: Circles and triangles. My God.

A. C.: Annie Desmond did that to you, pal. That's all I'm saying. There is a difference between being assertive and being pushy.

BARRY: God she's pushy.

A. C.: You think so?

BARRY: Don't you?

A. C.: I'm not good at making judgements about people. You're probably right.

BARRY: Of course I'm right. God she's pushy!

A. C.: You notice anything about the way she's been dressing lately?

BARRY: Well, not really. She looks nice.

A. C.: She used to look nice. Lately she's been wearing suits. She's trying to dress like a man.

BARRY: She is? I just remember the giraffes . . .

A. C.: Kiss those giraffes good-bye. It is going to be pinstripe from here on. Check her out next time you see her. She doesn't just want your job, man—she wants your closet.

BARRY: I liked the giraffes.

A. C.: Everybody liked the giraffes, Barry. But she's after bigger game now. It sort of reminds me of what you say about her.

BARRY: What's that?

A. C.: That she's pushy.

BARRY: She is, isn't she?

A. C.: I guess. *(Anne enters her office. Barry glares with hatred at her.)*

BARRY: God, she's pushy.

A. C.: *(He simultaneously gets Anne's attention while appearing to Barry to be talking confidentially; he is about to pass on the "very confidential orange document.")* Look, Barry, I got something for you. But, listen, this is very confidential. *Very confidential.* You're going to have to hide it somewhere. You got a place where you keep very confidential documents?

BARRY: Yeah. Of course.

A. C.: Great. Put this with them. This is very hot stuff. Top secret.

BARRY: *(Reading the document.)* He wears panty hose?

A. C.: Shhh! *(In a whisper.)* Under the suit—under the argyles—under the boxers—Sheer Energy. Shh! *(Anne snorts in disbelief.)*

BARRY: Right. I'll put this . . . uh . . . *(He is looking at A. C.)*

A. C.: Not now. Wait till I'm gone. I shouldn't know where you keep confidential documents. Only you should know.

BARRY: Right. *(He puts it on top of his desk. A. C. signals to Anne. Anne pointedly turns her back to A. C.)*

A. C.: Gotta get back to work. Make a few calls, you know? Talk to you later. *(He calls through the wall.)* Good-bye, Anne. *(A. C. exits.)*

BARRY: Annie, may I see you in here a moment? *(Anne exits her office, through her door and re-enters through Barry's door. She is toe-to-toe with Barry. And we can see now that she is wearing a more muted suit—much like A. C. described. Maybe a muted pinstripe. Maybe a muted herringbone. It's a muted something. And, whatever material it is made from, it is exactly—exactly!—the same material that was used to make Barry's suit. Probably cut by the same tailor. Both Anne and Barry are instantly aware of the fabric they have in common. There is an undercurrent of furor in the restrained dialogue they now have.)* New suit?

ANNE: Yes.

BARRY: Expensive?

ANNE: Yes.

BARRY: Didn't you used to wear dresses?

ANNE: Sometimes.

BARRY: With giraffes?

ANNE: Sometimes.

BARRY: Now you're into suits.

ANNE: Sometimes.

BARRY: I miss the giraffes.

ANNE: Maybe you can have a suit made out of giraffe fabric.

BARRY: Are you trying to be funny?

ANNE: No.

BARRY: Well, maybe the lining.

ANNE: Sure.

BARRY: I need my key back.

ANNE: What?

BARRY: I need my key back.

ANNE: What key?

BARRY: The key to my office. I need back your key to my office.

ANNE: What do you mean you need it "back"? You never had it before.

BARRY: Well, I want it now. May I have the key to my office?

ANNE: *(Anne pauses to consider her position.)* No.

BARRY: What?

ANNE: No. I don't want to give you my key.

BARRY: But, I asked you for it.

ANNE: Mr. Marlino gave me this key. I will give it back to Mr. Marlino, if he asks for it. But there's no reason I should give it to you.

BARRY: But, . . . but . . .

ANNE: It seems to me that this is pushing your authority a little bit hard, Barry.

BARRY: Are you saying I'm pushy?

ANNE: Get a grip, Barry. This shouldn't be a big deal. I didn't exactly call you pushy. I may have used the word push. I may have said that people who do what you're doing are pushy . . .	BARRY: You said I was pushy! I'm not deaf. You said I was pushy! That's a laugh, coming from you. You're the pushy one. Push, push, push. Don't you call me pushy.

BARRY: There's a difference between being pushy and being assertive, you know!

ANNE: Barry, calm down!

BARRY: *And get that picture out of my office!*

ANNE: The picture? Is there something wrong with . . .

BARRY: Circles and triangles! It's a picture of circles and triangles! Do you think I'm an idiot? Did you think I would just sit back while you put circles and triangles on my wall? I want 'em off. Off.

ANNE: I, uh, . . .

BARRY: I got kids, you know. Suppose my son comes up to see where his daddy works and sees a bunch of circles and triangles hung up on the wall? I want those circles and triangles gone! *(Anne is too stunned to answer. Her mouth is moving and noises are coming out but she cannot actually form words. Maybe if she had any idea what Barry was talking about . . .)* And is there some reason you can't get me a cup of coffee?

ANNE: Murp . . . blug . . . gup . . .

BARRY: One damned cup of coffee? I work hard. Sometimes I need a cup of coffee so I can keep going. Is it so hard for you just to get me a damn cup of coffee?

ANNE: Unk . . . klup . . . kurp . . .

BARRY: Me pushy! What a joke! I'm assertive; you're pushy. I don't go around hanging geometric shapes in your office, do I?

ANNE: Muggelbunken. *(She begins weeping softly.)*

BARRY: *Would it kill you to learn shorthand?!* *(Anne is silent.)* I'm leaving for a minute. Pull yourself back together. And when I get back I want the key on my desk and the circles and triangles off my wall! *(Barry storms out. Then he storms back in. He grabs the orange "confidential document" and looks suspiciously at Anne.)* Don't look! Go back to your office! *(Anne returns to her office.)* And stay there, okay? I don't want you poking around my office unless I'm here. *(Anne positions herself in a way that allows her to see where Barry hides the document. He puts it in the top drawer of his filing cabinet. Then he exits again, locking the door behind him. Anne re-enters Barry's office through her wall and crosses to the filing cabinet. A. C. appears on the window ledge. He has been listening to the fight. He peeks in and does not see Anne who is obscured by the filing cabinet. Thinking the offices are empty, he enters through the window. Anne sees him as he is tiptoeing toward the hallway door. She screams.)*

ANNE: Aaaaaa!

A. C.: Aaaaaa!

ANNE: Where were you? How did you get back in here? How do you do that?

A. C.: *(Coming over to her.)* I came in the door. It was open.

ANNE: You didn't come in the door. I would have seen you. *(Anne looks around the office and comes to the only conclusion that makes any sense.)* You were on the window ledge.

A. C.: What?

ANNE: You were on the window ledge. You were spying on us.

A. C.: The window ledge? It's twenty floors up! Who would be crazy enough to go out on the ledge?

ANNE: You are. You've been listening at windows. That's how you're able to get in here without a key. That's why you know everything that goes on. You are dangerously crazy.

A. C.: Anne, get realistic. Look out the window. *(Anne crosses to the window, looking suspiciously at A. C.)* Look down. *(Anne looks down. A. C. presses her face flatter against the window.)* Do you really think I would crawl out on that ledge?

ANNE: Well, . . .

A. C.: It's a twelve-inch ledge and it's three hundred feet down!

ANNE: Well, . . .

A. C.: Would you do it?

ANNE: Well, no. *(She thinks some more.)* How *did* you get in?

A. C.: I just came in the door. Your door. I was looking for you. *(Anne continues to stare.)* Really, Anne. Really. I'm not so crazy that I would go dancing around on window ledges. That's nuts. Look, I'll talk to you later, okay? After work?

ANNE: I know where he keeps his secret files.

A. C.: You do? Really?

ANNE: I do. I just found out.

A. C.: Where?

ANNE: I am not going to tell you.

A. C.: *What?!*

ANNE: Not until you tell me how you got in here.

A. C.: Through the door.

ANNE: Tell me how you got in here.

A. C.: Through the door.

ANNE: Tell me how you got in here.

A. C.: I came in through the door. Through the door. *Through the goddamned door! (Pause.)*

ANNE: Tell me how you got in here.

A. C.: I came in through the window. What's the difference?

ANNE: What were you doing on the window ledge?

A. C.: Anne, we got about two seconds before Barry comes back in here and the two of us are caught with no good excuses. Now just tell me where he hides his files.

ANNE: *You're a lunatic!*

A. C.: So I'm a lunatic? Who cares? Tell me where he keeps his files.

ANNE: Tell me what you were doing on the window ledge.

A. C.: I was spying on you. I wanted to hear how it was going. It went rotten. Anne, he hates your guts. Let's put him away. Tell me where he hides his files.

ANNE: What's in the file?

A. C.: I cannot believe this! Anne, we gotta move fast. Real fast. Very darn fast. I will tell you. I promise. But first tell me where the files are.

ANNE: What's in the file?

A. C.: It's a long story. Really. And we are out of time. *Tell me where the files are!*

ANNE: I don't like it when you yell at me.

A. C.: We don't have time.

ANNE: What's in the file?

A. C.: It's memos written between Zukasky and Barry.

ANNE: You're going to have to tell me a little more than that.

A. C.: They had a deal working on the Conklin bid.

ANNE: Keep going.

A. C.: Anne, there's no time.

ANNE: Then talk faster.

A. C.: *(He does. So does she.)* Barry was able to underbid everybody else on the Conklin Industries bid because Conklin asked for the wrong thing.

ANNE: More.

A. C.: Conklin specified stack architecture in their request for a bid. Do you know what stack architecture is?

ANNE: Sure. Stack architecture just means . . .

A. C.: *Don't explain it to me. I don't care what it is.* The only important part is that, for some reason, Conklin thought they wanted stack architecture. I don't know what that means, Barry doesn't know what it means and, apparently, Conklin

doesn't really know what it means either. But they asked for
it in the bid request.

ANNE: Okay. Keep going.

A. C.: So Barry shows the proposal to one of the programmers
who says that stack architecture is no damned good for what
Conklin wants. Conklin asked for the wrong thing.

ANNE: And . . .

A. C.: And every other company bidding changed the architecture for the purposes of their bid.

ANNE: That makes sense.

A. C.: To you and me, it makes sense. But Barry saw this as an
opening. He bid the job—*as requested*—and underbid everybody else. That is how we got Conklin Industries.

ANNE: But the system isn't going to work?

A. C.: Not with stack architecture. But, by the time Conklin
figures out they asked for the wrong thing, they will be into
us for millions. Millions. And when they ask us to make the
damn thing work, we will stick the screws to 'em. That was
what Zukasky and Barry worked out in order to get the
Conklin bid.

ANNE: Wait a minute! Wait a minute! We're building a system
that we know won't work?

A. C.: Right.

ANNE: That's illegal. It's fraud.

A. C.: Maybe, but hard to prove.

ANNE: They could sue us.

A. C.: Why? We're giving them what they asked for.

ANNE: But we know it won't work.

A. C.: How are they going to prove that? We'll say it's a hardware
problem. So tell me, Anne, in the two seconds we got left
before Barry comes in and has us fired, how is Conklin
Industries going to prove that we frauded them in order to
get their bid?

ANNE: I don't know.

A. C.: *They're going to prove it by producing the memos Barry wrote to
Zukasky as soon as you tell me where Barry hides his confidential
documents.*

ANNE: I don't know about this. I don't know about this. Is this
such a good idea?

A. C.: Don't start asking questions, Anne. The money is sitting on the table; all you gotta do is pick it up and put it in your purse. *Tell me where the files are!*

ANNE: What is it you are suggesting we do with them?

A. C.: God, you're as thick as Barry. We find the memos that went between Zukasky and Barry. We find the proof that Barry Mills bid that job knowing that the goddamn thing wouldn't work.

ANNE: You mean we find the file on Conklin . . .

A. C.: Right. The Conklin file . . .

ANNE: . . . and we show it to Marlino.

A. C.: *No!* Marlino sees that shit he'll give Barry a raise. How did you ever make it to Level Four?

ANNE: Then what do we want the Conklin file for?

A. C.: We're going to send it to Conklin. Once Conklin finds out he's been screwed—and he has the documents to prove it—he's going to call Marlino. Marlino is going to deny everything, they'll renegotiate the contract—maybe send it out for new bids—and, in order to save face with Conklin, Marlino will find a scapegoat. And the scapegoat will be . . .

ANNE: . . . Barry Mills.

A. C.: *Touchdown!* Now tell me where he keeps the file.

ANNE: Oooo. I'm not sure about this.

A. C.: Anne, why do you torment me like this? Just tell me.

ANNE: This is a bad thing you're suggesting. A very bad thing.

A. C.: What do I have to do? You want me to beg?

ANNE: This is a bad idea. Bad idea. We're going to get caught. We're going to go to jail.

A. C.: Anne, shut up.

ANNE: Bad idea. Bad, bad, bad. A security guard will catch us. We're going to get shot.

A. C.: Anne, stop it.

ANNE: We're all going to die. This is a bad thing. Bad, bad thing. Oh my God. We shouldn't be here.	A. C.: Anne, stop. We're not going to die. Stop babbling. Just tell me where the file is. Anne, the file. The file.

ANNE: *(A. C. slaps Anne to stop her from babbling. Anne, almost instantly, slugs A. C. in the face and sends him reeling. Then she resumes babbling.)* We're going to get caught. We're going to get fired. This is a bad thing we're doing.

A. C.: Hey! You hit me.

ANNE: You hit me first.

A. C.: I had to. You were getting hysterical.

ANNE: I am not hysterical. Don't you use that word with me. I am not hysterical.

A. C.: You were babbling.

ANNE: I still am. But I am not hysterical.

A. C.: You hit me hard.

ANNE: It was self-defense.

A. C.: I hit you softly. I barely even touched you.

ANNE: It wasn't that soft. You slapped me.

A. C.: You gave me a right cross.

ANNE: Slap me again and I'll kick your nuts up into your eye sockets. *(Back to babbling.)* Ooo, this is a bad thing . . .

A. C.: Okay. Okay. Take it easy.

ANNE: Let's just forget this whole thing and work for a different company. I can't deal with this. *(A. C. starts looking in preposterous places for the secret memos.)*

A. C.: Will you tell me if I'm getting close?

ANNE: God, make this work out. *(She opens the top drawer of the filing cabinet.)* Here.

A. C.: What?

ANNE: Is this what we're looking for?

A. C.: *(Peering into the drawer.)* In a filing cabinet? This man keeps top secret, confidential, news-of-this-will-end-your-career type documents in a filing cabinet?

ANNE: *(Removing the file.)* Well, this is it, isn't it?

A. C.: In a file folder labeled, "Confidential Files"?

ANNE: But this is it, isn't it?

A. C.: How can this be the same man who got the Conklin bid? Some days I think the man is a genius. And some days he's too stupid to tie his shoes.

ANNE: Is this it or isn't it?

A. C.: *Do you know how long I've been looking for this?*

ANNE: I found it, didn't I?

A. C.: All right. Put it in your purse.

ANNE: No. You take it.

A. C.: I don't have a purse. You take it.

ANNE: I'm not helping you anymore. You take it.

A. C.: *(Crossing to Anne's office and getting her purse.)* Just put the thing in your purse. I'll meet you after work. *(Barry is rattling his keys outside the door.)*

ANNE: Nnngaah! *(A. C. jams the file in Anne's purse and hides behind the drapes, closing them. Anne shoves the file in deeper just as Barry enters.)*

BARRY: What are you doing in here?

ANNE: Uh, uh, . . .

BARRY: What are you doing in here?

ANNE: I, . . . uh . . .

BARRY: You've closed my curtain.

ANNE: No. No I didn't. It uh . . .

BARRY: Yes you have. I left them open. Now they're closed.

ANNE: Well, that's true, it's just that . . .

BARRY: What have you been doing in here?

ANNE: Nothing. There's nothing.

BARRY: I think there's something.

ANNE: And seemingly there is. Something. Only it's not the case. In fact there is nothing. Even though it seems like something.

BARRY: You're babbling.

ANNE: I do that occasionally.

BARRY: And I think you're hiding something.

ANNE: No. Nothing to hide. It's nothing.

BARRY: *(Picking up his umbrella, he seems about ready to strike Anne.)* Something in this office, maybe.

ANNE: I'm telling you, it's nothing. You are making something out of nothing.

BARRY: *(He crosses to the exact location where we last saw A. C.)* Something behind the curtain? *(He winds up like a baseball batter and prepares to strike at whatever Poloniuses might be in hiding.)*

ANNE: *Hit the floor! (Barry swings his umbrella but hits only fabric. A. C. has apparently disappeared. Barry now looks toward Anne who is trying her best to cover.)* Wow. That was close. I thought you were going to break your window.

BARRY: You thought I was going to hit someone.

ANNE: Me? I thought you were going to break the window. Boy, would that be a mess.

BARRY: You shouted, "Hit the floor." You were trying to warn someone.

ANNE: No. I said that because, uh, I wanted you to hit the floor. Instead of the window. So I shouted out, "Hit the floor!" I was suggesting an alternative.

BARRY: You really want me to believe that?

ANNE: If you don't mind. *(He does mind. Persuaded that Polonius must have moved, he starts swinging furiously, up and down and from end to end until he has whacked every square foot of his curtain.)* Look out! *(But A. C. has vanished.)*

BARRY: You said, "Look out."

ANNE: *(As bewildered as Barry is.)* I did?

BARRY: I started hitting the curtains and you shouted, "Look out."

ANNE: I was worried about you.

BARRY: Who are you protecting?

ANNE: No one. Barry, get hold of yourself. You think there are spies hiding behind your curtains? That's ridiculous. The job is getting to you.

BARRY: Maybe. Maybe. Maybe it's the job. More likely, however, I think it is something else. *(He pauses a long time, waiting for Anne to respond.)*

ANNE: Are you getting ready to make a point?

BARRY: A man who lives with treachery learns to expect treachery, Ms. Desmond.

ANNE: I see.

BARRY: I left my curtains opened. I always leave my curtains opened. *(As he talks, he opens the curtains, revealing A. C. on the ledge. Barry's back is to A. C., however, so he does not see him. Anne, on the other hand, sees him all too well.)* Yet you insist that you did not close them.

ANNE: *(Trying not to panic.)* Mmmmaaaaa.

BARRY: No. Let me finish. In order for us to work together, I have to trust you. *(A. C. is tying a harness around his waist which he attaches to a safety line dangling from the floor above.)* But you lie to me, Ms. Desmond. So how can I trust you? This is a dangerous game you are playing.

ANNE: Nnngguh!

BARRY: Try to control yourself. I have asked you what you are doing here. *(A. C. begins to scale the wall up to twenty-three.)* Didn't I, Ms. Desmond?

ANNE: What?

BARRY: Didn't I ask you what you were doing here?

ANNE: *(Completely absorbed in A. C.'s ascent.)* Probably. I don't know. Is this important?

BARRY: Yes, damn it! I am making a point. Didn't I ask you what you were doing here?

ANNE: *(Before she can answer, she has to wait until A. C. has completely vanished from view. As soon as that happens, she relaxes and sits in the chair across from Barry.)* I'm sorry. What was the question?

BARRY: Ms. Desmond, what are you doing in my office when I explicitly told you I did not want you in my office?

ANNE: I, uh . . . *(She focuses on her purse which is open and sitting on Barry's desk.)* I left my purse in here. I just came to get my purse.

BARRY: Ms. Desmond, I demand a full explanation.

ANNE: *(In complete control now.)* Mr. Mills, you don't scare me. Why don't you just go about your job and leave me alone to do mine? You want to know the full story? The full story is, I came to get my purse and I resent being treated like a suspect. My conscience is clean.

BARRY: Is it?

ANNE: Yeah, Barry, it is. Is yours?

BARRY: *(Quite taken aback by the assertive Anne.)* Urg . . . bluk . . .

ANNE: If you are so paranoid that you think people are hiding behind your curtains, well, it sounds to me like that's a problem you're going to have to work out on your own. You know? Now, may I have my purse, Barry? Or is there something else you would like to discuss? *(Barry hands Anne her purse, but, before she can grasp it, A. C. falls past the window and is stopped violently when his safety line runs out of slack. He is left dangling by his line. Anne screams.)* Aaaaaaaaa!

BARRY: *(Bewildered.)* What? What?

ANNE: *(A. C. has recovered and is scaling the wall again.)* It was, uh, I thought I saw a spider on my purse.

BARRY: *(Dropping the purse, in a panic.)* Really?! Where?! God, I hate spiders. *(A. C. climbs out of sight again.)*

ANNE: He's gone now.

BARRY: What?

ANNE: He's gone now.

BARRY: What do you mean, he's gone now? Where did he go?

ANNE: He disappeared.

BARRY: To where?

ANNE: I don't know.

BARRY: Then he's still here.

ANNE: I don't think so.

BARRY: He's in the office somewhere.

ANNE: No. He went to a different office.

BARRY: How do you know that?

ANNE: I don't know. Does it matter? Just give me back my purse . . .

BARRY: *(Thinking as hard as Barry ever does.)* Ms. Desmond, I find your behavior to be suspicious. *(Abruptly.)* My curtains were open!

ANNE: I know, Barry. You've made that abundantly clear. Like the disappearing spider and Amelia Earhart, that is just going to be one of life's little mysteries.

BARRY: And I can't figure out why you would insist that you didn't close them when it's perfectly obvious that you did.

ANNE: Well, Barry, it's a brain buster, but what are you going to do? Can I have my purse now? *(Anne grabs hold of her purse. Barry grabs it too. They are now locked into a two man tug of war.)*

BARRY: *(Pulling the purse toward himself.)* And I don't recall your purse being on my desk.

ANNE: *(Pulling the purse toward herself.)* And, indeed, it shouldn't be on your desk. So if you can just give it back to me . . .

BARRY: *(Pulling the purse toward himself.)* So you're lying to me. And I want to know why.

ANNE: *(Pulling the purse toward herself.)* It's an imponderable, Barry. Can I have my purse?

BARRY: *(Pulling aggressively now.)* What's in here!

ANNE: *(Wrapping her body around the purse.)* Nothing! Nothing! It's my purse. Leave it alone! *(In the ensuing struggle, the purse bursts apart at the seams and the contents go flying. Those contents include, of course, the confidential file.)*

BARRY: Ms. Desmond, do you have an explanation for this?

ANNE: Ung, . . . blug, . . .

BARRY: This explains a lot. *(Kneeling by the strewn contents.)* This does not belong to you. It belongs to me. *(Anne is gasping for air.)* Mr. Zukasky gave this to me.

ANNE: Ulgh . . .

BARRY: *(Grabbing a pen from the contents.)* These cost a hundred and sixty-nine dollars a piece! This is not some plastic piece of Bic shit. This is a state of the art, air pump, steady flow fountain pen! *What the hell are you doing with my pen?*

ANNE: With your . . . *(Regular breaths.)* . . . pen?

BARRY: How can I trust you, Anne? How can I trust you? How can I trust you?

ANNE: I . . . *(Breath.)* . . . am . . . *(Breath.)* . . . not sure. *(Breath.)*

BARRY: Gather up your stuff and get out of here.

ANNE: You want me to . . . *(She gestures vaguely toward the stuff.)* . . . gather this stuff?

BARRY: Yes.

ANNE: *(She gathers all the contents, leaving the file folder for last.)* All this stuff, right? Gather it up and get out of your sight.

BARRY: Yes, Annie. *(She grabs the folder and heads for her office.)* And, Ms. Desmond . . .

ANNE: Yes, Mr. Mills?

BARRY: I feel I have to state that I am not at all sure how much longer you and I can work together.

ANNE: I guess . . . *(Breath.)* . . . time will tell.

SCENE 7

It is a few days later. Marlino is standing with his back to the audience, gazing at the south side. Someone—A. C., in fact—is sitting with his back to the audience, gazing at Marlino.

MARLINO: One of the Chinamen brings out this metal hoop. And all around the hoop were these knives. Big knives. And the sharp edge is facing the Chinaman. And the tips are all pointed at the center of the hoop. Then they set the whole damn thing on fire. And these Chinamen would jump through those knives and the fire with nothing to protect them from getting cut. Not even a shirt. They were amazing.

A. C.: Amazing.

MARLINO: Yes. Yes they were. *(Marlino turns to face A. C.)* Barry Mills no longer works here.

A. C.: You know, I heard that.

MARLINO: How would you have heard that?

A. C.: I keep my ear to the ground. *(Marlino regards A. C. for a while.)*

MARLINO: He was . . . disappointing. I mean, I think the world of Barry. He was tough. And shrewd. And a hard worker. But he . . . I don't know how to put it. He . . .

A. C.: He got caught, sir.

MARLINO: Well, yes. I suppose that's it. *(Beat.)* I just had a meeting with Anne.

A. C.: And how did that go?

MARLINO: I'm not sure. She was a little vague.

A. C.: Muddled thinking. It's the way she is. There's nothing you can do about it.

MARLINO: She sort of implied that you might know something about our problems with Conklin.

A. C.: Muddled thinking.

MARLINO: Do you know something about our problems with Conklin?

A. C.: We got a problem with Conklin. That's all I really know.

MARLINO: A big problem, don't you think?

A. C.: But nothing we can't handle.

MARLINO: You think we can handle it?

A. C.: Call Conklin. Tell him Zukasky's dead and Barry's on welfare. Tell him your new director of sales is A. C. Tattums and he is on a plane right now headed for Cincinnati. I'll tell Conklin we were stunned—absolutely stunned—to discover unethical behavior on the part of our recently departed sales department and that we will deliver a working system— as promised—with architecture that will work—at the price quoted. He'll stick with us. He's in too deep to back out now. That's what I'd do. *(Pause.)* If you're asking.

MARLINO: What would it cost us to develop a working system?

A. C.: We'll be okay.

MARLINO: You act like I'm going to offer you Barry's job. Did I say anything about offering you Barry's job?

A. C.: No. You didn't. I was guessing. Just a guess. It's your choice to make, of course. And appropriately so. Only, I think—just my opinion now—that I am really the only logical choice.

MARLINO: The only logical choice?

A. C.: Just my opinion.

MARLINO: You're saying that in this whole city, which is filled with guys, most of whom are salesmen, you think you are the only logical choice?

A. C.: If you just needed a guy, you could get a guy. You want a salesman; go hire a salesman. You don't need just a guy. You need a guy you can trust. That narrows the field of candidates considerably.

MARLINO: What about Anne, uh, you know . . .

A. C.: Desmond?

MARLINO: Yeah. Her. She's been here five years or something.

A. C.: Ten.

MARLINO: Ten. That sort of gives her seniority, don't you think?

A. C.: Well, Anne would be a good choice, if you think you can trust her.

MARLINO: You don't think I can trust Anne?

A. C.: I'll trust your judgement on that.

MARLINO: My judgement?

A. C.: I mean, she's been here ten years without a promotion; I'm sure you've had your reasons.

MARLINO: My reasons . . .

A. C.: I *know* it's not because she's a woman.

MARLINO: Well, no.

A. C.: So something else must have told you not to trust her.

MARLINO: Trust her? To do what?

A. C.: To keep your name out of this mess.

MARLINO: My name?

A. C.: That's why you need someone you can trust.

MARLINO: Why should my name be involved?

A. C.: It shouldn't. That's exactly my point.

MARLINO: Why would you say that I'm involved?

A. C.: I think I am saying exactly the opposite.

MARLINO: That I'm not involved. That's what you're saying?

A. C.: That's what I'm saying. You can trust me there.

MARLINO: I can trust you?

A. C.: Thank you, sir. I'm glad you think so.

MARLINO: No, that was a question. I was asking if I can trust you.

A. C.: I appreciate your asking. And I hope to earn your confidence in me.

MARLINO: My, uh, confidence . . . well, good.

A. C.: *(Putting his arm around Marlino.)* Can I tell you something, Henry? In confidence.

MARLINO: Well, uh . . .

A. C.: This is a really nice tie you're wearing. And I know you won't take this wrong . . .

MARLINO: I won't take this wrong?

A. C.: I know you won't, Henry, because you know you can trust me.

MARLINO: Uh, . . .

A. C.: The tie makes no statement. It's too conservative. If you wore a bolder pattern it would tell people you were a bolder guy.

MARLINO: A bolder pattern? You mean like . . .

A. C.: *(He hands Marlino a box from Marshall Fields.)* Now I know you won't take this wrong . . .

MARLINO: You bought me a tie?

A. C.: I knew you'd understand.

MARLINO: *(Looking at the tie.)* What are these?

A. C.: They're giraffes, Henry.

MARLINO: Wow. *(Holding the tie up to his neck.)* Certainly makes a statement.

A. C.: It's very nice, Henry. You have excellent taste.

MARLINO: Yeah? You don't think it's a little garish?

A. C.: Bold. It's bold. There's a difference between garish and bold, you know.

MARLINO: You think this is bold?

A. C.: Trust me.

MARLINO: Come see me this afternoon, A. C. We'll work out your contract.

A. C.: Yes sir.

MARLINO: You know, Barry was contracted at . . .

A. C.: . . . twenty thousand a year less than this position ought to pay.

MARLINO: *(Pause.)* Of course. *(Marlino exits. A. C. sits behind the desk and puts his feet up. Unseen, behind him, someone falls past the window and comes to a violent stop when she runs out of slack. It is Anne, dressed in her new suit. She dangles from her line for a while, trying to regain the ledge as the lights fade to black.)*

END

Jane Martin

Cementville

Cementville was directed in 1991 by Jon Jory with the following cast:

DWAYNE PARDEE	Jim Petersmith
TIGER	Suzanna Hay
NOLA	Corliss Preston
DANI	Annette Helde
NETTY	Adale O'Brien
LESSA	Kimberley LaMarque
BIGMAN	Fred Major
MOTHER CROCKER	Sally Parrish
DOTTIE	Peggity Price
DOLLY	Cynthia Carle
MISS HARMON	Jessica Jory
ONE-EYE DENEAUVE	Bob Burrus
KID	Lex Monson
EDDIE	Tom Stechschulte

Scene Design	Paul Owen
Lighting Design	Karl Haas
Sound Design	Darron West
Property Master	Ron Riall
Casting—NYC	Jay Binder
Costume Design	Marcia Dixcy
Fight Director	David Boushey
Stage Manager	Lori M. Doyle

| Assistant Stage Manager | Susan R. Fenty |
| Dramaturg | Michael Bigelow Dixon |

Cementville by Jane Martin. © 1991 by Jane Martin. Reprinted by permission of Alexander Speer, Trustee. All inquiries should be addressed to Actors Theatre of Louisville, 316 West Main St., Louisville, KY 40202-4218.

CHARACTERS

Dwayne Pardee: 45, a wolf in wimp's clothing.
Tiger: 35, at the end of a long rope.
Nola: 22, all the shrewd innocence of youth.
Dani: 35, a tough-talking frog in a small pond.
Netty: 40, mothers everything that moves.
Bigman: 40, promoter, wrestler, hustler, fool.
Lessa: 32, athlete in a cul-de-sac.
Mother: 50, don't tread on me.
Dottie: 28, wild beauty, bad karma.
Dolly: 26, sex and madness reconciled.
One-Eye Deneauve: 45, country nightmares.
Miss Harmon: 17, a little terrified order in chaos.
Eddie: 42, the Frankenstein monster.
Kid: 70, a boxer with a world view.

PLACE:

The locker room of a boxing arena in Cementville, Tennessee.

TIME:

The present.

Cementville

ACT ONE

An empty, run-down locker room in an unused boxing arena in a small industrial city in Tennessee. Peeling plaster, water stains. Portions of the ceiling bubble ominously. One door with a twist lock leads in from an outside hallway. One door leads into a shower room the delicate would avoid. One door stands open revealing a broom closet partially filled with rotten, rolled up venetian blinds and a decaying mop and bucket. Along the walls of the room stand lockers of two distinct periods. A ceiling fixture with three naked bulbs provides most of the illumination. Above the lockers there are posters ranging back to the 1950s naming fighters an aficionado might recognize. Some, mold has obliterated, some have inexplicably survived. The floor is littered with beer cans, Coke cups, newspapers and nasty dreck. Several lockers stand open, revealing their own distressing mess. A small man in his forties walks past the door. A moment. He returns and stands framed in the doorway looking in.

DWAYNE: Geez. *(Enters and stares around him.)* Geez, I don't know . . .

A woman's voice is heard in the outside hall.

TIGER'S VOICE: Anybody home?

Dwayne starts out the door, realizes he is trapped, moves into the broom closet and closes himself in. Tiger appears in the doorway. She wears a tank top and jeans with an Elvis Presley jacket that reads "Taking Care of Business" on the back. She carries a flight bag, a cat-carrying case and a beer. She has a rolled up comic in her back pocket. She is around thirty-five. She surveys the room.

TIGER: Son-of-a-bitch! *(She kicks a can.)* Hey, kid! *(Turns on light.)* Jeee-sus.

A young girl enters. She wears shorts and a heavy metal T-shirt. She carries a push broom. She is seventeen or eighteen.

NOLA: Yo.

TIGER: We supposed to dress in here?

NOLA: He said.

TIGER: We supposed to do it standin' up? *(Walking into the shower room.)*

NOLA: Huh?

TIGER: Benches.

NOLA: Right.

TIGER: You got benches?

NOLA: To sit down.

TIGER: Yeah.

NOLA: I don't know.

TIGER: *(Half pleased.)* There's a dead rat in the shower room.

NOLA: Showers don't work anyway.

TIGER: You seen a big man in a suit?

NOLA: On the pay phone two hours.

TIGER: Damn.

NOLA: Real agitated.

TIGER: Every time there's a man on a phone my life gets screwed up. You know was it a parole officer?

NOLA: No ma'am. *(Indicating the cat case.)* What's that?

TIGER: Family.

NOLA: *(Bending to look in.)* Kitty, kitty.

TIGER: It's a Chihuahua. French kisses better than a man. You got a cigarette?

NOLA: Sure. *(Offers one.)*

TIGER: They use this crap hole for anything?

NOLA: Not since Jesus was a pup.

TIGER: Yeah? Look, go find the big man and tell him I don't dress standin' up. And get me a beer. Make that a six-pack.

NOLA: You the one on the poster?

TIGER: No, I ain't on the poster.

Another woman enters. She is in her late twenties and prettier in a worn way. She wears a sweater and a beret. She carries a container of fast food, a Pepsi, french fries and a half-eaten burrito.

TIGER: She's on the poster.

DANI: *(Looking at the room.)* Are you kiddin' me?

TIGER: What's your name, kid?

NOLA: Nola.

TIGER: Nola, Tarzana Queen of the Jungle. Tarzana, Nola.

NOLA: Hey.

DANI: I'm not doing this.

TIGER: *(Experimentally opening lockers.)* Yeah?

DANI: I got a cleanliness clause.

TIGER: Rubbers. There's used rubbers in this locker.

DANI: Great.

TIGER: Well, I'm glad somebody was havin' fun.

NOLA: I was gonna, you know, sweep up, you know, but, whoa, he's got me hoppin'. *(No one speaks, she starts to leave.)* Six-pack.

DANI: Nola.

NOLA: Yo.

DANI: I'm Dani. You want my autograph?

NOLA: Yeah.

DANI: Clean this up.

NOLA: Yes ma'am. Soon as I . . .

DANI: Now.

NOLA: The big man, he . . .

DANI: I'm paid to hurt people, you understand.

A moment. Nola sweeps.

DANI: Tiger. You are drivin' me nuts.

TIGER: I like lookin' in lockers.

DANI: How's that rat doin'?

TIGER: Chihuahua. Bes' goddamn roommate I ever had.

DANI: Bigman says you bring her in here he's gonna eat her.

TIGER: Be the last bite he ever takes. She don't like that Motel 6. Got a nosebleed. *(She takes her out.)*

DANI: You get any sleep?

TIGER: Not a hell of a lot.

DANI: Eighth graders. They oughta electrocute 'em, not put 'em in a motel. Where's Bigman?

TIGER: On a pay phone.

DANI: Where's his brother, Eddie the asshole?

TIGER: Cruiserweight Champion of America?

DANI: Ain't that a bitch? Crowd loves them cruiserweights. I gotta see a gynecologist.

TIGER: Oughta cut down to two room clerks a week.

NOLA: Want me to wipe out some lockers?

DANI: Yeah. *(To Tiger.)* Where else am I gonna find a man by the time the bus gets in?

TIGER: Forget it.

DANI: I like to stay in working order.

TIGER: *(Short laugh.)* I'd rather rust.

DANI: There's a dead rat in the showers.

NOLA: Showers don't work anyway.

DANI: Great. You want the other half of this cardboard burrito?

TIGER: *(Takes it.)* Sure. What town are we in? *(Puts her dog back in the cat case.)*

DANI: Deepest Tennessee.

TIGER: No, really, what town?

DANI: Hey, Tiger, I really *don't* know. What town were we in yesterday?

NOLA: Cementville. You're in Cementville, Tennessee.

Dani and Tiger snort.

DANI: I'm in Cementville, Tennessee, with the All American Wrestling Federation Shower of Stars Tour. *(To Tiger.)* You got aspirin?

NOLA: How many stars?

TIGER: What was that, kid? *(Getting the aspirin.)*

NOLA: How many stars we in for tonight?

DANI: Well, kid, that's somethin' the rubes never know. You got five bucks?

TIGER: Hey.

DANI: This is a *fan,* Tiger. What separates the fans from the rubes is inside dope. You a fan, Nola?

NOLA: Yes ma'am.

DANI: You got five bucks?

NOLA: I got twenty bucks.

TIGER: Don't let her hustle you.

DANI: Five bucks I answer three questions. *(Takes the aspirin without water.)*

TIGER: I'm going for the big man. *(Stops by Nola. Gives money.)* This is for the beer. The buck's a tip. Keep an eye on that case. *(She exits.)*

DANI: She got a steel plate in her head.

NOLA: No.

DANI: Yeah. I fucked Tom Cruise.

NOLA: Yeah?

DANI: Yeah.

Nola pulls out her money, peels off a five, holds it out. Dani takes it.

DANI: O.K. The question was how many stars? You got a cigarette?

NOLA: Sure.

DANI: Cementville, Tennessee, huh? *(Nola nods.)* You ever heard of Madison Square Garden? *(Nola shakes her head "no.")* Well, I played there and now I'm playin' here.

NOLA: Wow!

DANI: O.K., we got the main event, right? Irish Bob McCarthy vs. Stosha "The Wild Man" Oronovsky.

NOLA: Whew!

DANI: That's Bigman doin' the Irish an his brother Eddie the asshole doin' the Ruskie. They fought for the championship eighty-three times this year.

NOLA: *(Shocked.)* Brothers?

DANI: Yeah.

NOLA: Irish Bob?

DANI: Well, he ain't Irish and he ain't Bob, an he owes me four weeks salary, the scumbag. Anyway, there's those two plus me, Tiger, Netty and Angelessa. O.K. We open up with me wrestlin' Tiger. Then Netty wrestles Angelessa. Then Tiger wrestles Angelessa masked. On like that 'til the combinations run out. Girls do tag team, then Bigman an the asshole do the Cruiserweight Championship, an we grab some showers an go out an get wasted.

NOLA: *(A pause.)* Just six stars?

DANI: Yeah, right.

NOLA: Doin' the whole thing?

DANI: Six, yeah.

NOLA: Who's the woman in the iron mask?

DANI: Sometimes Angelessa, sometimes me.

NOLA: Shoot. She was my favorite an she ain't even a person.

DANI: It's a bitch, ain't it? You got one more question for the five bucks.

NOLA AND DANI: How can I get started in professional wrestling?

DANI: One: it's major shit work for bad pay. Two: gives you foot fungus. Three: wrestlers got an attitude an bad knees. Now get the hell out of here, I'm tired of you.

NOLA: O.K.

As she starts to leave, Netty, a motherly woman in her forties, enters with Angelessa, a powerful black wrestler in her late twenties dressed in a sweatsuit with a college name and "Property of the Athletic Dept." emblazoned on it. She is carrying a large duffel bag. She wears a Walkman.

NETTY: Oh my God, did we have a good, good, good, good dinner. Country cookin'. Green beans, darlin', so much good bacon fat they kep' on slippin' out of my mouth onto the floor. Hi, Dani. *(To Nola.)* Who's this pretty thing?

NOLA: Hey.

DANI: Helpin' clean up this pigsty.

NETTY: *(Cheerful.)* Ooooooo, it's nasty, isn't it? What's your name, darlin'?

NOLA: Nola.

NETTY: Uh-huh, that's a pretty name. You straight or gay, honey?

NOLA: Huh?

NETTY: Boys or girls?

Nola stares at her nonplussed.

NETTY: Well, never mind, you'll get it figured out. You seen Eddie?

DANI: Haven't seen him.

NETTY: Well, I'm worried about that vicious ol' fart. No answer in his room.

DANI: Forgot to brush his teeth an died of the smell.

NETTY: Oh, now. He's our meal ticket an we got to worry over him. *(To Nola.)* Darlin', you gonna get us a bench to sit down on? I'm a big ol' fat lady, I got to have me a bench. Y'all want some Black Jack chewin' gun? Angelessa? *(To Dani.)* Angelessa ain't talkin', she's in a depression.

DANI: She's always in a depression.

NETTY: Oh, she is not. *(To Nola.)* Scoot. Shoo. You help us out now, O.K.?

Nola exits. Netty speaks loudly because of Lessa's Walkman.

DANI: What happened to your eye?

LESSA: Somebody messed with me.

NETTY: You smile, the ol' world smiles with you.

LESSA: I got about two hundred aggravated reasons to kill people. You smile.

DANI: *(Pushing Lessa's duffel bag with her foot.)* Goin' somewhere?

LESSA: Get your foot off my bag.

DANI: You cop a fade, you owe me fifteen bucks.

NETTY: You know, you got me thinkin' now . . . what if the asshole O.D.'s in his room? I mean, he's a freebaser, right? Wasn't he freebasin'? He was. Shoot. That just about gets me worried.

DANI: Bigman said he was clean.

NETTY: Well, they're brothers, honey. They got to speak well of each other.

Nola enters dragging two benches.

NETTY: You are a dreamboat, sweetie. That's a real nice bench. Have yourself some Black Jack Gum, it's refreshin'.

Nola takes a piece.

NETTY: *(To Nola.)* You seen the costume trunks, darlin'? *(To Dani.)* Didn't I just see them in the hall?

Lessa nods, Netty speaks to Nola.

NETTY: You wanta drag those trunks on in here, honey? See, I'm a fat lady an I got a bad back.

Nola goes to do her bidding. Tiger re-enters.

NETTY: Tiger, which way I go for the coin telephone?
TIGER: Bigman's on it.
NETTY: Only one?
TIGER: Only one I saw.
NETTY: You seen the asshole?
TIGER: Not since I screwed him.
NETTY: You did not?
TIGER: Two years ago.
NETTY: You saw him on the bus last night.
TIGER: I see him, but I don' *see* him. You know what I mean?

Nola drags a costume trunk into the room. Lessa takes off her Walkman. Tiger reads her comic.

NETTY: Well, nobody has seen him and that's what I'm talking about. You think I should get Bigman?
LESSA: *(Gets down to do stretching exercises.)* He usually on time.
DANI: Oooooo, you gettin' on that floor?
TIGER: There's bad shit on that floor, Lessa.
LESSA: I got to stretch.
DANI: Well, I'm not stretchin' on that floor.
LESSA: You never did.
DANI: Now don't get on my back, Lessa. I got infected ovaries. *(Dani lights up a cigarette.)*
NETTY: Well, you poor thing. *(Nola drags in a second trunk.)* Ain't that nice? You know we gonna be in bed without a vibrator the asshole don't show up.
TIGER: *(A crooked grin.)* Nice talk, Mama.
NETTY: Them fans wanna see them Champion Cruiserweights.
TIGER: *(To Nola.)* Wanna pull that thing over here? *(Tiger gets their first aid kit, a red fishing tackle box, out of the trunk.)*
NETTY: The rubes be wantin' their money back, we be in bed without a vibrator.
LESSA: Don't call 'em rubes.
NETTY: The fans . . .

LESSA: That's right.

DANI: They're rubes.

LESSA: Fans!

NETTY: Now you two, be nice.

NOLA: 'Scuse me.

NETTY: What's that, darlin'?

NOLA: *(To Tiger.)* I'm goin' for the beer.

LESSA: *(From the floor.)* No rat dogs or alcohol in the dressin' room.

TIGER: The dog goes where I go. I'm in Cementville, Tennessee. I got bad ribs, dog's got a nosebleed, I ain't been paid an I'm gettin' a six-pack. *(Tiger takes a large pill bottle out of the first aid box and swallows several, dry.)*

DANI: *(To Lessa.)* How come you carryin' your bag?

LESSA: Thought I'd let you do my laundry.

NETTY: See now, we're gettin' bad tempered 'cause of this money thing. I knew it.

DANI: Damn straight.

NETTY: So, I think Bigman . . .

DANI: I say we get cash before the show.

LESSA: An don't call it a show.

DANI: Lessa, you a real pain in the ass when you're depressed.

LESSA: I'm an athlete. I don't do a show.

DANI: O.K. I say we get cash before we do tonight's Olympics.

TIGER: He ain't gonna pay us before the show.

DANI: Well, if the asshole overdosed he ain't gonna pay us afterwards.

NETTY: Now, I think y'all ought to have a stick of Black Jack Gum . . .

DANI: I'm just tired of his kickin' our butts all over the lot.

LESSA: Kept you off the street for three years.

DANI: I told you I don't like that.

NETTY: Well now, Bigman, he got various traits . . .

TIGER: No kiddin'.

NETTY: There's good an bad . . .

DANI: I'm talkin' about . . .

NETTY: . . . Take into consideration . . .

DANI: Paychecks!

NETTY: . . . Nobody here . . .

DANI: Lessa?

NETTY: . . . Starvin' to death.

DANI: Four weeks, right Lessa? *(Lessa doesn't answer.)* Four weeks, right? *(Lessa keeps warming up.)* You didn't get a paycheck, right?

LESSA: I'm into my warm-up, O.K.? Gettin' my game face together, you dig? I like to keep my mind in the ring.

DANI: You better not have got a paycheck, Lessa. I don't care what Olympics you was in, you better not a got a paycheck.

LESSA: I had a paycheck, you'd be lookin' at air.

NETTY: All I'm sayin' is I'm worried about Eddie.

TIGER: Eddie?

DANI: The asshole.

TIGER: His name's Eddie?

DANI: I thought you screwed him?

TIGER: Yeah, I screwed him but I always called him asshole.

LESSA: *(A grin.)* You kiddin'?

TIGER: Seemed to energize him.

They laugh.

NETTY: 'Cause if he's hurt or sick or somethin', well . . .

TIGER AND LESSA: "We're just in bed without a vibrator."

They laugh.

DANI: O.K., but I got financial obligations.

LESSA: Still payin' your pimp?

Dani turns, infuriated. Tiger steps between Dani and Lessa.

TIGER: Enough, O.K. Jesus, I hate women.

NETTY: Must be a full moon, I swear. *(Netty goes about taping a mirror to the front of the locker she has chosen.)*

TIGER: Let's just get the card on an get us out of this pisshole.

DANI: Easy for you to say.

TIGER: *(Points to the dog.)* Gotta get her to a vet an get me some orthopedics, O.K.? An that sure as hell ain't here.

NOLA: *(Enters.)* Six-pack. Had to go a distance.

TIGER: *(To Lessa and Dani.)* Everybody cool?

NOLA: Wasn't hardly nuthin' open. Corona, O.K.?

TIGER: Corona? Damn. That ain't that Japanese stuff, is it?

NETTY: Ooooo, Corona, that's good.

TIGER: 'Cause they put sugar in that shit, it's nasty.

NETTY: Noooo, honey, ol' Mexico. Yes ma'am. I had some good times on that beer.

Tiger uncaps the beer with her teeth.

DANI: Now we got to hear about the Jai Lai player's wife.

NETTY: She had three breasts, and they were perfectly formed.

Bigman enters. He wears a green polyester suit. He looks like a wrestler.

BIGMAN: *(Taking over as is his want.)* O.K., ladies, we got to have a little powwow here.

NETTY: You havin' a hard day, honey? *(She pats his shoulder.)*

BIGMAN: *(Seeing the case. To Tiger.)* You got that frog-dog in here?

NETTY: *(To Nola.)* You want to get us some washin' water, darlin'?

BIGMAN: Goddamit, Tiger, hand it over.

TIGER: *(Low, eyes burning.)* You would regret touchin' this dog.

BIGMAN: *(Draws back.)* Hotel called, Tiger. Seems you forgot to pay a check in the coffee shop.

TIGER: The milk was sour, the roast beef was green, and the toast was wet.

BIGMAN: We got to be good citizens, dammit.

TIGER: I ate that sandwich, I'd be a dead citizen.

BIGMAN: Pay the friggin' bill, alright?

DANI: What she 'sposed to pay for it with?

BIGMAN: Look, I got a lot of problems, I don't wanta hear this minute shit.

DANI: Don't sweat the small stuff, right?

BIGMAN: Yeah, I . . .

DANI: Get to the heart of the problem.

BIGMAN: Tell me about it.

DANI: Paychecks.

Bigman, as if by reflex, hits her with his open hand across the head. Not on the face but above the ear.

TIGER: *(Knowing what's coming, leans her head against a locker.)* Damn.

DANI: You hit me, Bigman.

BIGMAN: No, I didn't.

DANI: You hit me in the head.

BIGMAN: *(To the rest.)* Sit down and listen up.

DANI: Nobody crosses that line. I don't take that from no fuckin' nobody. You hear me?

LESSA: Chill out.

DANI: *(To Lessa.)* Butt out.

Tiger sings a couple of snatches of "Me and My Shadow."

BIGMAN: Hey.

DANI: Hey, what?

BIGMAN: I didn't hit you.

DANI: Yeah?

BIGMAN: *(To the others.)* You hear this?

DANI: *(To the others.)* He hit me.

BIGMAN: You ever have a coach, Dani?

DANI: Get outta here.

BIGMAN: Football? Basketball? Any contact sport?

DANI: What the hell does that have to do with . . .

BIGMAN: You ever played a fuckin' sport you'd know what a coach was.

DANI: You hit me!

BIGMAN: I cuffed you.

DANI: Yeah, so?

BIGMAN: So the cuff is how the coach gets the athlete's attention. The cuff says wake up you are being communicated with with information.

DANI: The information is . . .

BIGMAN: Hold it . . .

DANI: You owe me four weeks' salary.

He cuffs her again. She goes after him and after a brief scuffle is subdued and held by Tiger and Netty.

DANI: Touch me again I'll tear your hand off.

BIGMAN: I got no time for this.

LESSA: Can I ask you a question?

BIGMAN: In a minute. Dani, Dani, your problem is inappropriate behavior. Like you don't pee in a blender.

DANI: *(To Tiger and Netty.)* Let go of me.

BIGMAN: An athlete lives physical, focused, physical. Your sprinter . . .

DANI: Off me!

BIGMAN: Your sprinter, short distance, waiting for the start, Chicago could fall down they don't hear it. You want to communicate mentally with an athlete . . . *(He touches her shoulder.)*

DANI: Don't touch me . . .

BIGMAN: . . . You gotta cuff 'em. That's all I'm sayin'. It's like an alarm bell, an idea is coming. *(He notices his suit.)* Look at that? You got oil or some crap on my jacket. For *this* I *should* hit you. Jeez. Looka this! I cuff you like a coach. I never hit you. Is that clear?

Dani walks over and hits the locker.

BIGMAN: Is that clear?

She hits it again.

BIGMAN: Is that clear?

DANI: Yeah, it's clear.

BIGMAN: Good! *(To Lessa. Nola enters with bucket of water.)* What's your question?

LESSA: We gonna wrestle?

BIGMAN: O.K., listen up. What is that, beer? *(No reaction.)* Is that a beer I see before me? What's my position on beer in the dressing room?

LESSA: No beer.

BIGMAN: That's right. Whose beer is this?

TIGER: My beer.

BIGMAN: O.K., I'm makin' an exception; gimme a beer.

Tiger tosses him one.

NETTY: *(Patting her.)* You doin' real good.

Nola exits.

BIGMAN: What is this, Bulgarian beer? Jeeminy. You don't buy American and you piss about the country goin' down the tubes. *(He takes a hit.)* Not bad.
NETTY: *(To Dani.)* Forget it.
DANI: *(Calmer, but still pissed.)* You forget it.
BIGMAN: O.K., you got your ears on? Hey, Lessa. *(She still stretches.)* Lessa. Jeez. Take a break, O.K.? *(More beer.)* O.K., you're all like family. You know that. You tour with me, you're family.
NETTY: O.K.
BIGMAN: O.K., right. We got a situation here.

Nola starts pulling in a dressing room unit with two mirrors surrounded by lights. It rolls.

BIGMAN: Hey! You?
NOLA: Yo.
BIGMAN: Not now.
NOLA: You said.
BIGMAN: Not now. Read my lips.

Nola pulls it back out.

BIGMAN: O.K., we got a situation. Now, we're in . . . where are we?
TIGER: Tennessee.
BIGMAN: I know we're in Tennessee. What am I, a moron? O.K., where in Tennessee?
TIGER: Cementville.
BIGMAN: O.K., Cementville. A good wrestlin' town. They had Wednesday night fights here . . . years, O.K., a town promoted by Bill Walla, O.K.? He don't take care of business, I get us the date. The strong survive, right?
NETTY: That's right.
BIGMAN: Right. O.K. We do big, or even we do good, I get his other Tennessee dates. See the picture? Maybe next year we

take all his dates get rich. You followin' me? O.K. We got a situation. My brother. *(He takes off his hat.)* An all-star. A man put six years in the big time . . . World Wrestling Federation . . . A man puts butts in the seats, a draw, in other words. A headliner . . .

Dani has put up her hand.

BIGMAN: What?
DANI: I gotta go potty.
BIGMAN: No.
DANI: No?
BIGMAN: Later.
DANI: Later what? I gotta go.
BIGMAN: Dani. The Gettysburg Address, Pearl Harbor there are times you don't go potty.
LESSA: Bigman?
BIGMAN: Yeah, what?
LESSA: They got no fights in here Wednesday nights.
BIGMAN: So?
LESSA: You said . . .
BIGMAN: I said in the town. Hertzburger Arena.
DANI: Yeah? So why aren't we there?
BIGMAN: 'Cause they bumped Billy Walla for a fuckin' ice show.
DANI: So you book the Hilton here?
BIGMAN: Hey, this is a famous fight joint. Jake Lamotta, Ezzard Charles.
DANI: So what are they, cavemen?
BIGMAN: Willie Pep, Kid Gavilan, Archie Moore. This here is a place for worship. Gods, I'm not exaggeratin', gods have spilled blood here.
DANI: *(Wrinklin' her nose.)* And apparently piss.

Tiger laughs.

BIGMAN: Knock that off. Hey, Dani. *(He ticks the following off on his fingers.)* Who the hell were you? Who the hell are you? And who the fuck are you gonna be when I dump you? *(There is silence in the room.)* We make the date work, next time we're in the Hertzberger Arena. *(He looks at his watch.)* What am I talking here? I'm bleedin' time here. My brother . . . *(He pauses, a strange look on his face.)* My brother is indisposed.

NETTY: I knew it.

LESSA: Damn shame.

DANI: Whatsa matter he can't fight drunk?

In one move, Bigman reaches down and puts Dani up against the lockers. Women scatter.

TIGER: Whoa!

NETTY: Bigman!

There is a frozen moment. Then, strangely, Bigman puts both fists to his forehead and sobs.

BIGMAN: Oh man. Oh man.

NETTY: Hey, baby . . .

TIGER: O.K., Dani?

BIGMAN: That man . . .

NETTY: Come on, honey.

BIGMAN: Oh man.

NETTY: Sit down, darlin' . . .

TIGER: Take a load off, Bigman.

BIGMAN: It's O.K.

NETTY: Take a hit on the beer.

TIGER: You want a shot?

BIGMAN: Gimme room . . . back off.

TIGER: *(To Lessa.)* Inside my bag there, half pint . . .

LESSA: Not me.

TIGER: *(To Netty.)* Wild Turkey.

NETTY: One-half pint.

BIGMAN: I'm O.K., get the hell off me. *(He stands up.)*

LESSA: *(To Dani.)* You O.K.?

NETTY: There.

TIGER: *(Bringing him the almost empty half pint.)* Try this.

BIGMAN: I'm in fuckin' AA, Tiger.

TIGER: You was drinkin' beer.

BIGMAN: Beer ain't booze. You don't hand a half pint to a man in AA.

TIGER: My mistake. *(Takes bottle.)*

BIGMAN: Have a little goddamned consideration.

NETTY: Well, she's sorry. She is. Now you sit down an drink your beer.

BIGMAN: This ain't booze. They give this to nursin' mothers.

NOLA: *(Enters dragging the makeup mirrors.)* Comin' through.

BIGMAN: Hey!

NOLA: Yeah?

BIGMAN: I said when I said.

NOLA: You said fifteen minutes.

BIGMAN: What are you? Hearin' things? Take it out in the hall. Smoke a joint. I'll call you.

Nola drags the mirrors back out.

BIGMAN: *(Getting emotional again.)* Jesus, Eddie, I don't know . . .

NETTY: Easy, big fella.

BIGMAN: My own brother . . .

NETTY: He's not dead is he, darlin'?

BIGMAN: Some bitch . . . I got one hundred bucks . . . no questions . . . anybody knows who was in his room last night.

Silence. Lessa turns back to her locker.

BIGMAN: Lessa?

DANI: Some escort whore.

BIGMAN: You saw?

DANI: A local. Blond wig.

BIGMAN: Where?

DANI: Saw her in the hallway, from the back.

BIGMAN: Yeah?

DANI: So?

BIGMAN: With him?

DANI: Yeah, he was tanked.

BIGMAN: I find her, she's dead. I find her I cut off her tits. I pull her inside out by her tongue. This is Eddie, my brother. Blood of my blood. *(He pounds his chest.)* I'm very full.

NETTY: Of course you are.

BIGMAN: I got feelings up to here.

DANI: O.K.

NETTY: Strong feelin's.
BIGMAN: Yeah.

A pause.

TIGER: We cancel?
BIGMAN: No, we don't cancel! Whatta ya mean cancel? I'm like
   Jackie-Fuckin'-Kennedy. I'm a professional.
LESSA: Let me wrestle you.
BIGMAN: Get outta here.
LESSA: Bikini. I'll do it in a bikini.
BIGMAN: Get outta here.
LESSA: I'll do it straight.

A pause.

BIGMAN: Straight?
LESSA: Real.
BIGMAN: Real? What are you, a brain transplant?
LESSA: I bench press 300. I'm an Olympic athlete.
DANI: Yeah, 19th in the shot put.
LESSA: *(To Dani.)* Yeah, well, I was there. Where were you?
BIGMAN: Ladies, demeanor, O.K.?
DANI: I just saved your ass, Lessa . . .
BIGMAN: Hey! O.K. Lessa. Number one, "real" looks like nuthin'.
   You seen "real" wrestlin'? The fans would rather watch paint
   dry. You know who comes to watch "real"? Mothers, mothers
   come to watch. And while they watch they knit. You're fuckin'
   screwy, O.K.? Number two, I win, who cares, you win, listen,
   you think two thousand morons in tractor hats wanna see a
   black chick ice the Cruiserweight contender? What, is this
   whole business lost on you? I got a brother in the hospital,
   unconscious. I don't have time for this.
TIGER: So we cancel, right?
BIGMAN: What'd I tell you?
NETTY: You said no.
BIGMAN: What is a promoter?
DANI: Don't ask.
BIGMAN: I'm serious. C'mon. What's a promoter?

TIGER: A guy with front money?

BIGMAN: No.

NETTY: Makes arrangements?

BIGMAN: No.

DANI: Fucks other people with promises?

BIGMAN: He's like a farmer . . .

TIGER: Get outta here.

BIGMAN: From piss he makes peaches.

NETTY: This is a nice thought.

BIGMAN: Thank you. No Eddie. This is like a huge, monster problem. Do we fold? No. I got responsibilities to my girls. I'm like your father.

DANI: Hand me that other beer, will ya?

BIGMAN: I get on the phone, I get a replacement.

TIGER: Yeah?

BIGMAN: But not on a plateau, you know? I see in the problem an opportunity. I make a big move and get a big payoff. So who, who do I get?

DANI: Gorgeous fuckin' George comes back from the dead.

BIGMAN: The Knockout Sisters.

NETTY: You're kiddin'?

TIGER: The blondes?

BIGMAN: *60 Minutes*. Connie Chung Saturday Night. Presenters on the goddamned Grammies!

TIGER: *(To Bigman.)* The blondes with tits?

Bigman nods, a long pause.

LESSA: They are coming here?

BIGMAN: Bingo.

Pause.

LESSA: Didn't they get picked up in a drug raid screwin' the L.A. mayor?

BIGMAN: Yeah, briefly, but, *People* magazine, *National Enquirer* . . .

DANI: Banned from wrestlin' for life?

BIGMAN: Hey, people forgive.

LESSA: They got film on them doin' crack.

BIGMAN: So?

DANI: *Screw Magazine* has them on the cover makin' a sandwich with the mayor.

BIGMAN: It's publicity.

LESSA: They barred for life.

BIGMAN: From W.W.F., from A.W.P. These are giants, these are corporation. I'm an independent.

TIGER: Hey, Bigman, they are in the slammer.

BIGMAN: Nah.

TIGER: Get your money out man, they are doing time.

BIGMAN: *(Unfolding a newspaper.)* What does this say?

NETTY: "The Knockout Sisters, free at last and home with Mama."

BIGMAN: Cairo, Tennessee. The mother lives in Cairo, Tennessee. So, I'm a genius or I'm a genius? Peaches from piss, right?

The women pass the paper around.

TIGER: You pulled that off?

BIGMAN: One phone call. Twenty-five cents.

DANI: Get outta here?

BIGMAN: *(To Dani.)* Tell me I'm good.

DANI: You're an animal.

BIGMAN: Tell me I'm good.

A pause.

DANI: You're good.

BIGMAN: You betcher ass. I am *good*.

TIGER: They travelin' with us?

BIGMAN: *(Nods yes.)* We treat 'em right.

DANI: What're you payin' 'em?

BIGMAN: O.K., I got a lot to do.

DANI: I don't get a check tonight, Bigman, I'm walkin'.

LESSA: I'm gettin' a check *and* I'm walkin'.

BIGMAN: Ladies, don't promise nuthin' you can't deliver. O.K. I'm makin' out a card. The sisters supposed to drive up here in ten minutes. First two prelims same as always. Get dressed. *(Starts for the door. Turns. Exuberantly throws his fist in the air.)* Yes! *(Does a little end-zone dance. Spikes his hat.)* Touchdown!

(Picks it up.) You wanta see a promoter, ladies? Bigman, he says, he does, it's done. Believe it! *(He exits. There is a pause.)*

TIGER: *(To Lessa.)* How much support wrap you got?

LESSA: Six-foot roll.

TIGER: I'll buy it off you.

LESSA: You can have it.

The women begin to put necessaries from their bags into lockers.

DANI: He's got to pay 'em what?

NETTY: Mucho dinero.

DANI: Man, it boils me!

LESSA: They get paid, we get paid.

NOLA: *(Enters with makeup tables.)* Comin' through.

TIGER: *(Pulling a comic book out of her bag to read.)* You seen their act?

DANI: Nothin', their act is nothin'.

LESSA: No moves, no skills.

NETTY: Y'all foolin' yourselves.

LESSA: Yeah?

NETTY: They got "it."

LESSA: They a couple crack-head whores. I'm embarrassed to be in the same locker room with 'em.

DANI: Stand around . . .

LESSA: Stan' around. Lie around. Hell, I hear they was doin' some Danish sex show and Man Mountain Montgomery zipped up his fly an discovered 'em. You know what their finishin' hold is? The Va-Va-Voom—it's a bump-and-grind makes their opponents faint.

Nola plugs in makeup table lights.

TIGER: What the hell is that?

NOLA: Dressin' table.

DANI: Where'd you get it?

NOLA: Rosemary Clooney's dressin' room.

TIGER: Say what?

NOLA: There's this room, see. Little room. Got about two inches of water on the floor an the lights don't work. Got a poster for Rosemary Clooney on the door an dead roses inside.

NETTY: Rosemary Clooney?

TIGER: Ol' time country singer, died when her plane hit a mountain.

LESSA: Yeah, right.

DANI: Some real singer played this dump?

NOLA: She looked real pretty on the poster.

TIGER: Started out singin' back-up for Chubby Checker.

NETTY: Oh, that one.

DANI: Well, who you think ol' Rosemary's dressin' table is for?

LESSA: He's givin' those bitches a dressin' table?

NETTY: Now y'all listen here now . . .

DANI: I don't . . .

NETTY: Dani . . .

DANI: Want to damn well . . .

NETTY: Mark my . . .

DANI: Hear it.

NETTY: I'm just an old Alabama waitress now but I'm makin' more wrasslin' three nights a week . . .

TIGER: When we're lucky . . .

NETTY: . . . than I did slingin' hash in seven, and I ain't the only one.

DANI: *(To Tiger.)* She's goin' now.

NETTY: Owe ol' Bigman for gettin' into show business . . .

TIGER: Jesus.

NETTY: . . . an havin' us a better life, praise the Lord. *(A moment.)* Just thought I'd speak up. People who ain't stayin' should get goin', and people who are stayin' should get dressed.

A pause.

NOLA: I saw 'em on television.

NETTY: *(To the wrestlers.)* Them girls is an *attraction*. Now let's *get down.* (She begins to tape herself up for the fight.)

NOLA: There's a tall one an a short one an the short one is mean an sneaky an, you know, hateful, an the tall one smiles an does, like, you know, dance steps an fluffs out her hair an has a pet tarantula.

DANI: *(Cold.)* Sounds great.

NOLA: An they're sexy as all hell with kinda Cher costumes, an they come on to the fans who go like boogaloo and love 'em.

LESSA: What's your name, girl?

NOLA: Nola.

LESSA: O.K., Nola, shut the fuck up.

NOLA: Sorry.

NETTY: Got me a bruise shape of an elephant.

LESSA: Hey, Netty, I'm a professional, you know? I got pride in my work. I do hard, dangerous stuff. I don't get hurt an nobody in the ring with me gets hurt. Now you put a couple showgirls in with me they gonna spend a lotta time on their ass. They screw with my timing I'm gonna take 'em out.

DANI: Well, I don't really think you got a problem.

LESSA: Yeah, why is that?

DANI: 'Cause you ain't gonna be in the ring with 'em.

LESSA: They gonna fight Bigman for the Cruiserweight Championship?

DANI: It's Tiger and me do the semifinal so it's Tiger and me move up.

LESSA: Tiger ain't got the moves, she on the injured list, plus they gonna be lookin' for bad guys, O.K.? An' you our little heroine.

DANI: Get it, I make fifty more a week. I'm on the poster. I got top girl's billing an do the top girl's fight.

LESSA: Yeah, well, you watch how it goes down.

DANI: I got the *contract!*

NETTY: *(To Tiger.)* How you feelin', honey?

TIGER: I feel like shit.

LESSA: All bets is off around here, you mark my words.

TIGER: Stifferen' hell an got about a third mobility.

DANI: You better pull in your horns, Lessa. You gonna need a friend with Bigman.

LESSA: What's that sposed to mean?

DANI: You know just what I mean, baby. Go on, tell me you don't.

LESSA: Screw you. *(Puts her Walkman back on.)*

DANI: Yeah, right. *(Goes to trunk.)* You want your stuff, Netty?

NETTY: I want romance.

Dani hands her a costume from the trunk. Netty starts to dress as "Pajama Mama."

DANI: Romance on the road. You want to suit up, Tiger?

TIGER: I want good drugs, a beach, an a hunnert comic books.

Dani hands her a costume. Tiger begins to dress as "Bloody Mary"—a red leotard with metal studding.

DANI: *(Tapes a mirror to her mirror.)* I want to win me a cruise vacation an marry any Arab we ain't shot. *(To Nola.)* Whatta you want, kid?

NOLA: I want to wrestle.

DANI: Yeah, it's a fuckin' paradise to be in wrestlin', kid. Travel opportunities, glamorous companions, luxurious surroundings, big money an the opportunity to meet crack-heads who went down on the mayor of L.A. *(She ruffles Nola's hair. Dani begins to dress as Tarzana, Queen of the Jungle.)*

NETTY: *(To Nola.)* I done twenty-six different jobs.

DANI: Oh man . . .

NETTY: I done dry cleanin', road work, cannin' line, store clerk, bartender,

NETTY: typewriter repair, phone company, re-solin', slaughterhouse, garbageman, dock loader . . . hotel maid, post office, fire fightin' . . . fast food, shirt factory, sewer sweep.

LESSA: Which trunk is my stuff in?

TIGER: Over there.

NETTY: 'Bout as close to a movie star I'm gettin'.

NOLA: I know the holds . . .

Lessa begins to dress as "Black Lightning," a superhero outfit with a lightning logo across the front.

NETTY: Uh-huh. That's good, honey.

NOLA: Backbreaker, pretzel, rope loop, double camel. I know all the holds.

NETTY: Well, sure, the holds is your basic . . . but you got your showmanship an your crowd work, see . . . *(Netty has finished dressing in a voluminous pair of striped men's pajamas.)*

NOLA: Boy, look at that! What you call that?

NETTY: Pajama Mama.

TIGER, DANI, LESSA: She puts 'em to sleep! *(Tiger begins to lace on boots.)*

NETTY: Say, you want to come up to the hotel after the show . . .

DANI: She'll show you a few holds ain't on your list.

NETTY: Now, that ain't nice.

DANI: True though.

NETTY: I don't work your side of the street, you oughta give me room.

DANI: Hell, there's enough hotel clerks for everybody. *(She starts to do her makeup.)*

NOLA: Sure.

NETTY: What's that, honey?

NOLA: I'd like to.

NETTY: Uh-huh.

NOLA: Get a few tips.

NETTY: Uh-huh. Well, O.K. then.

DANI: *(To Netty but half amused.)* Surgeon General oughta stick a message on your pussy.

NETTY: Now just knock that off.

Lessa, with her basic fight costume on, kneels briefly and bows her head. Netty begins to lace on boots.

DANI: Will you stop prayin', Lessa, I can't stand that!

LESSA: *(Rising and looking in the Knockout Sisters' mirror.)* How we supposed to do if the bitches got the only mirror?

TIGER: What the hell happened to Eddie? *(A pause.)* We talkin' about this, we talkin' about that, how come the man ain't wrestlin'? *(No answer.)* Yeah, sure he's an asshole, but he's *our* asshole.

NETTY: Well, you know Eddie . . .

TIGER: Yeah, I know Eddie . . . probably dropped some laced meth.

NETTY: Well, now, Eddie'd been saying he was clean.

DANI: Maybe you heard somethin', huh, Lessa? *(No response.)*

NETTY: He's been havin' that little numbness in his left hand.

TIGER: I seen Eddie wrestle real hurt. I seen him wrestle through a hamstring.

NETTY: Heart trouble?

TIGER: Bigman would have said.

LESSA: Somebody bit his dick off.

DANI: Yeah, sure.

LESSA: I'm tellin' you.

DANI: Bullshit.

LESSA: O.K. They didn't bite his dick off.

TIGER: You kiddin' or what?

LESSA: Two A.M. There's this screamin', Eddie's on the floor outside his room . . .

NETTY: Who would do a thing like that?

DANI: I would but you'd probably get food poisoning.

Tiger gives her the thumbs up sign.

NETTY: *(To Lessa.)* He was naked in the hallway?

LESSA: Pretty ugly, thrashing around, yellin'. I called the paramedics. Did a tourniquet.

NETTY: *(Horrified.)* You did a tourniquet?

LESSA: Used some dental floss. Shut down the blood but he fainted.

TIGER: Jesus!

LESSA: You said he was with some whore, huh, Dani?

DANI: Yeah, he was with some whore.

NETTY: I told that man, I told him stop messin' with strange all the time. God, how much got bit off?

LESSA: I forgot my ruler, O.K.?

NETTY: Shoot *I'd* service him he wasn't so mean.

TIGER: Jesus, Netty!

NETTY: Well, that poor man didn't have a thing in the world but that dick and now it's bit off.

TIGER: Maybe they can sew it back on. They tell you now you get a finger cut off in a lawn mower you wrap it up in a Kleenex bring it down to the hospital.

DANI: They wrap his dick in a Kleenex, Lessa?

LESSA: Put it in a sandwich bag.

NETTY: Now there's some men you can picture without a dick but poor Eddie just isn't one of 'em.

TIGER: He didn't pay her, or what?

LESSA: Or worse.

DANI: Life's just funny in't? Here you're the one hates his ass an you're the one there to help.

NOLA: You think he can come back an wrestle without a dick?

DANI: His dick didn't work when he had it.

NETTY: Now no speakin' ill of the man when he's bad off.

DANI: I'd speak ill of him on the best day he ever had. He's a schizoid scumbag. And there isn't anybody in here . . . except her . . . *(Points at Nola.)* doesn't know it personal.

TIGER: Well, whoever done it put us in a hell of a fix. Now that's straight.

LESSA: Whoever done it probably had a damn good reason. An that's straight.

TIGER: *(Pulling out a tin of gourmet dog food and an opener. As she talks, she feeds her dog.)* This tour folds, we a bunch of worn out ol' bitches on the street. An if the word is some one of us chomped his member they'd hire the Hells Angels before they'd hire us. I got no skills, an armed robbery conviction, an a sick dog. Now let's kiss ass an wrestle.

NETTY: On the money. *(A moment.)* Now Eddie did say it was a whore, right?

TIGER: Far as we hear Eddie ain't said shit, an Eddie won't say shit, he'll just kill somebody.

There is a crash behind the door between the lockers—the women turn.

DANI: You hear that? That's rats. We in this dressing room with rats!

NETTY: Now take it easy, honey . . .

DANI: No way. Noooooooo way.

Lessa opens the door. A small man in his early forties wearing jeans, a work shirt and Vietnamese Tiger jacket is revealed nervously clutching a thick autograph book.

DWAYNE: How you doin'?

TIGER: Son of a bitch.

DANI: You scruffy little maggot what you doin' in here?

LESSA: Step outta there, cracker.

DWAYNE: Yes ma'am. Yes ma'am. Dwayne Arthur Pardee. How you doin'?

LESSA: How'm I doin'? What're you doin'? You in the broom closet, Dwayne whatsit.

DANI: You in there lookin' for Rosemary Clooney, or what?

TIGER: *(Pulling him up in her face by the shirt front.)* You in there lookin' for poontang, Dwayne?

LESSA: You in there chokin' the turkey?

DWAYNE: No ma'am.

LESSA: No ma'am what?

DWAYNE: I ain't chokin' the turkey.

NETTY: Well, you been in there a hell of a long time, honey.

DWAYNE: Yes ma'am.

NETTY: *(Moving Tiger away from him.)* Well, you wanta tell Momma why you in there?

DWAYNE: Yes ma'am. See, I'm an autograph professional.

DANI: You a professional nutcase.

NETTY: *(To Dani.)* Now hush now. *(To Dwayne.)* You been in there a couple hours waitin' for our autograph?

DWAYNE: Well . . . see . . . I was in, you know . . . an ummm . . . an this uh big fellow he uh . . . uh . . .

NETTY: Kinda put you out?

DWAYNE: He did. He did. So I . . . you know . . .

NETTY: Come on back in?

DWAYNE: I did. I did. An he us . . . an he uh . . .

NETTY: Kinda put you back out?

TIGER: Netty, get him outta here.

NETTY: This is a fan, O.K.? This is a wrestlin' fan.

DANI: He's a fuckin' pervert.

DWAYNE: No ma'am, I'm an autograph professional. I got . . . I got every famous person . . . everyone been in Cementville since . . . see here . . . *(Opens the autograph book.)* 1972. Cass Elliott. Ol' Mama Cass. Year before she died. God bless her. See 1972. Gene Hackman. The Four Preps. Well, three of 'em. See this here this is American heroes, see, the American way right here, right here in Cementville. O.J. Simpson. See? Irene Ryan, you know, Beverly Hillbillies. Tony Boyle, United Mine Workers. See this here is goin' in a time capsule. Anita Bryant, God bless her. See here. This is my life work.

NETTY: Well, good on you.

DANI: Get him outta here.

NETTY: Now you want us to sign your book, honey, huh?

DWAYNE: Yes ma'am. I do. Yes ma'am, yes ma'am.

NETTY: Now Dwayne, you wasn't watchin' us get dressed through a crack 'er somethin' and jerkin' off in there, was you?

DWAYNE: No ma'am. No ma'am. I wouldn't do that.

NETTY: 'Cause then we'd have to kill you, Dwayne.

DWAYNE: Well, you know, the big fella . . .

NETTY: You was hidin' from the big fella?

DWAYNE: Yes ma'am, I wasn't . . . well, what you said.

NETTY: O.K., we'll sign your book then. *(She takes it.)*

DWAYNE: God bless you. You just an American Beauty Rose in my book. You American heroes, God bless yer pure hearts. You gonna be in the time capsule. You gonna be there when Jesus Christ walks again.

During his speech, the women, even Nola, sign his book.

DWAYNE: You the mothers of America. Umm, one to a page, ma'am. You the heart, the red heart of us men folks. You the arms that swing the cradle. You on a pedestal, a way high pedestal to Dwayne Pardee. Yes sir. You a hot lunch when the men's in the fields. Yes sir, you may be prostitutes an wrasslers but you mean home to me.

NETTY: O.K., Dwayne, we about got this together now.

DWAYNE: You cut from the cloth of Jesus Christ's momma. Yes ma'am. An I'm talkin' for the mens now. Speakin' for your daddies.

TIGER: *(The last to sign.)* O.K., Dwayne.

DWAYNE: For your husbands and sons an I say to you: Get you home an get me some dinner, bitch . . .

DANI: *(Head in her hands.)* Oh man . . .

DWAYNE: . . . Goin' to town in yer red lipstick, paradin' yourself like Jezebel with a tambourine, bringin' down the temple with your lascivious hips . . .

LESSA: *(Moving toward him.)* Let's take a walk, dude.

DWAYNE: *(Grabbing Tiger from behind.)* Touch me, Loretta . . .

She gives a sharp cry because of her ribs.

DWAYNE: Touch me, rub me, take me to heaven!

Lessa grabs him by the hair. He lets go. She throws a hammerlock on him and turns him to the door.

LESSA: Walk.

DWAYNE: My book . . . gimme my book . . .

LESSA: *(Taking him out the door.)* Move it.

DWAYNE: I'm a . . . ouch! . . . autograph professional . . . you hurtin' my arm . . .

LESSA: I'm breakin' your arm . . . *(And they are gone.)*

TIGER: . . . the damn ribs.

DANI: You O.K., Tiger?

TIGER: Don't touch me.

NETTY: Stand up.

TIGER: Hold on . . .

NETTY: Stand up, it's better, honey.

TIGER: Son of a bitch . . . ow . . . leggo . . . damn . . . mother-brother-son of a bitch kiss my ass dammit . . . *(Tiger's furious tirade finally reduces the rest to laughter.)* Hate this damn wrasslin' . . . ow . . . got up like some kinda . . . stupid . . . goddamn ribs . . . shoulda torn off that autograph bastard's balls, hung 'em on a rearview like goddamn cashmere dice . . . itchin' all over, fleas, head lice . . . get the goddamn bubonic plague in this goddamn shit hole . . . get the athlete's foot . . . what the hell are you laughin' at, you cross-eyed, knock-kneed, piss-ant, putrid, dick-lickin', flat-chested, slung-assed nowhere broads! *(She starts laughing too.)* Don't make me laugh!

DANI: You aren't mad, are you, Tiger?

More laughter.

TIGER: Hell, no, I'm happy!

NOLA: He left his book. *(Holds up the autograph book.)*

DANI: Gimme that thing.

NOLA: Well, but it's . . .

DANI: *(Taking it from her.)* I said hand it over. *(Rips out handfuls of pages, walks to door and flings them down the hall.)* Pervert!

TIGER: Son of a bitch.

DANI: You know they got celebrity insurance now. All these nutzoids trying to shoot movie stars. *(Finishing her makeup.)*

TIGER: We ain't movie stars.

DANI: You tellin' me.

NOLA: You think he was kind of crazy?

DANI: Yeah. An he ain't the worst. We the entertainment for fuckups. When you go crazy tryin' to live this life they send you over here for Wednesday night wrestlin'.

NOLA: *(Looking at the ripped-out pages.)* Who's Eugene McCarthy?

NETTY: *(To Tiger.)* Can you get up, honey?

TIGER: Yeah, I can, but not yet.

Lessa re-enters.

NETTY: *(To Lessa.)* O.K.?

LESSA: Yeah.

DANI: *(To Lessa.)* So?

LESSA: Said I was his Ethiopian Queen, said come over to his place he had musk oil.

DANI: What'd you do with him?

LESSA: Put him in the dumpster.

NETTY: How long you think he was in the broom closet?

LESSA: I think he grew there like a fuckin' mushroom.

NETTY: Talkin' the good book . . .

LESSA: An' humpin' parking meters. Yeah, I was married to a preacher once.

NETTY: Well, now, I didn't know that.

LESSA: It ain't your job to know, is it?

TIGER: *(To Netty.)* Give me a hand up.

LESSA: 'Bout the last thing I need me is a soulmate.

DANI: No problem.

LESSA: Zip my head.	RING ANNOUNCER:
Netty pulls Tiger up.	*(Offstage at a distance.)*
	(Ring bell.)
	Ladies and gentlemen,
	the all-American
	Wrestling Federation
	presents its Shower of
	Stars Tour.

BIGMAN: *(Enters.)* All right, lemme have your attention. *(Calls out to hall.)* Come on in here, Mother.

Mother Crocker, a rough-looking woman in her late fifties in a black church dress with a strand of pearls. She smokes a cigarillo. She enters and appraises the room and its inhabitants.

BIGMAN: This here is Mother Crocker, Mama and Manager for the Knockout Sisters . . . step in, Mother . . . she'd like to give us a little ground plan on how it's gonna come down tonight. Mother Crocker, I'd like to welcome you to the American Wrestling Federation. We got the finest up an coming girls in the sport. An I'd like to personally express my thoughts on the job you done makin' the Knockout Sisters a world-wide attraction. You done a great job. O.K., let 'er rip.

MOTHER: Pretty run-down lookin' bunch.

BIGMAN: Yeah, but wait 'til you see 'em in action!

MOTHER: Y'all are dead meat. You're a two-bit tour playin' morgue date and you got never-was, never-will-be talent on the way down. I wouldn't be caught dead puttin' my top attraction down this pisshole but I got me a public relations problem. See, we messed up, got ourselves into politics, put a crimp in our image. Now we got to lay low, stay in shape an make a few bucks. On the upside we probably goin' to get a film deal out of that mess, we're negotiatin'. The Knockout Sisters is A-One, U.S. prime horseflesh. While we're slummin' with you girls, you're going to have ace crowds an make the only decent money you ever made in your miserable lives. While we're together your sports pimp here . . . *(Indicating Bigman.)* . . . gets me coffee. You understand? I say fuck a sheep, he fucks a sheep, is that clear?

BIGMAN: *(A big smile.)* She got a great sense of humor, doesn't she?

MOTHER: Now think this over. How do you think a couple small-town girls became the fourth biggest wrestling attraction in the United States of America in two years? *(She pauses.)* That's right. Mobbed up. Just like Sinatra. You capice? Now this wrestlin' wears out an attraction, which is why we segue into film. But meanwhile, meanwhile don't bruise the meat. You understand me? You injure, deface or otherwise crumb up the dollar value on my attraction you're going to hear some fucking Sicilian. Got it? Dottie, Dolly, get in here.

The Knockout Sisters, one tall, one short, both attractive in a hard way with platinum hair, little bare-shouldered mauve dresses and spike heels, enter.

MOTHER: Say hello to the little people.
DOTTIE: I'm Dottie.
DOLLY: I'm Dolly.
MOTHER: Who are you?
DOTTIE AND DOLLY: We're the Knockout Sisters.
MOTHER: *(To the room.)* Remember what I said.

BLACKOUT

ACT TWO

The fights are on. The first prelim is over. Dani is changing from her Tarzana costume to her Texas Gold outfit, featuring gold sequins, gold cape and a gold cowboy hat. Tiger is still basically in her Bloody Mary outfit. Netty and Angelessa are upstairs working. The Knockout Sisters in little lavender dressing kimonos are heavily into their glamour makeup trip. Mother is out watching the fights, and Bigman is ranking out Dani and Tiger for the quality of their work. Dottie has decorated her locker with scarves, photos, dried flowers, and Eastern wisdom.

BIGMAN: I got seven hundred rubes out there laughin' their asses off while you pattycake.
DANI: Hey, I can't touch her ribs or put her on the floor, or if I get her on the floor she can't get off the floor, so what am I supposed to do?
DOTTIE: *(Stretching and preparing.)* Money, money, money, money, money, money, money . . .

BIGMAN: An athlete eats pain for lunch, Tiger.

TIGER: Dammit, where's that whiskey?

DOTTIE: Money, money, money, money, money, money, money, money, money, money, money, money.

BIGMAN: *(To Dottie.)* What the hell is that?

DOTTIE: It's my warm-up.

DANI: You got seven hundred rubes, huh?

BIGMAN: Yeah, six hundred, six fifty.

DANI: Three hundred, countin' people with a brain twice.

DOTTIE: See, life is a series of circles. One circle inside the next, inside the next.

BIGMAN: *(Trying to be polite.)* Circles, uh-huh. *(To Tiger.)* Got to get the rubes *hot,* Tiger. Get 'em wild and riled. They not *smokin'*, they get pissed.

TIGER: I don't know, Bigman.

BIGMAN: Put 'em on the edge. Keep 'em on the edge.

DOTTIE: Each one of us has a circle. See on that circle . . . *(To Bigman.)* Excuse me, I am talkin' to you.

BIGMAN: You got a circle. We got a circle. Everybody got a circle.

DOTTIE: You got two choices—get enlightened or die.

BIGMAN: Sounds real good. *(To Tiger.)* You got to go back out there with Lessa . . .

DOTTIE: Excuse me . . .

BIGMAN: An *turn it on.* They gonna be walkin' out!

DOTTIE: Excuse me.

BIGMAN: What!?

DOTTIE: Now I don't like that tone. Did you hear that tone, Dolly?

DOLLY: Yeah.

DOTTIE: Sometimes a tone such as that causes me to hyperventilate, and then I jus' have to go home.

BIGMAN: Listen.

DOTTIE: Yeah.

BIGMAN: Now I'm sorry . . .

DOTTIE: You're sorry what?

BIGMAN: Sorry Miss Crocker.

DOLLY: That's right, pig snot.

NOLA: *(Enters with a bottle in a paper bag. To Dani.)* Shoot. I am sorry. It's kinda, well, you know, boarded up around here. Shut down. No liquor store, no nothin'. I went . . . finally there was, you know, this guy, you know, in a doorway, I bought this from him. *(She pulls out a Smirnoff bottle about a third full of brownish liquid.)*

TIGER: What the hell is that?

NOLA: Said the vodka wasn't no taste so . . .

DANI: That is one suspicious color.

NOLA: So he kinda flavored it with sherry.

TIGER: Hell with it. *(Takes a hit.)*

DOTTIE: Now that is disgusting.

TIGER: Yeah, it's vodka and sherry.

DANI: Nasty.

DOLLY: I don't work with drunks.

TIGER: Lady, I'm numb or I'm gone. *(A long drink.)*

DOTTIE: So that each one of us has a circle. Like this . . . *(Makes a circle in the air.)* A path. Call it fate. Call it what you will.

DANI: I call it bullshit.

DOTTIE: I want this woman out of the dressing room.

BIGMAN: For Christ sake, Dani, shut up. *(To Dottie.)* O.K., a circle.

DOTTIE: Yes.

BIGMAN: Of fate.

DOTTIE: Yes.

NOLA: *(To Tiger.)* I had to give him the ten. 'Cause he was like a bum—like he couldn't make change.

DOTTIE: An Dolly an me, see, we are in the circle of sex goddesses.

TIGER: I gotta get dressed, doctor my dog. *(Tiger continues dressing as Pocahontas.)*

BIGMAN: Jesus!

DOTTIE: *(Snaps Bigman with a towel.)* I am expressin' myself.

BIGMAN: *(Suppressing growing anger.)* Sex goddesses.

DOTTIE: Nefertiti, Mary Magdalene, Marilyn, Madonna and us!

BIGMAN: *(Red in the face.)* Nefertiti.

DOTTIE: That's right. We gonna get good karma, give good head, get us ace parts in the horror flicks.

DOLLY: We gonna be dismembered in a close-up the size of this fuckin' room. You watch for it!

DANI: *(In the presence of some kind of madness.)* This is *real* interestin'. *(Pulling on cowboy boots.)*

DOTTIE: We carryin' forward, along the circle, the wisdom of the forbearers . . .

RING ANNOUNCER: *(Bell sounds.)* The winner, in 17 minutes, the pleasingly fat queen of the mat . . . Pajama Mama! *(Bell sounds.)*

DANI: And their tits, too. Right?

DOTTIE: That too.

DANI: It's very mystical.

DOTTIE: It is. You worked with Kad Ra Mas?

DANI: I'm like on the waiting list.

DOTTIE: "Know and embody your circle." He said that.

From above, there is the sound of the crowd stamping their feet. Some plaster dust drops down.

BIGMAN: *(Looks up.)* What the hell the girls doin' up there?

DOLLY: *(Slapping herself in the head as she looks in the mirror.)* This don't look right!

DOTTIE: Money, money, money, money, money, money, money.

DANI: Shut up.

DOTTIE: *(Immediately completely focused on her.)* Lace up my shoe.

DANI: You got granola for brains, bitch.

BIGMAN: *(Seeing Dolly rise meaningfully from her table.)* Lace up her shoe.

DANI: You lace up her shoe.

BIGMAN: Don't screw with me, Dani. Lace up her shoe!

Dani laces up Dottie's shoe.

DOTTIE: See some of us *are* desire, and some of us *serve* desire.

DANI: And some of us have our heads up our ass.

Bigman immediately kicks her in the behind with the flat side of his shoe.

DANI: Ow.

BIGMAN: You havin' a hard time understandin' me? You got a mouth ought to be washed out with soap.

DANI: I'll think it over.

Bigman turns away, she immediately kicks him. He turns.

DANI: I thought it over.

TIGER: *(To Bigman.)* Go easy.

At this moment Lessa re-enters, she is hot. Netty follows. You can hear crowd disorder in the background.

LESSA: Hey, Bigman! They got some guy out there shootin' crap at me . . . who knows . . . a blowpipe. Hit me with a rock or ball bearing or some low-down shit . . .

NETTY: Jesus, Bigman.

BIGMAN: *(To Tiger and Dani.)* You see what you got started out there?

LESSA: Coulda put my eye out . . .

BIGMAN: And?

LESSA: An I went out after him.

BIGMAN: Outta the ring?

LESSA: I'm tellin' you I went out after him so nobody else has to tell you, an I'll go out after him again . . .

LESSA: If I ever see him anywhere near ringside the rest of the night . . .	BIGMAN: I got one, only one rule, you don't go into the crowd under no circumstances no matter what.

NETTY: Got a bunch of animals out there, Bigman.

BIGMAN: Stay *in* the ring!

LESSA: Grabbed me out in the crowd started feelin' me up!

BIGMAN: . . . Got no business leavin' the ring!!

Suddenly there is a gunshot. Everyone turns. It is Dolly sitting at her dressing table holding a 9-mm pistol.

DOLLY: Y'all are makin' a lot of noise. I like it real quiet when I'm puttin' on my lipstick.

DOTTIE: You can smear lipstick.

DOLLY: Ordinarily we got a little room to ourselves. But if we got to be in the barnyard with the hogs, then we like to make it clear who's the head hog.

DOTTIE: See beauty is serene. I wonder could anybody go get me a little plain water in this cup?

NOLA: I'll get it.

DOTTIE: You are so sweet.

NOLA: Could I ask where's your tarantula?

DOTTIE: *(Touching her arm.)* I set it free.

TIGER: You want a hit, Lessa?

LESSA: *(Pointing at Dolly. To Bigman.)* You putting up with this crap?

Nola exits passing Mother who enters carrying a program. Lessa begins to change to "The Mercenary," dressed in jungle fatigues with a bandolier of ammunition.

MOTHER: We got dissatisfied customers, goddammit!

NETTY: Oh, oh.

MOTHER: What we got here is some piss poor *no control.* You got nut-bustin' males in a room, you got to dominate 'em!

BIGMAN: I am in knowledge of this.

LESSA: Nobody, Nooooobody shoots shit at me when I'm workin'.

MOTHER: *(To Bigman.)* One rule only, keep the dogs on a leash.

BIGMAN: What I'm gonna do . . .

MOTHER: . . . is toss 'em raw meat.

LESSA: *(Emphatic but to herself.)* Nobody!

MOTHER: Who's on next?

BIGMAN: Tiger goin' on Lessa bein' "The Mercenary."

MOTHER: Well, that's real smart!

BIGMAN: I believe so.

MOTHER: *(Slapping him sharply.)* That oughta set off a riot, get us all killed.

TIGER: Hey, we do this every night.

Nola re-enters with Coke cup of water for Dottie.

BIGMAN: They ain't gonna . . .

MOTHER: You think you're in goddamn Minneapolis? *(Crowd roars.)* You probably got Klan out there, probably got skinheads, neo-fuckin' Nazis, general all purpose defectives, got you a nice mix.

LESSA: You got you a nice mix.

MOTHER: What's your name, honey?

LESSA: What's your name?

MOTHER: My name is Sara Mae Louellen Crocker, originally from the Crocker auto repair Crockers before I saw Fantasy Entertainment was the growth industry of the 90s.

LESSA: Angelessa.

MOTHER: You wanta get hurt?

LESSA: I done my job in fifteen states.

MOTHER: Well, Lessa, you can either bleach yourself white or buy yourself some permanent rest in Cementville, Tennessee. These people pay good money to see people they don't like get beat up by people they do like *inside* the ropes. They don't like smart people, they don't like rich people, they don't like Arabs, they don't like Jews, and they don't like you. So they come down here to drink beer an yell shit at you an then everybody goes home happy. Fantasy Entertainment. Well you broke the rules an went *outside the ropes* . . . you went an got real an now you're fucked. *(Crowd roars.)*

Dani chuckles.

MOTHER: *(Hands Lessa a ten.)* Go back to the hotel, buy yourself some skin cream an a magazine and let me get this straightened out. *(Big crowd roar.)*

BIGMAN: O.K., get us some wrestlers.

MOTHER: Shut up.

BIGMAN: Shut up?

MOTHER: This crowd won't sit through much more, they want my girls.

BIGMAN: Shut up?

DOLLY: This eye shadow, Mama?

MOTHER: Needs more.

DOLLY: *(Angry with herself.)* I keep on gettin' it wrong!

DOTTIE: I'm gettin' a headache, Mama.

BIGMAN: This is *my* friggin tour! Now . . .

MOTHER: *(To Bigman.)* Send 'em out naked.

BIGMAN: *(Appalled.)* Do what?

MOTHER: Send some of your talent out naked, get the rubes' minds on their cocks. We're not workin' while their blood's up. I got inves*tors*. I got invest*ments*.

BIGMAN: I can't send my girls out naked!

MOTHER: Why not?

BIGMAN: Why not? Why not? This is America, that's why not!

MOTHER: *(To the Knockout Sisters.)* Pack it up and move it out. We're goin' home.

BIGMAN: We got a verbal contract!

MOTHER: Dream on, sucker!

BIGMAN: Those rubes'll get nuts.

DOTTIE: *(Passing him.)* You got her upset now.

BIGMAN: Give me five minutes . . .

DOLLY: You think we need this? We did a fuckin' hairspray commercial.

DANI: You got any balls, Bigman?

BIGMAN: Give me one miserable minute here . . .

DOTTIE: You couldn't peddle this act to a dog show.

TIGER: Watch it!

BIGMAN: *(Grabbing Dolly's purse off the makeup table.)* Okay, ladies, let's see what we got here . . . *(He dumps the contents on the ground.)*

DOLLY: Hey, dickwad . . .

BIGMAN: *(Snatching something up.)* Oh, yes.

DOLLY: Hey!

BIGMAN: Seems to be . . . *(Taking it out of her reach.)* Uh-uh. Seems to be white powder . . .

DOLLY: You dumped my personal items . . .

BIGMAN: In a little bitty glassine bag.

DOLLY: . . . out my bag.

MOTHER: Bigman . . .

BIGMAN: Might be say an illegal substance . . .

MOTHER: You got both feet in your mouth . . .

BIGMAN: . . . be a real no-no seein' you're one day outta the joint.

Dolly slams trunk lid closed.

MOTHER: Gettin' Dolly excited . . .

BIGMAN: See just who is *head hog!*

DOTTIE: What you are holdin', sir, is a personal memento.

BIGMAN: What I'm holdin, bitch, is a trip back inside. *(To the wrestlers.)* You girls ever seen this shit before?

TIGER: *(Seeing Dolly pull out the pistol.)* Watch it!

DOLLY: *(Moving toward him with her pistol.)* You ever seen this shit before? *(Dolly jams the gun against Bigman's nostrils.)*

DANI: O.K., O.K., we're messin' around while the rubes is trashin' the joint.

Lessa laughs.

BIGMAN: You think this is funny?

LESSA: Uh-huh.

DOLLY: Let's see you eat it.

BIGMAN: I ain't eatin' this.

MOTHER: Dolly, you are so unstable, honey.

DOLLY: Eat it.

DOTTIE: You want him to eat your precious memento?

NETTY: You think maybe we could get past the gun part?

DOLLY: Eat it!

TIGER: She's got fucked up eyes, Bigman.

NOLA: I could get us all some Coca Colas.

DOLLY: I been in a snuff film, pig snot. It was widely distributed.

DOTTIE: Money, money, money, money, money, money, money.

DOLLY: One, two . . .

Crowd roars.

BIGMAN: *(Tosses the powder back, immediately chokes and spits it out.)* Choking . . .

NETTY: Pound him.

Dani and Nola whack him on the back.

DANI: Spit it out. Get rid of it.

Dolly has gone back to the makeup table lowering the pistol.

NETTY: Whack him some more.

BIGMAN: Sand.

NETTY: Say what, honey?

MOTHER: You a little accident-prone, Bigman.

BIGMAN: That shit was sand. What the hell you carryin' sand around for in a little bag?

DOTTIE: May I share with him, Dolly?

DOLLY: You share with him.

DOTTIE: On July 16, 1985 . . .

BIGMAN: *(To Nola.)* Get me some water.

DOTTIE: I was at Daytona Beach with Dolly's husband Earl. Now the sky was real pure teal blue . . .

BIGMAN: *(To Mother.)* We need wrestlin', for God's sake, what are we doin'?

DOTTIE: . . . just that single instant between day and dusk when time is suspended . . .

A young woman, perhaps sixteen, in an Andy Frane usher's uniform with a thin line of blood coursing across her face from a cut in her hairline, appears in the doorway. She smiles.

MISS HARMON: Mr. Vague?

BIGMAN: Holy Jesus.

MISS HARMON: Paging Mr. Vague, please?

BIGMAN: What?

MISS HARMON: Mr. Vague?

BIGMAN: Vag.

MISS HARMON: Mr. Vag? Oh boy, oh boy, Mr. Vag.

NETTY: You're bleeding, honey.

MISS HARMON: *(Oblivious.)* Uh-huh.

DOTTIE: Oooooo, I hate that.

MISS HARMON: Mr. Vag, Mr. McClendon, the referee, he said, oh boy, here I wrote it down . . . we better get him some wrasslers pretty pronto, because that crowd, it's ugly, it's a real ugly crowd. It is. So, oh boy, that's the whole thing, the whole message. From Mr. McClendon. 'Cause they're about to shit a brick, Mr. Vag, they really are. So perhaps I could . . . I could bring him your perspective.

BIGMAN: Godammit, I'm just tryin' to make a living!

MISS HARMON: *(Writing.)* . . . Make a living.

BIGMAN: I got my brother in the hospital with his dick cut off!!

MISS HARMON: . . . Cut off.

BIGMAN: I got the Knockout Sisters from Screw Magazine feedin' me sand and the Cosa Nostra tellin' me to send my stable out naked an I got tanked up rubes trashin' uninsured property I'm gonna be responsible for . . .

MISS HARMON: Rubes?

BIGMAN: Now you tell me what the hell to do!?

Irate crowd sound.

MISS HARMON: Well, I'm not sure, but they're throwing chairs.

NETTY: We ought to think this over, Bigman.

MOTHER: *(Steps forward. Wipes blood off the girl with her handkerchief.)* You tell him there is wrestlers comin'. Go on. Go on.

MISS HARMON: I will. Yes ma'am. Y'all, oh boy, y'all have a nice day, ya hear.

Big crowd sound. She disappears. A moment.

DOTTIE: *(Serenely.)* An I looked at Earl split by the horizon, with his history of impotence problems, standing there kind of give out, and I said, "Earl, I am Dolly and Dolly is me, we are the circle, we are the earth for you." An I lay down on the dusky beach and took him inside me and he cried out, "Dolly, Dolly, I'm home, Dolly." An then he had a heart attack and dropped dead.

DOLLY: Pretty much the way it always went.

DOTTIE: So I took some of that white sand from under his head and brought it home to Dolly as a memento which you have swallowed.

DOLLY: You hurt my heart.

TIGER: You got you some live ones, Bigman.

BIGMAN: I'm in charge here!

MOTHER: *(To Bigman.)* You want to know what to do?

BIGMAN: No!

Big crowd sound. A moment. He paces.

BIGMAN: O.K., maybe.

NOLA: *(Entering.)* I got the water.

BIGMAN: *(Knocking the cup out of her hand.)* I never asked for any damn water.

NETTY: Biggie . . .

MOTHER: You get the Indian . . . *(Pointing at Dani.)* An the cowboy . . . *(Pointing at Tiger.)* Out there in their underwear.

BIGMAN: I said that, I said underwear.

MOTHER: *(To Dottie.)* Hold it! We still got those garter belts?

DOTTIE: Oh, I'm just a little pack rat.

MOTHER: You announce you a specialty bout . . . what did we call it that one time?

DOLLY: Bra wars.

DANI: Forget it.

DOLLY: You the Virgin Mary, huh?

DANI: I fuck but I don't tease.

MOTHER: Extra fifty dollars?

DANI: You can't find a whore for fifty dollars.

MOTHER: A c-note?

She tosses it on the floor. Lessa reaches for it. Dani picks it up.

DOLLY: Hard to find a *good* whore for a *hundred* dollars.

She hands Dani two garter belts and stockings. Dani now changes from "Texas Gold" down to underwear, garter belt, stockings, and a sheer cover-up Dottie hands her.

DANI: *(Mildly.)* You don't know what a whore is, babe. You livin' in blonde world. We just aren't playin' off the same sheet of music, toots. See, I'd rather be a hundred-dollar whore than a thousand-dollar blank. *(She walks away.)*

BIGMAN: *(Turning to Tiger.)* Tiger.

TIGER: You saw the bout. I been leanin' on this locker 'cause I can't get off it.

BIGMAN: O.K., Netty.

MOTHER: Those boys aren't lookin' for no ugly fat people in a G-string.

He turns to Lessa.

NOLA: I can wrestle.

MOTHER: Yeah?

NOLA: I can wrestle good.

MOTHER: How old are you?

NOLA: Nineteen.

MOTHER: Where you worked?

NOLA: The Whale.

MOTHER: Where?

NOLA: It's an independent gas station with skateboard service.

MOTHER: Wrestled. Where have you wrestled?

NOLA: No place. Since I was twelve I saw all the bouts in three hundred miles. Thursday nights I practice with Jadine.

BIGMAN: Jadine who?

NOLA: My cousin. She weighs one ninety.

MOTHER: What kind of underwear you got on?

NOLA: Black with a red heart.

MOTHER: You're in the ring . . .

NOLA: Yeah.

MOTHER: She takes you down with a flying leg scissors . . .

NOLA: Yeah?

MOTHER: You do what?

NOLA: Counter with the grapevine, slip into a chicken wing and drop the heck out of her with a Carolina slam.

MOTHER: *(Holds out bills.)* Thirty bucks.

NOLA: I'm in? I'm in the bouts?

NETTY: You wanta do this, honey?

Crowd roar.

NOLA: I wanta wrassle. I wanta wrassle my ass off.

LESSA: Your mama oughta *whip* your ass.

NOLA: My mama already whips my ass. She whips my ass with a coat hanger.

BIGMAN: You do a good job there might be somethin' temporary on the tour.

NOLA: *(Beside herself.)* On the tour?

BIGMAN: See me up in my hotel room after the bouts? Number's ten-zero-six.

NOLA: *(Looks at Netty.)* O.K., I'll be there. *(Leaps in the air, arm and fist extended.)* I am in! Yes! Get down!

BIGMAN: Right, that's settled.

NOLA: *(To Mother.)* What's my name?

MOTHER: Frenchy.

NOLA: All right!

Nola begins to undress. She gets ready to go out in her underwear plus garter belt, stockings and sheer cover-up handed to her by Dottie.

TIGER: *(To Nola.)* Have a hit.

Nola takes one.

LESSA: *(To Bigman.)* I got to have my money.
NOLA: Yes!
MOTHER: Let's get us some wrestlers in the ring.

There is a flurry of activity as Nola and Dani get ready.

MOTHER: O.K., main event . . .
BIGMAN: Yes ma'am, now what we're gonna do is . . .
MOTHER: Shut up.
BIGMAN: I'm just saying . . .
MOTHER: Shut up. You tried to leverage me, now you're warm piss. You wanta wake up in your water bed with a fresh cut horse's head, you keep talkin'.
DOLLY: That was a good movie. *(Angry.)* I could *be* in that movie!
MOTHER: *(Pointing at Nola and Dani.)* I want the same two . . .
LESSA: Wait a minute . . .
MOTHER: . . . in the main event.
DANI: *(Gives Lessa the finger.)* Hey, Lessa?
NETTY: *(Points at Nola.)* Now, Frenchy gonna be tired, and she's green.

The usher appears again in the doorway. A thin man in a black suit, white shirt, black string tie with a haunted face and a burr haircut has her by the hair.

MISS HARMON: Mr. Vag, there is a gentleman to see you, Mr. Vag.
THE MAN: How y'all doin'?
BIGMAN: Get your hands off my staff.

The Man flicks open a switchblade in his free hand.

MISS HARMON: Oh, no.

THE MAN: I'm Mr. One-Eye Deneavue down from Lecher County, Kentucky for the wrasslin'.

MOTHER: *(Moves up beside Bigman.)* Hello, One-Eye.

THE MAN: I drove a distance to see me some gut-pumpin', butt-bumpin', airborne wild pussy in a good family entertainment type show. See I hump two-hundred-pound cartons all week so I'm seekin' an action attraction an I got squat zip right to this point.

MOTHER: I'm Mother Crocker, One-Eye, you probably seen me on the T.V.

THE MAN: Yes ma'am.

MOTHER: Seems like you got some sweet child by the hair there.

THE MAN: Could be. Now we don't get us some fine tits an see us some body fluids on the mat pretty quick, we gonna have to come down here cut out your pumpin' heart an eat that sumbitch like a nacho.

MOTHER: *(Walks up to within two inches of the man's face.)* One-Eye, we got some fine tits comin' up, an y'all aren't a hunnert percent satisfied you can have any woman in this room in a heart-shaped bed with mirrors on the ceiling all expenses paid an no questions asked, but you cut the girl here you gonna be one dead fuck. How's that sound?

THE MAN: You got a deal. *(He releases Miss Harmon. He winks and clicks his tongue, looking at Dottie.)* You a fine woman, Mama. I'll check on back. *(He's gone.)*

MISS HARMON: *(Nervous but determined.)* I could have handled the situation. I got personnel training.

The crowd begins stamping and clapping.

DANI: Why do I do this?

MOTHER: You want to stay down here?

MISS HARMON: Well, they need me in B Section non-reserved.

There is a burst of screaming from above.

MISS HARMON: Oh, boy . . . *(She exits, closing the door behind her. People exhale.)*

DOTTIE: I'm not fuckin' him. I got standards.

LESSA: *(Steps forward.)* Lemme do the main. I got the know-how.

I got the experience. I can handle your girls like they was marked fragile. I'm not goin' out in the crowd again. I will . . . I will apologize to . . . to the crowd. I'm a professional athlete, that's all I am and I need this work. I can make your girls look good. I can take punishment. If I have to do it I can take a straight punch. I uh . . . I know how to take orders, do what I'm told. I'm askin' for the fight.

MOTHER: Angelessa?

LESSA: Yeah?

MOTHER: If you're in tennis, you're a professional athlete . . .

LESSA: Yeah?

MOTHER: . . . if you're in track and field, you're a professional athlete, even if you catch on with the Harlem Globetrotters, you're a professional athlete, but if you're in Fantasy wrestling in the main feature attraction they pay for, you are nothing in this world . . .

DOLLY: But a nigger.

Lessa steps toward her but Bigman gives her a two-handed push that sends her crashing into the lockers.

NETTY: Lessa! Go easy now, go easy!

LESSA: *(Steadies herself against the lockers and leans there.)* I'm cool.

MOTHER: *(To Bigman.)* Take the girls out there.

NETTY: I don't know, Bigman.

BIGMAN: Dani, Frenchy, let's move it.

Crowd roars. He exits. Dottie and Dolly remove their cover-ups, revealing red, white and blue sequin peekaboo outfits with five-inch heels.

DANI: *(Hesitates a moment, then:)* O.K. We pull hair, kick each other, stuff like that. Work the crowd. You pull off my top. I pull off yours. I mess you up with the Argentine. I full press, it's over. We grab the clothes, we're out of there. Six, eight minutes max.

NOLA: Just lead me.

DANI: You got it.

NOLA: *(To Tiger.)* Thanks.

TIGER: Don't mention it.

Nola and Dani exit.

NETTY: I don't know . . .

MOTHER: She's got tits, how bad can it be? *(Handing Bigman a xeroxed sheet.)* When they come off, hand 'em this. Breaks down how they wrestle my girls.

Bigman takes it, starts to leave.

MOTHER: Dottie doesn't work off her feet. I got those legs insured for thirty thousand.

DOTTIE: You said fifty.

MOTHER: Fifty. Nothin' in the face. They don't go through the ropes. Crowd gets messy, they split.

Bigman starts out again. She stops him.

MOTHER: Do right.

Bigman exits.

DOTTIE: How do we look, Mama?	RING ANNOUNCER: Gentlemen, we got a little change of program here . . .

MOTHER: Turn around.

DOTTIE: Do we look like queens, Mama? Are we sweet as pie?

MOTHER: I could eat you for breakfast.

DOLLY: Tryin' Passion Flower on my nails.

MOTHER: You look good.

DOTTIE: You look good too, Mama. You are part of the circle.

MOTHER: Stay away from the young one, she doesn't know shit.

DOLLY: No problem.

MOTHER: Stay off the ropes. I don't want you marked.

DOTTIE: Yes, Mama.

MOTHER: Smile to the crowd, they fans.

DOLLY: Yes, Mama.

MOTHER: *(Handing them miniature American flags.)* Wave the little flags.

DOTTIE: We will.

MOTHER: You are stars in the Fantasy Entertainment field.

DOLLY AND DOTTIE: Yes, Mama.

MOTHER: We are just workin' out a little political setback . . .

DOLLY: Yes, Mama.

MOTHER: Usin' drugs was a bad thing, a bad, bad thing.

DOTTIE: Yes, Mama.

MOTHER: But fuckin' the Mayor of Los Angeles was a good thing.

DOTTIE: Yes, mama.

MOTHER: That's part of a career. That's networking.

DOLLY: Yes, Mama.

MOTHER: All right, go on up there and get ready. Get inside yourselves.

DOTTIE: You didn't say we were goddesses, Mama.

MOTHER: You are motherfuckin' goddesses.

DOTTIE: *(Hugging her.)* You sweet ol' thing. *(Turns to the room.)* Bye, y'all. You keep evolving now, y'hear?

She blows them a kiss and they are gone. We hear music and crowd cheering.

MOTHER: *(To those still in the room.)* Let me give you a little personal advice. Get yourself a husband and a shit job. You don't have it. You never will have it. You got no future on T.V. *(She leaves.)*

NETTY: How you feelin', Tiger?

TIGER: I'm feeling bad.

NETTY: You look bad. You want some morphine?

TIGER: You got?

NETTY: I got. *(A crowd reaction. She reaches into her bag and pulls out a small commercial vial.)*

TIGER: Where you get it?

NETTY: Well, darlin', we have our little ways. *(Crowd roars.)*

TIGER: You always a surprise, ain't ya?

NETTY: Girl's got to live, honey.

TIGER: Hard as that may be. You got a syringe?

NETTY: *(Handing her one in a packet.)* Fresh as a daisy.

TIGER: *(Feeling her ribs.)* Makes my day.

NETTY: Cementville, Tennessee. I'm too fat for Fantasy Entertainment.

TIGER: An I'm too far out there. *(Tiger starts changing from Poca-hontas back into street clothes.)*

NETTY: What about you, Lessa?

LESSA: Just fine.

NETTY: What you doin'?

LESSA: Gettin' dressed. *(Lessa puts on her Olympic warm-up suit.)*

NETTY: Never saw you pull that out.

LESSA: Just seemed like what I wanted to wear.

TIGER: *(To dog.)* You sweet sweet thing.

NETTY: You want to catch a beer tonight?

LESSA: I'm catchin' a bus.

TIGER: Shit, Lessa, cool off.

LESSA: I'm cooled off. I'm way, way cooled off.

NETTY: Where you catchin' a bus to?

LESSA: Wherever seventeen dollars and change gets me.

NETTY: Probably Memphis. Shoot we're all goin' to Memphis. Get the bus with us in the mornin'.

LESSA: I don't think so.

An old man, in his late sixties, early seventies, cane in hand appears in the doorway. He is African American.

KID: Good evening.

NETTY: *(Caught off guard, she startles.)* Good Lord!

KID: Didn't mean to make you jump. *(Takes off his hat.)* Pay my respects.

LESSA: What do you need?

KID: Well, ladies, I don't have much and I don't need much.

TIGER: This here is a dressin' room. We got a show on, Granpa.

KID: *(Points to a poster.)* Willie "The Kid" Cayman, that's my picture.

They look. He laughs.

NETTY: This is you, honey?

KID: Light on my feet. Lookin' real sweet. TNT in both hands.

NETTY: Honey, you got million dollar charm.

KID: Much obliged.

NETTY: Don't mention it. *(Roaring and whistling from the crowd.)*

KID: Could I bother you ladies to step in? On my way from Key West, Florida to Catafalque Bay, Alaska in a '79 Cadmium Red Pontiac Firebird. Stoppin' here, stoppin' there.

NETTY: Come on in, darlin'.

KID: Just call me Kid. *(Turns to Tiger.)* Kid Cayman.

TIGER: Tiger.

KID: Tiger who?

TIGER: Just one name.

KID: *(Smiling.)* Uh-huh, I can understand that. *(Sees cat case.)* I got me a small yellow dog. *(Turns to Lessa.)* Seems to me I know you, sister.

RING ANNOUNCER: . . . winner of our lingerie interlude, lusty, busty Dani Malowsky!

Crowd reaction.

LESSA: I don't think so.

KID: Sure I do. I got a memory they come miles for.

LESSA: Angelessa.

KID: Oh, it'll come to me. I'm workin' on it. *(The crowd breaks into applause.)* You're all in the wrestlin' bouts, huh?

NETTY: That's right, honey.

KID: Now I had one hundred seventy fights, featherweight to middleweight, but I still got my brains 'cause they couldn't hit me. I was kinda here, kinda gone at the same time. What you'd call a will-of-the-wisp. *(To Lessa.)* Your daddy wasn't the cut man for Sugar Ray Robinson, was he? *(She shakes her head.)* Fought here two times. Once with Jose Higuera, an old veteran with a good left hand. Carried him eight rounds so he could set up another payday. Once with Sandy Sadler. Oh, he was the dirtiest fighter alive, thumbed me so bad. Took forty-six stitches 'round my left eye. Knocked me down seven times. It's in the book. Fought Sandy three times. *(To Lessa.)* You ever won a beauty contest?

LESSA: Kid, I never won a beauty contest.

KID: Well, the fix musta been in. You ever married to a high hurdler?

Crowd roars, applauds and whistles.

LESSA: *(Smiling.)* You ought to move on pretty soon, Kid.

KID: Oh, I plan to. Yes, you got to keep movin'. *(Looks around room.)* Oh my, ladies . . . memory lane.

At this moment Dani and Nola enter like whirlwinds. They have covered themselves with the kimonos. They change into ninja costumes for the main event. They have masks.

NOLA: Whoa! Hot patootie, was that somethin'?

DANI: Into it, honey! I'll say that for them.

NOLA: . . . Throwin' money . . .

DANI: Bills . . .

NOLA: Change, bills, I didn't have a . . .

DANI: Five dollar bills . . .

NOLA: . . . Have a place to tuck it . . .

DANI: *(Passing Kid.)* Who's he?

KID: Bonjour, how you doin'?

TIGER: Used to fight here.

DANI: Pop, you got my sympathies. *(Handing money to Netty.)* Eighty bucks off the floor. Split it up.

Tiger starts humming "Me and My Shadow," occasionally singing a few words of the lyric.

NOLA: Am I gettin' this on straight?

NETTY: Come over here, honey.

DANI: How you doin', Tiger?

TIGER: Feelin' no pain.

DANI: *(Holding up xeroxed sheets Mother gave Bigman.)* You see this shit? The Dolly & Dottie Show.

NETTY: How it goes?

DANI: Yeah, how it goes. They parade around, we fall down. They writhe around on the floor, we're amazed. Va-Va-Voom, we collapse unconscious.

LESSA: Damn.

DANI: Fuckin' stupid. Tiger, dammit! *(Tiger stops singing.)* Well, you got to play it like it lays.

LESSA: Get goin'.

DANI: I'm gone.

NOLA: *(Tying the laces.)* One minute.
DANI: *(Exiting.)* Catch you up there.

NOLA: *(Finishing.)* I am sweatin' buckets.
LESSA: Lemme look you over.

RING ANNOUNCER: And now our featured bout of the evening . . . the fine, fabulous femmes fatales of American wrestling . . . direct from national television . . .

NOLA: *(Moves over to her.)* I hope I can do this.
LESSA: Turn around.

Nola does. Lessa pushes her into the broom closet and slams the door, turns the twist lock. Tiger chuckles.

NOLA: Hey!
NETTY: Now, Lessa . . .
NOLA: *(From inside.)* Come on, Lessa. I got to get up there. Stop playin' around.
LESSA: The bitch as called me a nigger is mine.
NOLA: Let me outta here! I got to be wrasslin', I can't be in here.
NETTY: Lessa, what the hell . . .
LESSA: Payback.
NETTY: Don't be crazy now.
LESSA: I'm gone.

She moves rapidly to the outside door. Just as she gets there, two hands fasten on her throat and drive her back into the room. It is Eddie. He wears a hospital robe over hospital pajamas. There is some blood staining through his bandages and onto the robe. Eddie is big. His face is gray. His voice a gurgle in his throat. He's a little like the Frankenstein monster only he moves faster.

EDDIE: You bit my dick off. *(He drives her up against the wall.)* You . . . bit . . . my . . . dick off.
NETTY: Eddie . . . come on, Eddie.

Lessa fights, but he maintains the grip.

EDDIE: Bit . . . bit my . . . dick.

TIGER: *(Trying to move.)* Get him off her.

Eddie makes only a gurgling roar now. He bends Lessa backward over the bench.

NETTY: Come on, Eddie. Come on, Eddie.

A very loud voice cuts across the ruckus. It is Kid.

KID: Stosha!! Stosha "The Wild Man" Oronovsky!

Eddie throws Lessa down and turns. The Kid opens his arms with a radiant smile.

KID: You the cream in my coffee, man.

Kid slaps his own hand and holds it out. Eddie, trancelike, slaps it and they are into a six or eight beat streetshake at the end of which the Kid drives his knee upward into Eddie's groin. Eddie lets out pain that lasts an eternity. When he stops the Kid says:

KID: You slicker than a snake on ice, baby.

Eddie crashes to the floor insensate. Unfortunately he falls on Tiger's cat box. Tiger doesn't see it. Netty does.

NETTY: Oh God!

TIGER: You O.K., Lessa?

LESSA: Yeah. I'm fine. Stay off me.

The Kid turns to Lessa who has stumbled to her feet.

KID: Did you ever put the shot in Seoul, Korea?

LESSA: *(Nods.)* Down in Seoul, Korea.

KID: Ooooooo, you were fine! Now you go on up there and have a good time. I like to see people enjoy themselves.

Lessa nods and moves out of the room.

TIGER: How'd you know his ring name?

KID: Read the poster on the way in. I got me a memory I could point out the same fly five days apart.

TIGER: You think he's hurt bad?

KID: *(A big smile.)* He might be if she bit his dick off.

TIGER: *(Sings lightly.)* "Walkin' down the avenue . . ."

NETTY: Tiger honey, I got bad, bad news.

TIGER: What?

NETTY: Well, he fell on your dog.

TIGER: Where?

NETTY: Kind of flush, direct *on* her. *(She kneels by Eddie and lifts his upstage side a little.)* Oh my. Tiger darlin', I'm afraid she passed.

TIGER: Yeah? *(Netty nods.)* O.K.

NETTY: Honey, I'm sorry.

TIGER: *(Tears rolling down her cheek.)* O.K.

NOLA: *(Pounding on the door.)* Let me outta here!!

NETTY: Oh my God, I forgot. *(Heads for the closet.)*

KID: Let her cool down.

TIGER: *(Trying to get up.)* Whoa, got the nods.

KID: No last name, huh?

TIGER: No name.

KID: You know what I see when I look in your eyes, Tiger?

TIGER: Yeah, what?

KID: Morphine. Morphine, am I right?

TIGER: Yeah.

KID: Oh, that's a sweet low, isn't it? I had me several months of that down in Calcutta. Oh I'd cry and I'd cry and I'd sleep like a baby.

There is an ugly roar from the crowd upstairs.

TIGER: We're all fucked.

NETTY: We are.

KID: Not me, I got Florida real estate.

NETTY: I hope Bigman don't hurt her.

TIGER: Yeah.

NETTY: *(To Tiger who is throwing stuff in a bag.)* What are you doin'?

TIGER: Movin' out. *(Starts tossing stuff in the flight bag.)*

NETTY: You got no place to go.

TIGER: I can go where that crowd ain't. *(Another roar.)* Fuck this place.

NETTY: *(Looking down at Eddie.)* One thing, Lessa, she'll be gone.

TIGER: Eddie don't look like he's wrestlin' in Memphis.

NOLA: Tiger? Somebody? *(There is a tremendous roar from upstairs.)*

KID: *(Looking at the ceiling.)* Uh-huh, they like it.

TIGER: *(Looking around the room.)* Ain't much works out.

KID: I had an uncle lost his greeting card business, on the next day, the next day he won an *all expenses paid vacation* for two in Hawaii.

NETTY: That ain't us, oldtimer.

KID: Outside his hotel he put fifty cents in a machine to get a papaya juice an the can got stuck. He shook that machine and it tipped over on him, broke both his legs.

TIGER: Sure, it works that way.

KID: In that hospital he met a beautiful nurse who a year after became his wife . . .

NETTY: You're kiddin'?

KID: That's right, two years after that she poisoned him for his insurance. Oh, you never know what's coming off next.

There is shrieking in the hall and moments later Dottie appears holding one hand over her face. Her head and face seem covered with blood.

DOTTIE: My face! Oh God, my face. My eye. Where's my eye?

NETTY: Jee-sus.

DOTTIE: *(Trying to see the damage in the makeup table mirror.)* I'm ruint. Ruint in the race wars. My God, I can't see out of my eye.

NETTY: Let me look.

DOTTIE: *(Raging.)* I got to be in the movies!

NETTY: Sit still! Where's your sister?

DOTTIE: Went under. Some thyroid giant drug her into the crowd by one leg. I seen somebody rip off her G-string an eat it. They've gone crazy.

NETTY: Looks like it's mainly the nose.

DOTTIE: *(Shrieking.)* Oh Jesus, I'm disfigured!

> *Lessa enters, she has Mother, her dress ripped and completely disheveled, in a headlock.*

MOTHER: Three hundred dollars.

> *Lessa bangs Mother's head into a locker.*

MOTHER: Six hundred dollars.
TIGER: Hi there, Lessa.

> *Lessa bangs Mother into the lockers again.*

LESSA: *(To Tiger.)* How you doin'?
MOTHER: You bitch, you tore my artificial breast off. *(Mother pulls free.)*
LESSA: So long, Mama.

> *She hits her cleanly with a punch. Mother goes down.*

NETTY: Godammit, stop roughhousin'!
TIGER: Bye, Netty.
NETTY: Hold on.
TIGER: Adios, Bigman.

> *Bigman enters, his shirt is torn, his suit jacket a collage of spilled Coke, Cracker Jacks and beer. He's obviously been on the floor in the arena.*

BIGMAN: *(Acknowledges her without thinking.)* Yeah.
DOTTIE: Is that a broken nose?
TIGER: Lef' three cans of gourmet dog food.
DOTTIE: My God, that's a broken nose.

> *Tiger exits. Bigman focuses on Lessa.*

BIGMAN: You have screwed with my hustle. You miserable slimeball, five-way cunt.

Lessa charges him, knocking him down. For the first moment of the fight she seems to dominate him. She gets him in a hammerlock. He breaks it. Slowly the fight begins to change. Soon Bigman dominates. Then he begins to administer a real beating. He brutalizes Lessa. It must look like he might actually kill her. During the fight other dialogue takes place.

NETTY: Lessa! Lessa, for Christ's sake, blow it off! Lessa!

DOTTIE: *(Over to the fallen Mother.)* Mama, she broke my nose, Mama.

NETTY: Bigman!

BIGMAN: *(To Netty.)* Off me.

DOTTIE: There'll be media, Mama. We got to go. We can't be on the T.V. all ruint. Come on, Mama. *(She pulls at her.)* My God, it's the apocalypse. *(Pulling her to the door.)* They ate Dolly, Mama. They like cannibals, Mama.

BIGMAN: *(Beating Lessa.)* Yes. Oh yes. Oh yes.

DOTTIE: Come on, Mama. I got you. I got you, Mama. *(Pulls her out the doorway and exits.)*

Bigman slams Lessa against the lockers. She falls down. Without warning, and from where he sits, the Kid shoots him with Dolly's gun. Bigman sits suddenly down, awkwardly, as if surprised. The room freezes. Sound from the arena where a full-scale riot is in progress rocks around them.

BIGMAN: Who shot me? *(He focuses on the Kid.)* You shot me. *(He sees Eddie.)* What's Eddie doin' here? Christ, he shot Eddie. You're a serial killer.

Lessa lurches to her feet; feels if she's in working order; crosses to bucket of water. Throws some on face.

NETTY: *(Looking at the carnage.)* You O.K., Lessa?

DANI: *(Enters.)* The rubes they . . . unbelievable . . . on the floor, in the ring, like a bee swarm . . . broke pipes, water gushin' in . . . I'm tellin' ya . . . the rubes gone apeshit . . . *(Sees Bigman, Eddie.)* What the hell?

BIGMAN: I'm shot. I'm shot down.

NETTY: Let me see.

BIGMAN: Get off me!

Lessa still in a rage trashes the sisters' makeup tables. Sweeps tubes and bottles onto the floor. Rips tables away from the wall and upends them.

LESSA: Yes!!!

DANI: Goddammit, Lessa.

Lessa opens the Knockout Sisters' trunk, goes through the clothes, flings them around room.

DANI: *(To Bigman.)* Who shot you?

BIGMAN: *(Vastly irritated.)* Who gives a shit? I'm shot.

DANI: *(Indicating the Kid.)* Are you still here?

KID: Just passin' through.

DANI: Is that Eddie? Eddie, is that you?

NETTY: Jesus.

LESSA: Sequins, man. I hate sequins.

DANI: *(She checks Eddie.)* Jesus. This ain't my style. We got to blow, Netty, we got to blow now. *(Glass breaks somewhere outside the door.)* You hear that? The rubes are comin'. *(Turns to Kid.)* Don't shoot. Don't shoot me.

KID: *(Chuckling.)* O.K.

LESSA: *(Surveying the damage she has wrought.)* Lookin' good.

Nola pounds on the door. Dani startles.

NETTY: Oh, God.

DANI: Who is it? What is that?

NETTY: I completely . . . *(She unlocks door.)*

DANI: We got Dwayne again?

NOLA: *(Emerging.)* I been . . . no air . . . banging. I been yelling . . . *(She sees.)* Jeeminy, holy cow, boy-Friday.

Lessa packs her stuff.

DANI: Now. Out now.

More crashes outside. Dani throws stuff in her bag. She scoops up the money from her fight with Nola. Netty kneels by Bigman.

DANI: There's gonna be cops and bad shit.

NOLA: We're gonna die, we're all gonna die.

NETTY: You want me to stay, Bigman? *(She touches him, he yells.)* Sorry.

BIGMAN: That hurt, O.K.?

DANI: *(To Netty.)* Let's roll. Come on, Netty.

NETTY: *(Back to Bigman.)* Poor darlin'.

BIGMAN: Will you get your fingers out of the bullet hole?

NETTY: Bigman.

BIGMAN: You could kill a fuckin' tree.

DANI: *(Pulling Netty away.)* Cops, Netty, freaked out rubes . . . *(Gestures at the fallen bodies.)* They gonna pin this shit on us.

KID: Say . . .

DANI: *(Whirling.)* Don't even look at me.

KID: Kid Cayman . . . How you doin'?

DANI: Screw off.

Angry crowd burst.

DANI: *(A sudden thought.)* You got a car, Pop?

KID: A car, huh?

DANI: A drivable car.

KID: Got me a '79 Cadmium Red Pontiac Firebird parked right out front in a handicapped zone.

LESSA: You lookin' for company?

KID: Always lookin' for company. Got a workin' radio, a part-time clock, and she seats six comfortable. *(Tosses her the keys.)* Pull it in the back; I'll be along.

LESSA: *(Looking at him.)* O.K.

KID: Don't mention it. Ooooooo, you was poetry in motion!

People are standing around.

DANI: Are you all like *deranged*? Let's split.

NETTY: Where?

DANI: When the hell did we ever know where?

Lessa moves out without speaking.

DANI: Move it. Hump it. Move it.
NETTY: *(Taking the terrified Nola's hand.)* Come on, honey. Mama take care of you.
DANI: *(Pulls and pushes Nola and Netty out.)* Move it. Move it. Beat it. Go! Go! Beat it. Beat it!

Nola and Netty exit.

LESSA: Eddie. Hey Eddie.

He suddenly shoots out a hand and grabs her ankle.

LESSA: Let go.

He doesn't. He tries to pull her over. She stamps on his wrist. He lets go with a grunt. She goes down on one knee just outside his grasp.

LESSA: I hope you don't die, but I hope you come goddamn close. Amen. *(She rises.)*
DANI: *(Speaks to Kid.)* Hell, that oughta make him feel better.

Lessa exits.

DANI: So long, Bigman.
BIGMAN: Get me some help.
DANI: *(Ambivalently.)* Sure. *(To Kid.)* Move it out, Pops. *(She exits.)*

Kid rises and closes the hall door. He twist-locks it. We hear the sound of the approaching crowd.

BIGMAN: You snuffed me.
KID: You won't die. I didn't hit you in the right spot. *(Looks at Eddie.)* I hit him in the right spot.
EDDIE: . . . My dick.
KID: Uh-huh. *(To Bigman.)* You Jack Vag's boy, used to be a coffee kid down to Joe Louis Gym.

Bigman looks at him amazed.

KID: Now you doin' this trash.
BIGMAN: What the hell are *you* doin'?
KID: Keepin' you company.

Crash from outside.

BIGMAN: Don't ditch me.
KID: You want a smoke?
BIGMAN: Yeah.
KID: Hurtin' people, now that's a serious gig, see. I don't play with it. I don't fool nobody. *(Big smile.)* When I hurt 'em, I hurts 'em. *(Puts the cigarette in Bigman's mouth.)* I ever tell you I fought Sandy Sadler three times? Second fight a woman come to the dressing room, bare shoulders, ball gown, took off a diamond bracelet, give it to me, said, "You, sir, gave a fine account of yourself." *(He tips over a bank of lockers, stage right. Points at a door behind the locker which has been revealed.)* Come right through there in that China silk dress. Took me to her home on a bluff overlooked a wide turn in the Mississippi and there we danced the Samba to a sixteen-piece all-girl orchestra from Venezuela. Sandy Sadler, he was there. Two-Ton Tony Galento, he was in town. Ooooo, he was light on his feet. The referee, he danced with the governor's wife and a secret service man. Ol' Jake Lamotta, he slow danced with a nine-year-old girl standin' on his shoes. Oh, that was a sight. The waiters in their white coats, they joined in. All of us laughin', hummin' along, all doing the rumba, while the moon went down. *(He heads out.)* There was a girl playin' clarinet in that band later left a camelia on my pillow. *(His voice recedes down the hall.)* 'Course those were different times. Different times. Different times.

A moment. Someone begins pounding on the hall door. We hear, "Y'all in there . . . you're road kill, you hear me." Bigman startles awake.

BIGMAN: Eddie?

EDDIE: Yeah?
BIGMAN: You there?
EDDIE: Yeah?
BIGMAN: How much you got left?

> *No answer. The lights start to fade. A fire axe breaks through the panel of the door. Once, twice, a third time. The lights are out.*

END

Regina Taylor

Watermelon Rinds

For Novella Nelson and the Louisville cast—and special thanks, Mom

Watermelon Rinds was directed in 1993 by Novella Nelson with the following cast:

JES SEMPLE.............................. Roger Robinson
LOTTIE SEMPLE .... Kalimi A. Baxter
WILLY SEMPLE .... Donald Griffin
LIZA SEMPLE .... Regina Byrd Smith
PINKIE SEMPLE............................. Elain Graham
PAPA TOMMY SEMPLE .... Ray Johnson
MAMA PEARL SEMPLE .... Yvette Hawkins
MARVA SEMPLE-WEISSE........................ Judy Tate

Scene Design............................... Paul Owen
Costume Design .... Toni-Leslie James
Lighting Design.......................... Marcus Dilliard
Sound Design .... Casey L. Warren
Property Master....................... Mark J. Bissonnette
Stage Manager......................... Frazier W. Marsh
Assistant Stage Manager..................... Lori M. Doyle

Second Assistant Stage Manager . . . . Emily Fox
Movement Supervisor . . . . Ervon Neely
Production Dramaturg . . . . Michael Bigelow Dixon
Casting arranged by Judy Dennis

FOR CAUTION NOTICE SEE PAGE OPPOSITE TABLE OF CONTENTS.

PLACE:

A household in an urban neighborhood.

TIME:

The present.

Watermelon Rinds

SCENE 1

Jes stands in spotlight DR.

I don't like to go to plays. I'd rather sit on the corner and play poker, a little dominoes, talk loud at passing women, watch cats copulating on the sidewalk, turn up the volume and do the loose goose . . . or do the nasty with a lady whose butt costs less than the price of a g-d theater ticket.

I bought a theater ticket once. The paper said it was a black comedy. I went inside. I sat there for two hours. I didn't see one black. And it sure wasn't a comedy. Just a bunch of white people talking about throwing babies out with their bath water and putting hedgehogs up their you-know-whats. (Excuse me, ladies.) But as I said, this ain't no black comedy. This is absurd. Then I got up and walked out.

BLACKOUT

SCENE 2

Lights come up on a living room stacked high with articles of living . . . clothes, books, furniture, a candelabra, old toy baby carriage . . . everything including the kitchen sink. Boxes are scattered. Some empty, half-full, and full, taped, and labeled—pottery, Lottie's clothes, bar-b-que grill, Sam, etc. There is a clearing that leads off R to the kitchen. Another path leads to a door UL to the other parts of the house. Off L is the door to the outside. DL is a window.

Lottie, fourteen years old, wearing a white slip that shows her newly-budding form, is standing on that table doing a barefoot softshoe.

LOTTIE: *(Singing cheerfully.)* YANG YANG YANG YANG. YANG YANG YANG. *(A knocking on the door.)* I'll get it.

WILLY: *(Offstage.)* Don't touch that door. Nobody lives here. We're moving.

LIZA: *(Offstage.)* Are they here already? Everything isn't prepared yet.

WILLY: *(Offstage.)* You never know who's on the other side—

LIZA: *(Offstage.)* Lottie, are you dressed yet?

WILLY: *(Offstage.)* Damn BEAN EATERS.

LIZA: *(Offstage.)* If they're here and you're not dressed yet . . . *(More knocking.)*

LOTTIE: Who's there?

JES: *(Offstage.)* Jes.

LOTTIE: Jes who?

JES: *(Offstage.)* Jes me and my shadow . . . Let me in.

Lottie opens the door. Jes is there.

JES: *(His best Groucho Marx imitation.)* This country club once refused me entrance. I said—Fine, I don't want to join any club that would have me for a member. They said—their swimming pool was for whites only—I said my great-great-grandmother was raped by her slave master—I'm part white—can I go in up to my knees?

LIZA: *(Offstage.)* Is anyone here yet?

LOTTIE: No, ma'am.

JES: I'm hungry. When we were growing up we were so po'—our parents had to sleep in the same bed. We were so po' . . .

Willy enters from UR carrying a bundle and box. He begins sorting.

WILLY: They'll all come, they'll eat, they'll leave, we'll move. Get off the table, Lottie.

LOTTIE: Guess who I am. *(Tapping and singing.)* YANG YANG YANG YANG. YANG YANG YANG.

WILLY: You're my daughter, is who.

JES: Though a man can never tell for sure—

LOTTIE: No. Not your daughter.

JES: A woman can tell a man anything.

LOTTIE: Shirley Temple. Get it?

JES: Shirley Temple Black.

LOTTIE: Shirley Temple in *The Blue Bird of Happiness*.

WILLY: Shirley-going-to-get-her-butt-beat-for-dancing-on-the-table-when-I-told-her-to-get-off-Temple. *(Lottie gets off the table.)*

JES: You may be Shirley but your hips are Monroe. Girl, you are getting as big as your mama.

LIZA: *(Offstage.)* I know I'm not known for my cooking but this is a special occasion. I can feel it. *(Then:)* Lottie, are you dressed yet? You're getting too big to run around with nothing on. *(Lottie takes two nickels and drops them down the front of her slip and sticks out her chest.)*

LOTTIE: TA-DA! They didn't fall down. Get it?

JES: Do you know another one?

LIZA: *(Offstage.)* They'll be here any minute and if you're not dressed yet . . . *(Jes takes a glass, puts it to Lottie's elbow, pumps her arm and the glass fills with milk.)**

LOTTIE: How did you do that?

LIZA: *(Offstage.)* Heard of a girl abducted, half-naked from her own house . . . *(Jes drinks the milk.)*

LOTTIE: How?

LIZA: *(Offstage)* . . . never seen again.

JES: I'll tell you the secret when you get older.

LIZA: *(Offstage.)* Found out later that it was a member of her own family.

LOTTIE: I don't want to ever grow up. Do you remember Shirley Temple in *The Blue Bird of Happiness*?

JES: *Blue Bird of Happiness?* Isn't that the one with Bill "Bojangles" Robinson? She used to do a lot of films with old Bojangles. He was one of the best tap dancers in the world. They attributed it to his big feet. What else can you do with feet that big? I heard he taught little Miss Shirley everything she knew about dancing. And how she loved to dance with her Bojangles. Sweet, black, big-footed Bojangles. Always smiling, both of them together—dancing and smiling—That's why they took him away.

LOTTIE: Who did?

JES: When they found out why they were always grinning—they dragged him away, kicking, and cut off his—

---

*Check with a magic shop. One suggestion might be to use a two-sided glass.

WILLY: JES!

JES: His feet. Nigger with all that rhythm and no feet—what's he going to do?

LOTTIE: That's not funny, Uncle Jes.

JES: Bojangles didn't think it was funny either. Can't tap with your hands—though some have tried—just can't get the same kind of satisfaction. *(We hear a round of firecrackers. Lottie runs to the window.)*

WILLY: Damn bean eaters!

JES: Blow your hands off—Don't come crying to me.

WILLY: That's why we're moving.

JES: "Don't come crying to me." That's what they used to say.

WILLY: Lottie, get away from that window.

LOTTIE: It was so pretty. It shot straight up—a bright red ball— and exploded in mid-air. It sprinkled down like rain. Red rain . . .

JES: "Blow your hands off. . . ."

WILLY: I don't want you going out of this house today, Lottie.

LOTTIE: You never want me to go out.

WILLY: Damn neighborhood. BEAN EATERS—try to find any excuse for disturbing my peace of mind. *(To Lottie.)* I don't want you to talk to them, touch them, look at them directly. *(Then:)* That's why we're moving.

LOTTIE: When are we moving?

WILLY: Soon. Very soon. Leave everything behind. It's just going to be good things for my little bluebird. *(Tying up the box he has been filling.)* Boxes. Everything I own, memories, conversations—in these boxes. Shit. Tombs. I've been sitting in the same spot, the exact same spot for the last twenty years and steadily progressing backwards. How can that be? This used to be my favorite shirt. What's left of it . . . rags . . . pieces of something else . . .

JES: Heard you got King Tut's tiara stashed away up in there.

WILLY: Maybe . . . but damned if I can remember which box.

JES: Ain't that the way it goes?

WILLY: One day real soon we're going to move—move forward—move out and get us a big mansion for my little bluebird. Sacrifices have been made and it's any moment now.

JES: People can't move forward without some sacrifice.

WILLY: Mortgages, loans, scraping, saving, hard work.

JES: Man knew from the beginning. While beating on their drums, and getting high on mooloo juice—they dipped their bodies in monkey fat and danced—danced until the earth gave way to valleys. While praying to their gods they burned sacred offerings . . .

LIZA: *(Offstage.)* Fried chicken . . . bar-b-que ribs . . . smoked ham . . .

JES: . . . the fatted calf, the lamb, the first-born male, the virgin.

LOTTIE: Everybody is coming today. YANG YANG YANG YANG.

LIZA: *(Offstage.)* . . . pickled pig's feet . . . ox-tail stew . . . hog head cheese . . . I know I'm not known for my cooking but I've really outdone myself today.

WILLY: She used to be able to cook.

LIZA: *(Offstage.)* Mmmm. It smells good in here.

WILLY: That's why I married her.

LIZA: *(Offstage.)* Get out of here. I don't want anyone peeping into my kitchen until I'm ready. You're going to be so proud.

WILLY: Every Friday and Saturday, this was before I proposed, she would lure me into her kitchen with a promise of a taste from her pot.

LIZA: *(Offstage.)* Remember those things I used to fix for you, Willy? I'm feeling it again.

WILLY: Yes, Liza.

LIZA: *(Offstage.)* You don't believe me, do you? Man doesn't believe anything until it's rolling around on his tongue. You'll see.

WILLY: *(Hopeful.)* It is beginning to smell . . .

LOTTIE: I smell something.

JES: I'm hungry enough. *(Willy picks up another bundle and exits.)* When we were growing up, we were so po'—our termites reported us to the Better Housing Bureau. We were so po'— we'd wait until the lights went out and stole the leftovers from our rat's pantry. We were so po'—No, po' ain't funny, there is nothing funny about being po'—We were so po' that fourteen of us had to sleep in one bed while the rest slept on the floor—which was pretty difficult considering that we were so po' we couldn't afford a house with indoor plumbing—so po' we lived in the outhouse. We lived in an outhouse so small that those sleeping on the floor were likely to fall into the hole if they weren't careful. Those sleeping on the floor learned to hold on to each other and the walls. But every once in awhile you would be awakened in the middle of the night by a surprised echoing scream and you'd know another brother or sister had let go or was pushed and was lost in that bottomless stinky pit. They said that if you were lucky that you would fall straight to China. If you were lucky. We were so po'—we had a dog once. We named him Lucky. He starved to death. Lucky—we ate him. I did keep a pet cockroach. He was as big as a dog. Named him Rex. Walked him on a leash. Ever try to teach a cockroach to roll over and play dead? Ever try to curb a roach? Which leg does he raise? Listen, Lottie—we were so po'—we had to devour our own in order to survive. Do you know what c-a-n-n-i-b-u-l-l spells?

We hear firecrackers. Jes falls to the floor and convulses as if he were repeatedly shot. Willy re-enters, carrying another box.

WILLY: Damn bean eaters.
LOTTIE: *(Watching Jes convulse.)* Are you dead yet? Uncle Jes is such a riot.
JES: *(Finally.)* Hear that?—'NAM.
LOTTIE: Were you in 'Nam, Uncle Jes?
WILLY: That's why we're moving.
JES: The summer of '68. Hot, white beach. Beirut.
WILLY: You were never in Beirut. Shooting, killing, raping.
LOTTIE: That's what it's like in Beirut?
WILLY: This neighborhood. Bean eaters with their ghetto blasters and uzis.
JES: If I wasn't in El Salvador—then—what happened to my hands? *(Jes loses his hands up his sleeves and chases Lottie—screaming—around the room.)*
WILLY: The real estate man said that we were buying into a good solid middle-class neighborhood. We moved in. The first on the block. Fine. A couple of families moved out. Fine. Next thing you know—another black family wants to move in. White flight. They flew. Mass exodus. The next thing you

know—any kind of nigger and his pit bull is moving in. Drug dealers, bean eaters and their pet cockroaches big enough to walk on leashes. If I wanted to buy into a ghetto—I would never have moved. This is not what was promised. Sacrifices have been made.

JES: When we were growing up, we were so po'—

WILLY: We were never *poor.* Yes, we had to struggle, but we were never poor. Anything worth anything is worth some sacrifice. Remember that, Lottie.

JES: We weren't poor. We were so po' we couldn't afford the extra o and r. Ever been to a all-white beach in Alabama with a sign on it—"No dogs or coloreds allowed"?

WILLY: . . . can he go in up to his knees . . .

LOTTIE: That's how it was in the old days?

WILLY: They don't have beaches in Alabama.

JES: 1968. Hot, white beach. Alabama. He said, "Boy, what you doing on this here beach?" I said, "Boy? Who are you talking to?" And he and his friends took out these knives, long enough for shish ke-babin', and he says, "I'm talking to you, nigger." And that is how I lost my hands down a white woman's bikini in Alabamy. *(Jes loses his hands up his sleeves and chases Lottie—screaming—around the room.)*

WILLY: First on the block.

JES: No, I've never been to Iraq.

WILLY: Should have been the last.

JES: But I know how it feels.

LIZA: *(Offstage, singing.)*

There is a fountain filled with blood,
Drawn from Emmanuel's veins . . .
And sinners plunged beneath that flood, lose all their guilt and stain.
Lose all their guilt and stain, lose all their guilt and stain.
And sinners plunged beneath that flood, lose all their guilt and stain.

WILLY: *(Hopeful.)* It's been a long time since I heard her singing in the kitchen. *(We hear a knocking on the door.)*

LOTTIE: Who's there?

PINKIE: *(Offstage.)* The big bad wolf. Let me in.

LOTTIE: Not by the hair on my chinny, chin, chin.

PINKIE: *(Offstage.)* Your chin, my ass. Girl, open this door.

Lottie opens the door and Pinkie enters. She is very pregnant.

WILLY: Well look what the cat dragged in.

PINKIE: Boy, don't get started with me. I came here to celebrate, to have a good time. This time I'm going to have a nice time with my family. *(To Lottie.)* Look at this girl, getting so healthy and fat. I see the bees done bit.

JES: You can't talk about getting fat . . .

PINKIE: *(Rubbing her belly.)* . . . any minute now.

WILLY: What's the count up to now? Every time I see you, you're pregnant. What do you do, Pinkie?

PINKIE: Well if you don't know—I'm not going to tell you.

JES: Where are the rest of them?

PINKIE: Left them at home. You know my kids . . .

WILLY: Wild and untamed.

PINKIE: I see you redecorated the place.

WILLY: We're moving any day.

PINKIE: I heard that before. When are we going to eat?

LOTTIE: You know how slow Mama is.

PINKIE: Ain't you fast? Why aren't you in there helping?

LOTTIE: She said that she didn't want any help. *(We hear a crash of pots and dishes.)*

PINKIE: Liza, are you all right in there?

LIZA: *(Offstage.)* Pinkie! I'm just fine. Everything is fine in here. Never mind me. Any minute, and we'll be feasting at a banquet.

PINKIE: All right, then . . . *(Lower.)* I hope you got a McDonald's nearby. I'm hungry. My feet hurt and my back. *(She rubs her stomach.)* I might name this one—Jessee.

WILLY: I don't want to hear it.

PINKIE: I didn't say nothing. Let me hush. But this one is going to turn out.

WILLY: Just like your other ones.

PINKIE: They just weren't inspired. They had it in them but they just weren't inspired.

WILLY: Where is little Lumumba?

PINKIE: Big Lumumba. He hasn't written to me in a long time.

WILLY: And coke-head Marion? Heard Eldridge went crazy—

PINKIE: He was a hyperactive child . . .

WILLY: Carmichael fled the country . . . George was in a shoot-out in prison.

PINKIE: He's dead. They were just born in the wrong time, is all. That's what I figure. The time wasn't right. Not for them. But this one—by the time he gets through puberty . . . *(She notices Lottie staring at her belly.)* You never seen a pregnant woman before? Do you want to rub my belly? *(Lottie places her hands on Pinkie's stomach. Then, startled, Lottie jerks away.)* Don't be scared. That's just him saying hello. *(To her belly.)* What's that? You saying, "Who's that rubbing on Mama's belly?" That's your cousin, Lottie . . . No, you haven't met her before.

LOTTIE: He can hear you?

PINKIE: Of course he can. Talk to you too—if you want to get to know him better. He'll talk your ear off.

LOTTIE: *(Her head on Pinkie's belly.)* I can hear him breathing.

WILLY: Unborn babies don't breathe, Lottie.

PINKIE: Who are you—Dr. Spock? The girl knows what she hears.

LOTTIE: I think I can make out . . . he's saying something . . . but it's too low.

PINKIE: He can be a bit soft-spoken.

WILLY: I may not be a pediatrician but most fetuses don't speak.

PINKIE: That's brilliant, Sherlock. Most don't. I think I'll name him X.

JES: X. I like that.

WILLY: First, Jessee and now—X. As far as I know Malcolm X died a long time ago. Just who are you claiming this child is by?

PINKIE: Do you really want to know? I didn't think so.

JES: X Semple. I like that.

PINKIE: Thank you.

WILLY: And how do you know it's going to be a boy?

PINKIE: How does every mother know?

WILLY: Oh, he told you.

PINKIE: He didn't have to . . . He isn't just kicking up in there . . . I can feel him. Three-inch erections pounding against my womb, four or five times a day. That's how I know.

WILLY: Three inches! . . . Four or five . . . Pinkie!

PINKIE: I suppose you're going to tell me that it's not possible. How would you know? You've never been pregnant.

WILLY: My wife has and she never told me . . .

PINKIE: How would she know? The only child she had was a girl. X Semple. Finally, a manchild to do credit to this family.

WILLY: And what does that mean?

PINKIE: I mean, that not since our brother Sam, as stupid as he was, has there been a Semple man in this family worth the salt he pees.

WILLY: Wait a minute . . .

PINKIE: Let me hush. I came here to celebrate and have a good time with my family.

LOTTIE: I can feel it. It is a boy . . . Daddy . . . it IS a boy!

WILLY: Lottie, take your hands off this second.

PINKIE: Yeah, that's him. Just humping away.

LOTTIE: I felt him!

WILLY: Didn't your mother tell you to go get dressed? Go get dressed, Lottie.

PINKIE: *(Rocking.)* Um-um . . . that's my boy . . . mmm-hmm. *(Lottie reluctantly exits.)* Why do you want to send Lottie out, Willy? She's a woman now. There are things she needs to know. You always have been protective.

WILLY: She's still a child.

Lottie is in her room, dressing.

LOTTIE: When the hens come home . . . Sometimes the voices come from outside. My parents. At night I can hear them through the walls. Sometimes I hear the walls quaking, banging. Their voices rise and fall in arias. On the other side. Of the wall. The sheets flapping. Flapping above them. And the beating of bird wings against its bars. In those mornings I sneak into their room. After they've risen. And search the room. The closets, between the bedcovers . . . searching for signs . . . feathers of the slaughtered birds. Sometimes I find a spot of blood and always the fresh smell of death. Yang, yang, yang, yang, yang, yang, yang. When the roosters come home? When the chickens . . . What Pinkie's baby whispered in my ear . . . Sometimes the voices come from outside. On the other side. Out there. Like low-flying helicopters, their voices. One day—looking out. Three boys talking loud and throwing bottles against the wall. One was black as midnight. One with coiled snakes hissing all over his head. And the third tall and sinewy like a swaying palm. The first one saw me spying and smiled at me. His teeth glistened with gold. Rapunzel, Rapunzel, let down your golden hair. And he climbed up to her ivory tower . . . Sometimes the voices come from inside me. Clear as a bell. She was a poor peasant girl and barely thirteen when she saw the visions and heard the voices that told her to pick up the shield and sword and march to . . . New Orleans? One day my voices will tell me what and when. My voices will explode. The walls will be knocked down. And you'll see freedom flapping its wings and crowing. When the morning comes.

WILLY: Some things she doesn't need to know. Not now.

PINKIE: Then when?

WILLY: Some things she doesn't ever have to know about. Not like we knew them. No need. Some things she never needs to hear, see or touch.

PINKIE: No pain, no gain.

WILLY: The things we went through—I went through so she would never have to. I cherish her, protect her, fight for my destiny.

PINKIE: One day she'll have to learn to fight for herself. Locking her in her room isn't going to help. It's just going to make the lessons she's going to have to learn just that much harder.

WILLY: Yeah, you know all about it.

PINKIE: That's right. I have the proof of my life experience written all over my body. From stretch marks to razor scars from a drunken lover . . . I still have the welts on my back which were the gifts from our dear parents.

WILLY: Our parents never beat us.

PINKIE: That's how bad they beat you—BRAIN DAMAGE. You can't even remember. I remember—Mama tried to break my neck, one time.

WILLY: If only she had broken your tongue.

PINKIE: You know it's true.

WILLY: The only time our parents laid hand on us was in love.

PINKIE: They loved to lay hand on me, fist on me, extension cord . . . frying pan.

WILLY: It wasn't so bad. Though, there was this time when Daddy chased Jes with a baseball bat.

JES: *(To audience.)* Yeah, yeah . . . I gave him a good run. He was fast back then. I ran into the park and lost him around the lake.

WILLY: You had to come back home sometime.

PINKIE: Daddy sat patiently on the porch.

JES: *(To audience.)* For three days.

PINKIE: Three hours. Dinnertime, you came home.

WILLY: Slunk home with your tail tucked between your legs.

JES: *(To audience.)* He said, "Boy, are you ready?" "Yes, sir." "Then, get in the house and let down the shades and then let down your pants."

PINKIE: *(Sarcastic.)* They only laid hands on us in love.

JES: *(To audience.)* "This is going to hurt me more than you. I'm only starting what the MAN is going to finish."

WILLY: *(To audience.)* He always said that we couldn't afford to be lazy and undisciplined. That's what *they* expected from us. And he came down harder on us living up to their expectations. That was the world. That's what I learned from the whuppings.

PINKIE: *(To audience.)* Your own will treat you as bad or worse than anyone else. That's what I learned.

WILLY: Pinkie . . .

PINKIE: Sam never got any licks.

JES: I sure do miss Sam.

WILLY: He was always the favorite.

PINKIE: He should have been. He was a saint, as stupid as he was.

WILLY: Like the time he fell out of the treehouse.

JES: *(To audience.)* . . . Some got lost down the hole . . .

PINKIE: *(To audience.)* Jes pushed him.

JES: *(To audience.)* He jumped.

PINKIE: I was in the house cleaning up after you lazy lunkheads, as usual, when I heard his scream. I never will forget it.

WILLY: I had gone to the candy shop and left Jes up in the treehouse with little Sammy. I heard him five blocks away . . .

PINKIE: I ran to the backyard, yelling, "What's going on?" and there was little Sam lying flat on the ground.

JES: He just jumped.

PINKIE: And Jes was up in the treehouse, looking down, laughing.

JES: I told him not to.

PINKIE: Just laughing your head off.

JES: *(To audience.)* We were playing—Tarzan—and he was Cheetah. I lost my balance and the next thing I knew—he had flung himself off. He said something about wanting to cushion my fall. I told him not to.

WILLY: Carried that big old bump on his head for years.

PINKIE: Just laughing your head off.

WILLY: That was just like little Sam.

JES: Saigon.

PINKIE: He volunteered.

JES: *(To audience.)* I was a conscientious objector.

PINKIE: How was Canada?

JES: 1968. Hot, white beach. The Bahamas.

WILLY: One of my legs is longer than the other.

PINKIE: He was a real hero. Worth his salt. Stupid as mud, but a hero just the same. Blowing up like that. He should have died over in Vietnam for his country. What'd he die for? Should have been blown to bits on some land mine, fighting someone else's battle. Instead of blowing up for . . . What did he die for? *(Silence.)* Don't look at me like that. You're the one with all this stuff. *(Indicates box marked "SAM.")* Look at this. What's in here?

WILLY: Don't start stirring things up, Pinkie. Everything's packed down and ordered . . .

PINKIE: *(In Sam's box.)* His uniform. His football trophy, basketball trophy, baseball . . . track . . . honor roll pin, medals of honor, dog tags . . . his varsity jacket . . . *(Cradling the rag.)* He blew up and wasn't enough to piece together for a decent funeral.

WILLY: Hush, Pinkie.

PINKIE: And everybody knew and nobody said a word. He said he was going to die.

WILLY: This isn't the time, Pinkie.

PINKIE: When? When, then? What did our brother die for?

WILLY: Too late now to look back. Time now to look to the future.

PINKIE: Keep your eye on the prize . . . And what a sweet crackerjack prize you got. Big old house, two car garage, a fence for them junkies outside to lean up on . . . and now you're moving to a bigger, brighter, white neighborhood. Leave all us po' dunk Negroes behind. You and Marva. Especially Marva, living fat.

WILLY: Everyone got theirs. You grabbed your share with both hands . . .

PINKIE: My children were hungry—

WILLY: Weren't we all. Enough said.

PINKIE: Let me hush.

JES: All of that is past and done. Let it go. Spit it out like a old woman's dried up tiddy. No use sucking on that. Set your teeth on the future's firm, sweet breast.

We hear a clear, sweet bell. A light comes up on Lottie in her room.

JES: Look at this—Aunt Celine's iron, Great-grandma Semple's quilt . . .

PINKIE: My first baby carriage . . .

JES: Uncle Matt's lucky horseshoe . . . Marva's straightening comb . . . Shaka Zulu's spear, I expect. And these . . . *(Holding up shackles.)* You're taking these?

WILLY: I'll sort things out once we get there.

Lottie enters in a white dress.

LOTTIE: We are gathered here today, though everyone isn't here yet . . .

PINKIE: I hope that Marva heifer doesn't show.

LOTTIE: . . . to celebrate the death of . . .

PINKIE: BIRTH.

LOTTIE: . . . to celebrate the birth of the King. "His life was the manna that fed the soul-weary masses." I read that in a book.

JES: *(Overlapping.)* K-A-N-I-B . . . I may not be able to spell it—but I know what it means.

LOTTIE: I don't remember the King. I wasn't born back then, but from the films in schools I saw the marches and the people in dashikis and 'fros, carrying signs and singing those

old Negro spirituals. Those were the days of King, of Came-
lot, when legendary heroes arose. Women like Angela . . .
Angela . . . something . . . Angela and her brothers in prison
. . . Soledad. Angela Soledad.

PINKIE: Angela DAVIS.

LOTTIE: Angela Davis? Angela Davis and her sister, Patricia Lumumba.

PINKIE: *(Remembering, longingly.)* PATRICE Lumumba was a man.

LOTTIE: It reminds me of when we studied that French woman
who fought alongside her brothers and she heard voices and
bells and was burned at the stake for her beliefs.

JES: A steak sounds good. I'm hungry.

LIZA: *(Offstage.)* Any minute now we'll be sitting at the table. The
day of feasting has arrived.

LOTTIE: And the king and his knights sat around the table . . .

PINKIE: What knights?

JES: Ku, klux, and klan.

LOTTIE: Jackson, Bond, and Young Andrew the lionhearted . . .

PINKIE: And Toto and Dorothy flew over the cuckoo's nest . . .
Willy, I told you to let this girl grow up.

LOTTIE: In the days of Camelot there came forth a king whose
holy quest took him to the mountaintop. And he looked over
to the other side and heard the voices and saw the visions
which he brought back to his people. He brought to them a
dream. But before he could lead them to the promised land,
he died. But "his life was the manna that fed the soul-weary
masses."

BLACKOUT

SCENE 3

We hear voices in the blackout.

VOICES: *(Overlapping and repeating.)* YANG YANG YANG YANG.
YANG YANG YANG. It is a far, far better thing I do than I
have ever done before. All for one and one for all . . .

Ungawa! Kings are not born: they are made of universal hallucination. Fight the power. Free Mandela. Viva Zapata. Remember the Soledad Seven. I have a dream.

Voices are drowned out by bells. Spotlight up on Jes.

JES: I'm not bitter. I'm not hostile, I'm not angry. I'm not going to sneak into your house at night and slit your throat. I'm Jes Semple—I like white people. There are two kinds of white people. The kind-hearted liberals who subscribe to the *Village Voice, Jet Magazine,* and *Town and Country.* And then there are those that still believe Gerry Cooney is the Great White Hope. Not that the white folk can't fight. But you put a black man, who's either consciously or unconsciously aware of his over one hundred years of oppression, in the ring with a white man and he's going to beat the shit out of the white man. And he's getting paid for it, too. Just as if you put a Latino male in the ring, he's going to beat the shit out of that white man and depending on what oppressed dictatorial regime he might have come from—he'll give that black man a good whupping too. You take an American Indian—and this is the fight I personally want to see—he'll beat the shit out of all of them . . . with his hands tied behind his back . . . blindfolded. I'm not bitter, I'm not hostile. I'm not angry. Call me Jes Semple.

Lottie enters the spotlight, laughing.

LOTTIE: You're so funny, Uncle Jes.
JES: Come here, my sweet naive. Let Uncle Jes whisper in your ear. *(Lottie goes over to Jes and he begins whispering in her ear. She laughs and laughs and laughs.)* Oh, stop, Uncle . . . oh, don't, stop . . . oh . . . oh . . . *(Lottie laughs until she cries . . . then laughs some more.)*

BLACKOUT

SCENE 4

Lights up on living room. Mama Pearl has entered and takes C stage. Lottie is at the window watching Papa Tommy. Everyone else is in their usual positions.

PEARL: I started out as a singer. Most of my first engagements were in the cotton fields. I was a healthy alto. I could sing. I can't anymore. *(Tries singing.)* Brighten the corner where you are . . . You could hear me a mile away. They used to call me Big Mouth.

LOTTIE: He's wearing a bow tie! He just got into the gate.

PEARL: Then I started sneaking to Bubba's at night—singing the blues, yeah. I was my mama's only child and this man says to me—"Girl, you sound good. Let me take you to Louisiana with me." I was sixteen at the time or I was fifteen . . . His name was Floyd. A piana player. He said, "Girl, you can be a great singer. Come on with me." And I said that I would first have to ask my mama.

LOTTIE: He's up to the garden.

PEARL: Next morning I told Mama that I could become a great singer if she would just let me go with Floyd to Louisiana. Don't you know that woman played those evil blues upside my head, that I will never forget. First, for sneaking out at night. Second, for wanting to sing that nasty, evil, low-down blues. Thirdly, for hanging around shiftless, lazy musicians— My daddy was a musician and had run out on Mama and me for some no account, hulley-gulley gal. And lastly, for wanting to leave her alone—me, being her only child. She beat me for seven days and seven nights.

LOTTIE: He's past the zinnias.

PEARL: After she finished beating me, she was so tired, she went to sleep. While she slept, I packed my things took the next bus to Louisiana. I caught up with Floyd and we teamed up. We called ourselves—Big Mouth and Ivory. We toured Mississippi, Virginia, Florida and all the way up to Chicago. That's where I met your daddy. A tap-dancing fool. Talk about some quick pepper feet! As big-footed as that man is, it's amazing how fast he could move them. I met him in this club and I said, "Hey, fool, where you learn to dance like that?" He said that he knew how to tap before he learned to walk. Shoot, people remember Bojangles, the Nicholas Brothers, Sammy Davis . . . Sandman . . . your daddy was the best.

LOTTIE: He stopped.

PEARL: I quit Floyd and teamed up with your daddy. Big Mouth Pearl and Mr. Pepper Feet. We went to New York in '41 or '42.

JES/PINKIE/WILLY: '41.

LOTTIE: He's taking off his hat and pulling out a handkerchief.

PEARL: '41. We were in love. He said that he loved me more than anything in the world and that was good enough for me. So we got married and the same night we debuted at the Apollo.

LOTTIE: He's wiping his head and looking around.

PEARL: Mama wrote to tell me that she was coming up to see the fool I had married.

LOTTIE: He's at the foot of the steps.

WILLY: Maybe I should help him up.

PEARL: Let him be. He said he didn't need any help, the fool. *(Continuing.)* I met her at the train station and she beat me over the head with her suitcase. "When I woke up that morning you were gone." She moved in with us and prayed for our souls every night we went on stage.

LOTTIE: He's on the second step.

PEARL: I got pregnant with Marva, swell up so bad, I was laid up in bed. Tommy was tapping at the Cotton Club and packing them in. Mr. Pepper Feet.

LOTTIE: He's still on the second step.

PEARL: He felt it would help the act if he had a partner. I was laid up in bed. So he hired this stringy-haired, skinny gal by the name of Lola.

UNISON: Lola.

There is a knocking on the door. Lottie opens the door and an ancient, shuffling, Tommy enters.

WILLY: Come on in. How are you, Pop?

TOMMY: Umm-hmmm. Umm-hmm.

JES: Let me rub your head for luck, old man.

TOMMY: Rub my butt.

PINKIE: *(Offering a seat.)* Sit over here.

TOMMY: Naw. *(He continues his slow shuffle, flapping walk past Pinkie and sits on the box labeled SAM.)*

PEARL: She thought that she was cute—that skinny, hulley-gulley child. *(Tommy wheezes and laughs.)* Yeah, you know who I'm talking about. Lola. And she sure was LOW, wasn't she? Mr. Pepper Feet.

TOMMY: *(Enjoying himself.)* Dem was de days.

PEARL: Yes they were. Living in a two-room, heatless apartment with a evil mother, laid up in bed swollen to the size of a cow, and you tap-dancing at the Cotton Club with LOW-LA.

TOMMY: Yowsah, yowsah, yowsah.

PEARL: I was singing them Saint Louis Blues . . . Blue as I can be . . .

TOMMY: Dat de way. Yo' moms was a sanging fool. Bi' Mouf . . .

PEARL: Big Mouth and Mr. Pepper Feet.

TOMMY: De Apollo—19 and 40 somethin'.

PEARL: I told them already.

TOMMY: '41. And de Cot-tone Club.

PEARL: And LOW-LA.

TOMMY: Yowsah, yowsah, dem was de days. *(Then:)* I gots to pee.

PEARL: Who's stopping you?

TOMMY: Woman, I's tie-ud.

PEARL: And I's a bony-backed mule.

WILLY: I'll take him, Ma.

PEARL: When did he become *your* husband? *(She stands, wide-legged in front of Tommy and squats so that he can climb on her back.)*

PINKIE: Mama, you're going to break your back.

PEARL: It'd take more than this fool to break my back.

TOMMY: *(As they exit.)* Can't you go no fast-uh?

PEARL: Man, don't you pee on me.

WILLY: Mama, I'll take him.

PEARL: I can take him.

WILLY: I'll take him.

TOMMY: Bony-back woman. Let he take me. You too slow.

PEARL: Gone, take him. The fool. *(Willy and Tommy exit.)* Calling somebody a bony-backed woman. That's the second time. We couldn't find a parking spot in front of the house. Too many people out front running back and forth. I parked a block away. Started walking with him on my back. His feet ain't any good anymore. He know. He called me a bony-backed woman. Said it was too slow. You talk about somebody bony . . . Lola was bony. She was the skinniest thing I'd ever seen. The only thing big on her was her knees. She was so skinny you could thread her through the eye of a needle except for them knees. She was as skinny as a toothpick. Looked like somebody had used her to clean the gunk from between their teeth. She wasn't that clean. Always smelled of that toilet of Paris. She smelled like she poured that stuff all over herself to hide the fact that she didn't bathe regular. It must have gotten pretty funky up there on stage with her. Especially doing them highkicks. They must have smelled her all the way in the back row balcony. She was a skinny, musty-smelling, hulley-gulley gal. That was a long time ago. I don't know why I'm thinking about her now for. Haven't thought of her in a long time.

Willy re-enters.

PINKIE: Didn't Marva buy Dad a motorized wheelchair, Mama?

PEARL: You know your father. He doesn't go for them newfangled, electricized contraptions. He didn't want to sit in it. He didn't want to sit comfortable in somebody else's electric chair and then get fried and served up with mashed potatoes and corn bread. He said, "What did God make strong-backed womens for?" I have lost a few extra pounds but my back is still strong. We all have our crosses to bear. And as long as I'm able . . .

PINKIE: All I'm saying is that you shouldn't have to carry a grown man on your back.

PEARL: I didn't have to bear five big-headed children and raise them up. But I did. I didn't have to buy you new clothes and shoes while I wore the same Sears and Roebuck dress that I patched for twelve years and stuff my shoes with newspaper.

But I did. I didn't have to take an extra job scrubbing floors at the Sheridan Hotel at night scraping knees on the tiles so you could get your teeth fixed and get you that saxophone you begged me for and then played it once, deciding that you'd rather take up bongos.

UNISON: BUT I DID.

PEARL: But I did. Who stayed up all night wiping your snotty nose and giving you mustard compresses to ease the fever when you had the flu? Changed your diaper and gave you my tiddy when you were a bawling baby girl? Not that I'm complaining. You do what you are able, to provide the best for your family. Your daddy ain't heavy. Compared to the burdens I've had to shoulder in my lifetime—He's light. When are you getting married?

PINKIE: Who said anything about getting married?

PEARL: That baby sitting in your belly. I swear, Pinkie, you should give at least one of your children a name.

PINKIE: All mine have names.

PEARL: Your daddy told me that he loved me more than anything in the world and that was good enough for me. None of my children had to wonder where they came from.

PINKIE: Nobody has to wonder about mine. The truth is . . .

WILLY: Hush now, Pinkie.

PINKIE: Let me hush. I came here to have a nice time. Let me close my mouth. My child will speak for me one day. I'm quiet, now.

PEARL: I've been with one man for fifty years. Promised to love only me to the day he died. None of mine had to wonder.

PINKIE: Let me hush. (*We hear voices outside:* "hungry"—"I'm hungry," "Spare some change . . ." "I want a VCR, a Porsche, and chicken in every pot . . ." "I feel hungry . . ." "My children need food." *Then a rapid knocking at the door.*)

MARVA: (*Offstage.*) Let me in . . . please, open the door.

Willy grabs a baseball bat and opens the door. Marva rushes in. She looks like a white woman with heavy makeup and disheveled but expensive clothes. Willy runs out with bat.

PEARL: What happened?

MARVA: They tried to kill me . . . they were going to kill me. Three black boys. They surrounded me at my car. Pulling at my purse . . . my hair . . . my suit. Calling me names. They don't know me. They don't know who I am. Calling me out of my name. Who the hell are they? Who do they think they are? No count, worthless . . . my hair . . . my suit . . . my car.

Willy re-enters.

WILLY: Scattered like rats. That's why we're moving. This isn't what was promised.

MARVA: They tried to kill me. They shot at me.

LOTTIE: Firecrackers.

PINKIE: No one bothered me when I came up.

MARVA: Well, I guess they wouldn't bother you.

PINKIE: And what do you mean by that?

PEARL: Marva didn't mean anything by that. You've always been so high-strung, Pinkie.

MARVA: I didn't mean anything by that, surely.

PINKIE: Surely, let me close my mouth.

PEARL: Let me look at you. What'd they do to my baby, my bright morning star . . . oh . . . *(Surveying and smoothing out the damage.)*

MARVA: It was terrible, Mama. And I wanted to look especially nice for this occasion . . . my nails . . .

PEARL: Mama kiss it. All well again—see. *(Pearl kisses Marva's hands and face. Marva laughs. They hug.)*

MARVA: Jonathan couldn't make it today—he was on call. He sends his regards.

JES: How is Doctor Hatchet?

PEARL: Now, Jes . . . never mind him. One child crazier than the other. But he's crazy for sure. Always has been, always will be. But the Lord never gives you more than you can handle and sometimes he sweetens the pot. *(To Marva.)*—My chocolate drop, on the cover of *Essence Magazine* this month, and once again voted Black Woman of the Year. I save the articles, put them in the scrapbook . . .

WILLY: I was voted Manager of the Month . . . gave me a plaque with my name on it.

PEARL: And your eyes—hazel?

MARVA: Blue.

PEARL: You looked so beautiful on the cover of *Jet Magazine*.

MARVA: That was the first cover I did.

PEARL: That was back when you looked like Dianne Carroll. Then for *Ebony* you looked more like Diana Ross.

MARVA: Before Diana Ross looked like Diana Ross.

PEARL: By the time she did *Vogue* she looked like a young Lena Horne.

MARVA: That was around the sixth operation. And I had just started the chemical peels. They burn away the darker outer layers . . . the nerve endings become so sensitive that you can't touch or be touched. They wrap you in a cocoon until you heal.

PINKIE: When you were little, they used to call you tar-baby. Big-lipped, flat-nosed, tar-baby, remember?

MARVA: I remember.

PEARL: My daughter was named "The Black Woman of the Year," three years in a row.

MARVA: I take pride in setting a standard.

PEARL: And married herself a doctor.

PINKIE: Who burned, tucked, cut and sucked all the black out of you years ago.

UNISON: HUSH, PINKIE.

PINKIE: Let me hush.

TOMMY: *(Offstage.)* Gits me off dis shit house.

WILLY: I'll get him. *(Exits.)*

MARVA: And how is Father?

PEARL: You know your father . . .

TOMMY: *(Offstage.)* OOOHHH, Lordy . . . de pain, de pain, de pain o' him-roids.

MARVA: Have you thought of a home?

PEARL: He's got a home.

LOTTIE: *(Who's been looking out the window.)* Sometimes I sneak out and give them things. The homeless. I give them handouts. Leftovers . . . bread, rice, beans . . . fruit to their children. Dried fruit keeps longer. Raisins.

JES: Next thing you know . . . they'll want a seat at the table.

LOTTIE: It makes me sad to see them. We can spare a little.

Willy enters carrying Tommy.

WILLY: We don't have enough to feed the whole damn neighborhood . . .

MARVA: *(Adjusting her face.)* Of course we do contribute to various charities . . . SAVE THE POOR . . . UNICEF . . .

WILLY: The whole crippled, mangy-assed breed. They're no kin to me.

MARVA: . . . The Negro College Fund . . . NAACP . . .

WILLY: They're no kin to me.

MARVA: I'm a life member of the NAACP.

LOTTIE: Some live in subway tunnels . . . the children . . . I give them raisins . . . they give me smiles . . .

WILLY: I pay taxes so welfare mothers can sit at home watching the VCR.

MARVA: Just last year we adopted a boy from Ethiopia and a girl from Somalia. They're in the finest boarding school in Europe. The question is "What is to be done?" and "When have we done enough?"

TOMMY: *(Looking at Marva.)* Who is you?

MARVA: Who am I? I'm your daughter, Father.

TOMMY: Youse ain't mine.

MARVA: I'm not yours? I'm your daughter, Marva, Father.

PEARL: Your eldest girl.

TOMMY: Eldest? Cain't be mine. Naw, uh-uh, cain't be mine.

LIZA: *(Offstage.)* All that's left is the garnish and then I'm done. Set the table everyone . . . the day of feasting has arrived.

UNISON: HALLELUJAH! *(All begin to set the table, finding tablecloth, dishes, and silverware among the rubble.)*

LOTTIE: We are gathered here today to celebrate the birthday of Reverend Martin Luther King.

MARVA: I was there. 1963. The march on Washington.

WILLY: I had work to do that day.

MARVA: Thousands of us walking hand in hand to the great lawn. Reverend Martin Luther King uttered his famous speech. He was a beautiful orator. Black as coals. In the heat of the revolution. America had lost its innocence—our sons were in a foreign land fighting strange battles for causes we couldn't understand. This was before the assassinations. Before LBJ threw up his hands and wept. Before the fall of Nixon, the peanut farmer, the movie star, and the lessons of Bush tactics. Back when America lost its first blush, King spoke of a vision, a dream. In the midst of bombings and fires he spoke of his vision of the future. They killed the man but his memory burns on in an eternal flame. His dream burns on in the minds of the survivors. In those frightful days, America lost its innocence in the jaws of the revolution. (And with that thought some might argue that it was our innocence that fed the revolution.) Point taken. And with the devouring of that innocence came hope. Reverend Martin Luther King Jr. had a dream. And he passed that dream on in a voice that rang out to all on that fateful day. And on that day we were all brothers and sisters . . . in that moment in time we were all family and holding hands. White man, Black man, Gentile, Jew, Arab, Indian . . . I remember sitting on that great lawn and listening to a man, a king as he cast bread upon the waters. And we sang "We Shall Overcome" . . .

UNISON: WE SHALL OVERCOME
WE SHALL OVERCOME SOME DAY
DEEP IN MY HEART
I DO BELIEVE
WE SHALL OVERCOME SOMEDAY.
(Humming as . . .)

PINKIE: Yes. I remember that day. I was there. I can still hear his voice. Our dream was one. It was as if he was speaking only to me, looking only at me. He knew he was going to die. The death threats were common knowledge. Who could carry on his dream? Rev. Abernathy had told me to come to the motel *(Humming stops.)* that night and I could meet him, speak with him . . . It had always been my dream to conceive a child that would lead his people . . .

UNISON: Lies . . . that's enough . . . hush!

PINKIE: And that night with the revolution burning in my thighs . . . *(H/)** . . . you know it's the truth . . . *(H/)* . . . I laid down . . . *(H/)* . . . the truth will set you free . . . *(H/)* . . . when I laid down . . .

UNISON: *(Overlapping.)* HUSH! HUSH! HUSH! *(They sing* "We

---

*(H/) indicates UNISON. HUSH.

Shall Overcome" *with fervor as Willy, Marva and Pearl tie Pinkie up and tape her mouth. Willy places her in a box. Song stops at . . .* I DO BELIEVE.)

PEARL: She always was high-strung.

MARVA: Fantasies . . .

PEARL: I always told her to settle down. No telling who all those children of hers are by. *(Willy tapes up the box and labels it.)* No telling.

TOMMY: I's just regusted.

PEARL: I cried when Kennedy died. I don't pay any attention to all that sluttish gossip. I don't care what anybody says . . . I cried when King died. *(At Tommy.)* Lord, seems like he takes the good ones early.

TOMMY: Where's Sambo?

MARVA: Who?

TOMMY: Li'l black Sambo. Now he could dance. Only one of my chirren who could feel it. Feel where he come from.

PEARL: You know he's dead, Tommy. Been dead for a while now.

MARVA: Sam.

TOMMY: That's right. Mmm-hmmm—he was good. Mmm-hmm. Lip-smacking good served up with them pancakes.

MARVA: What?

TOMMY: Pancakes. With pancakes. That's how we ate 'im.

LOTTIE: *(Laughing.)* Pancakes and Aunt Jemima's syrup.

WILLY: Shut up.

LOTTIE: But, Dad, it's just a joke—get it?

WILLY: Go to your room.

LOTTIE: You can't send me to my room for the rest of my life—

WILLY: Shut up. Shut him up.

MARVA: He's just an old man, talking out of his head. Sam had a proper funeral. Just close your ears, child.

JES: Though there wasn't enough of him to piece together for a decent funeral.

PEARL: He was the one that wanted to be cremated.

LOTTIE: SAMBO! PANCAKES—FRIED . . .

WILLY: SHUT UP! This is not the time to get into this. This is not the time.

PEARL: It was an accident. He's the one that bought the insurance.

JES: Blow your hands. Don't come crying to me.

MARVA: It was declared by the authorities as an accidental death.

JES: Don't come crying to me.

WILLY: Not murder. Not suicide.

JES: We each got a piece.

TOMMY: Legs, thighs, wings . . .

PEARL: He was a saint.

LOTTIE: You're joking, right? Aren't you?

JES: Some got more than others.

MARVA: We all got the same inheritance. Some used it more wisely than others. He's the one that bought—

JES: Life insurance.

MARVA: *(Continuing.)* No one pushed him.

WILLY: *(To Jes.)* For the lives of our children.

TOMMY: Paid in blood. Still gnawing on his bones.

MARVA: He was cremated.

JES: What was left of him.

TOMMY: Burnt offerings.

LOTTIE: *(Covering her ears and singing loudly.)* Yang yang yang yang yang yang yang yang . . . *(Beat.)*

MARVA: *(Pulls up her face.)* How do you put up with it, Mother?

PEARL: Put up with what?

MARVA: *(At Tommy.)* Him.

PEARL: That's your pa, Marva.

WILLY: He's our father.

MARVA: I was the one that was called to pay the bills when he needed the new kidney, the bladder operation . . . the hip joint . . . the gallstone operation . . . the bypass . . . the new teeth. You're trying to tell me that what's left of him is my father . . . this babbling, illiterate, incoherent, shuffling, head-scratching, dinosaur used to be my father but ceased to exist with Amos and Andy reruns. Yet he attaches himself to our hems as we drag him into the next century and we're supposed to continue to pay tribute by calling him our father. *(Breaking.)* You can't be my . . . oh . . . Daddy . . . *(Sits on his lap.)* Dad.

TOMMY: *(Low.)* Bastid. *(Pushes her out of his lap.)* And y'all— BASTIDS. Cain't be mine. *(Getting up.)* No ridim. No ridim. Cain't be mine. Uh-uh.

PEARL: Calm yourself.

TOMMY: Damn bastids. Git outta my way. Yeah, I feel it. Feelin' it. *(Begins to tap.)* Dat de way. Uh-uh. Dat de way. Dem was de days. *(His whole body comes to life.)* Yowsah. Dem was de days. All uh God's niggah chirren had ridim. Yeah. Dat de way, yowsah. Day knew where it come from. Day could feel it. Don't feel nothin' now. But I ain't dead . . . I ain't dead . . . naw suh . . . *(He taps faster and faster then drops.)*

PEARL: Tommy . . . Tommy.

TOMMY: *(Whispering.)* Dem . . . was . . . de . . . days. Pepper Feet . . . and *(Clutches his heart.)* Lo-la.

PEARL: Lola? Lola? *(Shaking his lifeless body.)* I'll kill him . . . I'll kill him.

MARVA: *(Trying to keep her face from falling apart.)* He's dead. He's dead . . . *(Willy gently places Tommy in a box, tapes the box and labels it. Lottie covers her eyes.)*

JES: *(To Lottie.)*

What happens to a dream deferred?
Does it dry up like a raisin in the sun?
Does it fester like a sore and then run
Does it stink like rotten meat
Or sugar over like a syrup sweet
Does it sag like a heavy load—
(Lottie uncovers her eyes.)
Or does it explode?

(We see smoke coming from the kitchen.)

LIZA: *(Offstage, hysterically repeating.)* Everything is fine. I don't need any help. Soup's on. *(Smoke billows from the kitchen as everyone runs in.)*

EVERYONE: Water, more water . . . *(Lottie, hearing Joan of Arc bells, runs out the front door with armful of food to the clamoring masses.)*

LOTTIE: *(As she exits, singing.)* YANG YANG YANG YANG . . .

WILLY: More water . . . more water. Save the turkey. *(Jes echoes.)*

PEARL: . . . the ham . . . *(Jes echoes.)*

MARVA: . . . Save the chitlings . . . *(Jes echoes.)*

PINKIE: *(From inside the box.)* What's going on out there? Somebody let me out. I came to celebrate.

JES: Save the house, but not the mouse. Save the kitchen, keep that water pitchin'. Save Lottie, she gonna be somebody. Save the dolphins. No one can save us, from us, for us, but us . . . save yourself.

MARVA: I don't know what else I can do here.

PINKIE: *(From inside box.)* OH! I feel him . . . OH . . .

MARVA: Lottie! Lottie! *(Marva exits after Lottie.)*

We hear gunshots from outside. Pearl enters from kitchen and lays herself across Tommy's box. A huge bone is thrown through the window, shattering the glass.

BONETHROWER: UNGAWA! BLACK POWER!

PINKIE: *(From inside box.)* He's coming . . . Jesus . . . Jesus . . . Jesus . . . HE'S COMING!

BLACKOUT

SCENE 5

Spotlight up on Jes. He's eating a whole pie.

JES: You can only slice an apple pie so many ways. Somebody is always going to go home hungry.

SCENE 6

The room is cleared except for a few boxes—including those labeled LINEN, STEREO, PINKIE, MA, PA, and MARVA. Liza sits in the living room wrapped in gauze from head to toe. Lottie sits, her white dress ragged, soiled and bloodstained.

WILLY: Signed the papers. Ha ha. Highland Hills. This is the open door we've been waiting for. That step into the future. My little bluebird's future. We're moving. *(Willy picks up a box and exits outside. Lottie gets up on the table and begins to do a lewd grind-dance.)*

LOTTIE: *(Singing, bitterly.)* YANG YANG YANG YANG. YANG YANG YANG.

Willy re-enters.

LIZA: *(From inside bandages.)* Don't forget my good china.
WILLY: Yes, Liza. *(Willy picks up a small box next to Pinkie's box. As he exits he stops, measures its weight and then seriously shakes it. Sound of a baby crying comes from within.)*

Spotlight up on Jes—he puts on a record—and watches Lottie's dance. We hear a recording of Martin Luther King.

MLK: Today I want to tell the city of Selma, today I want to say to the state of Alabama, today I want to say to the people of America and the nations of the world: We are not about to turn around. We are on the move now. Yes, we are on the move and no wave of racism can stop us. The burning of our churches will not deter us. The bombing of our homes will not dissuade us. The beating and killing of our clergymen and young people will not divert us. The arrest and the release of known murderers will not discourage us. We are on the move now. Like an idea whose time has come, not even the marching of mighty armies can halt us. We are moving to the land of freedom. *(Lottie silently continues grind-dance.)* However difficult the moment, however frustrating the hour, it will not be long because the truth crushed to the earth will rise again. *(Lottie's dance becomes a stomp shuffle stomp. She picks up spear and continues with her warrior dance which evolves into a summation out of space and time evoking spirits past and present from child to woman.)*
LOTTIE: HOW LONG?
MLK: Not long, because the arc of the moral universe is long but it bends toward justice.
LOTTIE: HOW LONG?
MLK: Not long, because mine eyes have seen the glory of the coming of the Lord.
LOTTIE: HOW LONG?

BLACKOUT

END

Richard Dresser

Below the Belt

Below the Belt was directed in 1995 by Gloria Muzio with the following cast:

HANRAHAN............................. William McNulty
DOBBITT............................ V. Craig Heidenreich
MERKIN....................................... Fred Major

Scene Design................................ Paul Owen
Costume Design .... Marcia Dixcy
Lighting Design............................T. J. Gerckens
Sound Design .... Martin R. Desjardins
Property Master............................... Ron Riall
Stage Manager...................... Kieran Jason Hackett
Assistant Stage Manager................. Janette L. Hubert
Dramaturg........................ Michael Bigelow Dixon

154

CHARACTERS

Hanrahan: a man
Dobbitt: a man
Merkin: a man

PLACE:

An industrial compound in a distant land.

SET:

We see a room with two beds, an office, a little bridge over
a stream, and a bit of the surrounding area.

Below the Belt

ACT ONE

In darkness we hear Hanrahan attempting to type. He responds to each keystroke, which echoes in the silent room.

HANRAHAN: Excellent.
(Another keystroke.)
Good. Very good.
(Five quick keystrokes.)
Beautiful. *Beautiful.* Keep it up. Nice and steady.
(Three quick ones.)
Damn you! Damn you to hell! Bastard!
(The sound of paper being viciously crumpled and another piece of paper being put in the typewriter. A pause, then a hesitant keystroke.)
Okay, alright, that's the idea. Easy does it.

The lights slowly come up on Hanrahan's room, which is small and makeshift, with two small beds, a simple cooking arrangement, an old radio, and a door to the bathroom. Hanrahan is laboriously typing at a desk with a large, old-fashioned typewriter.

Dobbitt enters, carrying a suitcase. He stands there a moment, not wanting to interrupt. Hanrahan doesn't acknowledge him.

DOBBITT: I'm Dobbitt.
(Pause, then louder.)
I'm Dobbitt.
HANRAHAN: *(Not looking up.)*
Can't you wait 'til I'm done?
(Hanrahan stares at the typewriter. Dobbitt puts his suitcase down as quietly as possible, barely making a sound. Hanrahan turns and glares at him.)
What's all this ruckus? I'm busy. I'm looking for the "y."
(Dobbitt goes over and hits the "y" on the typewriter which makes a loud echoing sound. Hanrahan stares at Dobbitt.)

Well, well, well. Very impressive. He knows just where they keep the "y."

(Hanrahan stands up, takes the paper from the typewriter, puts it in an envelope, seals the envelope, puts the envelope in a manila folder, puts the folder in a large envelope which he seals, then puts the large envelope in a drawer, which he locks. He puts the key in his pocket, which he buttons.)

DOBBITT: I was just trying to help.

HANRAHAN: I don't like people looking over my shoulder, passing judgment. There's going to be trouble if you pry into my affairs. Who are you, anyway?

DOBBITT: I'm Dobbitt. You must be Hanrahan.

HANRAHAN: I *must* be Hanrahan? I don't have a choice?

DOBBITT: Are you Hanrahan?

HANRAHAN: Who are you to barge into my room and tell me who I must be?

DOBBITT: You're not Hanrahan?

HANRAHAN: As it turns out, I *am* Hanrahan, but not because it happens to suit your purposes.

DOBBITT: I'm sorry. It was an endless flight and then we drove for hours through the desert. This is where they told me to stay.

HANRAHAN: You're staying here? In my room?

DOBBITT: It's a two-person room. They told me there was someone in here before.

HANRAHAN: Haney. He left early.

DOBBITT: Why did he leave? Did something happen?

HANRAHAN: *(A long look at Dobbitt.)* Which bed?

DOBBITT: Oh, it doesn't matter.

HANRAHAN: Yes it does. This one in the corner gets an icy wind off the desert snapping right through it. The window doesn't close. A man could freeze to death in this bed.

DOBBITT: If it's all the same to you, I'll take the other bed.

HANRAHAN: Suit yourself.

(Dobbitt throws his suitcase down on the bed and starts unpacking. Hanrahan pours himself a mug of coffee.)

That one's a sweatbox. Right next to the radiator, which clangs in your ear like a train wreck all night long. You'll be begging for mercy by morning.

DOBBITT: Why don't we move the beds?

HANRAHAN: That's an idea. That should solve everything.
(Dobbitt tries to move the bed.)
Except they're bolted to the floor. Lots of thievery on the compound.

DOBBITT: They're stealing beds?

HANRAHAN: Not since the bolts went in.

DOBBITT: Which bed do you sleep in?

HANRAHAN: Both. I start in the one next to the window. When I start to freeze I climb in the other one. Then, when I can't breathe I get up and start the day. I guess that's all gone now that *you're* here.

DOBBITT: I seem to have caught you at a bad time.

HANRAHAN: Oh?

DOBBITT: I fear I've upset you.

HANRAHAN: *You've* upset me? That's a bit grandiose, don't you think?

DOBBITT: You seem disgruntled.

HANRAHAN: Gruntled or disgruntled, it has nothing to do with you.
(Dobbitt watches Hanrahan sipping from a cup. He yawns.)

DOBBITT: Is that coffee?

HANRAHAN: Yes.
(Hanrahan doesn't move.)

DOBBITT: I feel as though I've been traveling forever. I should either sleep or try to revive myself. If there's any more coffee.

HANRAHAN: There's plenty more coffee.
(Hanrahan still doesn't move.)

DOBBITT: I could get it myself.

HANRAHAN: Are you asking for coffee?

DOBBITT: Only if it's no bother.

HANRAHAN: Well of course it's a bother!
(Hanrahan angrily starts clattering around the coffee pot.)

DOBBITT: Then please, forget it.

HANRAHAN: Now that I'm knee-deep in it you don't want any?

DOBBITT: If it's easier to continue . . .

HANRAHAN: *(Turning on him.)* See here. I'm not a puppet on a string. You'll have to make up your mind and you'll have to do it right now.

DOBBITT: No coffee. I don't want to put you out.

HANRAHAN: I'm already put out. The only question is whether or not you want coffee.

DOBBITT: Everything else being equal, I would say yes to coffee.

HANRAHAN: Very well.

(He pours a cup of coffee.)

It just means I have to make a whole new pot for myself.

(He hands it to Dobbitt who tries to refuse the coffee.)

DOBBITT: Then you take this, please—

HANRAHAN: No!

DOBBITT: I insist!

(As they struggle, the coffee spills on Hanrahan, who bellows.)

My God! I'm terribly sorry—

HANRAHAN: Look what you've done!

DOBBITT: It was an accident—

HANRAHAN: If you'd made up your mind this never would have happened.

(Hanrahan dries himself with a towel. There's a beep from a small intercom on the wall. Hanrahan stops and glares at it.)

Well. That's Merkin. And he sounds upset.

(Grimly.)

Come on, Dobbitt, it's time to meet the boss.

(Hanrahan hurries from the room with Dobbitt following as lights fade.)

Lights up on Merkin's office, which contains a desk, a desk chair, and one other chair, which looks none too comfortable. A window with drawn blinds looks out on the compound. Merkin peers out through the blinds. Dobbitt and Hanrahan enter. Dobbitt comes forward and shakes hands with Merkin.

MERKIN: Welcome, Dobbitt. I'm Merkin.

DOBBITT: I'm thrilled to be here, Merkin.

MERKIN: Thrilled? That seems a bit extreme.

DOBBITT: It's my very first off-country assignment. I've had extensive experience in-country, however—

MERKIN: Yes, yes, we've read your file. We frankly know more about your life than we'd like. Make yourself comfortable.

(Hanrahan quickly sits in the one chair. Merkin sits at his desk.

Dobbitt looks in vain for another chair, then assumes what he hopes is a casual stance.)
We're in a fix and there's no time to waste. On November fifth we're delivering the largest order this company has ever received. The work must be meticulously checked if we're to avoid penalties and crippling lawsuits and a tarnished reputation that could bring the corporation to its knees. Unfortunately, until this moment, we've been short one Checker.

DOBBITT: What happened to the last Checker?

MERKIN: Why don't you ask your friend Hanrahan?

DOBBITT: *(Turning to Hanrahan.)* Well?

HANRAHAN: He's no friend of mine.

MERKIN: It's enough to say we need you, Dobbitt. You come highly recommended.

DOBBITT: My assignments have been serendipitous to date, and I have no reason to believe this will be any different.
(A sudden laugh from Hanrahan. Dobbitt turns but Hanrahan is staring at the floor.)

MERKIN: All three plants are operational twenty-four hours a day. You'll tour the compound and see. We turn out seven thousand one hundred and eighty-six units per eight-hour shift. Which means with all three shifts we do—

HANRAHAN: Twenty-one thousand five hundred and fifty-eight units a day.

MERKIN: So over a six day work week we do—

HANRAHAN: One hundred twenty-nine thousand three hundred and forty-eight units.

MERKIN: Factor in a loss of three percent based on our checking—feel free to jump in, Dobbitt.

DOBBITT: Uh, let's see . . . I'm just so tired from my trip . . .

HANRAHAN: Twenty thousand nine hundred and eleven units a day, one hundred twenty-five thousand four hundred and sixty-six units per week.

MERKIN: Thank you. I'm glad *someone* is paying attention. Our delivery date is November fifth, which means at our current rate when will we be done? Dobbitt?

DOBBITT: Oh . . . I think we'll make it in plenty of time.

HANRAHAN: We'll finish November third at 10:30 P.M.

MERKIN: Why do I have November second?

HANRAHAN: Aren't you forgetting the holiday?

MERKIN: Quite right, quite right. Human error. In any event, we have a gun aimed at our head and without a system our brains will be trickling down the wall when November rolls around. While Hanrahan is out checking, Dobbitt will be typing his reports. While Dobbitt is out checking, Hanrahan will be typing his reports. Any questions?

DOBBITT: It sounds like a perfect arrangement.

MERKIN: That's not a question. This is where you're allowed to ask questions.

DOBBITT: I have none. Thank you.

MERKIN: No questions?

DOBBITT: Most people would have a question here?

MERKIN: Frankly, I'm surprised.

DOBBITT: Alright, alright . . . my question—

MERKIN: Don't ask a question just for the sake of asking a question. Ask only if you want to know the answer.

DOBBITT: I'm fine with no questions.

MERKIN: On the other hand, there's no such thing as a stupid question.

DOBBITT: Tell me, what exactly are those units you spoke of?

MERKIN: Pardon me?

DOBBITT: The units would be . . . what? What are we making in these factories?

MERKIN: Hear that, Hanrahan?

(Merkin and Hanrahan laugh.)

DOBBITT: I'm just very—

MERKIN: We're well aware of how tired you are. I'd like the two of you to function as a team. Personalities—such as they are in this case—rank a distant second.

DOBBITT: That's my philosophy. I'll do anything I can for the team. While I may not be quite as quick with figures as some, I'm an excellent typist.

MERKIN: Which is to say?

DOBBITT: It might speed things up if Hanrahan helped me with the calculations and I pitched in on his typing.

HANRAHAN: That's not necessary, Dobbitt.

DOBBITT: I just meant in the heat of battle—

HANRAHAN: I said it's not necessary, Dobbitt!

MERKIN: Hanrahan, you're free to go on your merry way. I'd like to tell Dobbitt how we do things on the compound. *(Hanrahan gets up to leave.)*

DOBBITT: Thanks, Hanrahan.

HANRAHAN: *(Turning on him.)* For what? For what, Dobbitt?

MERKIN: Alright, Hanrahan, that's enough.

HANRAHAN: I demand to know why Dobbitt is thanking me.

MERKIN: Dobbitt, why are you thanking Hanrahan?

DOBBITT: For welcoming me to the compound.

HANRAHAN: I never did that.

DOBBITT: For sharing your room.

HANRAHAN: I did it under duress.

DOBBITT: For what I just know will be a wonderful partnership.

HANRAHAN: If the platitudes have abated, I'll take my leave.
(Hanrahan leaves. Merkin gives Dobbitt a long look.)

MERKIN: So. What has Hanrahan said about me?

DOBBITT: Nothing at all.

MERKIN: I'm not worthy of mention?

DOBBITT: He *mentioned* you. There hasn't been time for more than that.

MERKIN: Does he hate me?

DOBBITT: Please! Of course not!

MERKIN: How do you know?

DOBBITT: To be honest, I don't *know.*

MERKIN: Then there's a possibility he hates me?

DOBBITT: I am completely unfamiliar with the situation, and after all that time in the air—

MERKIN: I've heard all I can stomach about your damnable flight!

DOBBITT: Well . . . I suppose technically there's a possibility . . .

MERKIN: Of what?

DOBBITT: That Hanrahan . . .

MERKIN: What?

DOBBITT: Hates you.

MERKIN: Dear God.

DOBBITT: Although I have no reason to believe it's true.

MERKIN: If you have no reason to believe it's true then why do you dangle it in front of me, like some terrible carcass rotting on a meat hook? Why, Dobbitt, why?

DOBBITT: I . . . I don't know . . .

MERKIN: There's something you should know. Hanrahan and I have served here together for nearly one year. In that time we have grown to be close friends. I trust you'll respect that.

DOBBITT: Of course. No harm was intended.

MERKIN: It never is. Do you know, I am responsible for everything that happens in this entire department? It's a lonely and treacherous job.

(He gets a large, imposing stamp from a desk drawer.)

I make the hard decisions. The people decisions. Who goes up, who goes down. And who stays locked in place, shackled in bureaucratic leg irons until all hope is lost.

(Merkin slams the stamp on a piece of paper. It echoes ominously. He turns the paper to Dobbitt.)

What does that say?

DOBBITT: "Void."

MERKIN: Exactly. I expect we'll get along fine, Dobbitt. *(Merkin starts going through papers. Dobbitt is unsure what to do.)*

DOBBITT: Am I . . . dismissed?

MERKIN: You may come and go as you please. You're a highly skilled professional and that's exactly how you'll be treated.

DOBBITT: Thank you. *(Dobbitt starts for the door.)*

MERKIN: Oh, Dobbitt? Entre nous, I'd be careful, razzing old Hanrahan about his typing.

DOBBITT: I wasn't razzing!

MERKIN: Sounded like razzing to me. You razzed him up and down and back and forth. You're quite the razzer, Dobbitt.

DOBBITT: I'm no razzer! I wouldn't know how to razz!

MERKIN: He's damned sensitive about his typing. Hell, you might as well have razzed him about his *dancing.* I'd hate to have you discover that the hard way. Consider yourself dismissed.

Lights fade as Dobbitt leaves.
Lights up on a little bridge over a stagnant, polluted river. Dusk.
Hanrahan is standing on the bridge, smoking a cigar. Dobbitt comes up wearing a name tag and carrying a brochure.

DOBBITT: I just finished my tour! What an exhilarating glimpse at modern industry!

HANRAHAN: Will you be standing there long?

DOBBITT: Here?

HANRAHAN: Yes, there. That's exactly what I meant when I said "there."

DOBBITT: Is there someplace else I should stand?

HANRAHAN: This is my favorite time of the whole day. Night coming on. Having a smoke. Looking at the river. All by myself.

DOBBITT: I don't know where else to go. There are limited vistas for observing the sunset.

HANRAHAN: But this is *my* view. It cheapens it if you're looking at the exact same thing as me.

DOBBITT: I'd be happy to look at something else. Over there, for instance.

HANRAHAN: You won't know what *I'm* looking at so how will you know what's safe for *you* to look at?

DOBBITT: I'll look over this way and you look that way.

HANRAHAN: But some of my favorite things are over on your side. You look upstream. It's the only solution if you're to remain here.

DOBBITT: Alright.

(Dobbitt goes to the other side of the bridge and looks upstream, his back to Hanrahan.)

Is the river always like this? I don't believe I've ever encountered such a color in nature before.

HANRAHAN: The colors vary according to our manufacturing schedule. By Thursday it positively glows. *(They watch in silence.)*

DOBBITT: Look, Hanrahan, I'm sorry for anything I might have said about your typing.

HANRAHAN: What did Merkin say about my typing?

DOBBITT: He said you were . . . sensitive about it.

HANRAHAN: Well I'm not! He's feeding you garbage like you're some kind of barnyard animal. Now he's having a good laugh, watching you root and snort in his rancid trough.

DOBBITT: But why would he say something like that if it isn't true?

HANRAHAN: You'll learn that Merkin's brain has a mind of its own.

DOBBITT: In any event, I never would have brought it up if I'd known.

HANRAHAN: Do I seem sensitive to you? Do I?

DOBBITT: I think it's best not to discuss it.

HANRAIIAN: But we *are* discussing it, Dobbitt. My penmanship was an inspiration to Checkers of every stripe. Then word comes down our reports must be typed. *Typed!* Why did you bring it up in front of Merkin, anyway?

DOBBITT: Hanrahan, I'm a world-class typist. I can help you.

HANRAHAN: But then you'd get the credit.

DOBBITT: Oh, no, I wouldn't take credit.

HANRAHAN: If you didn't take credit you'd be a fool. Are you a fool?

DOBBITT: I'm nobody's fool.

HANRAHAN: You'd be *my* fool if you did my work for no credit. Are you my little fool, Dobbitt?

DOBBITT: No!

HANRAHAN: Then you're trying to steal credit for my good work. You're either a fool or a thief, which is it, Dobbitt?

DOBBITT: Are those my only choices?

HANRAHAN: And still, not a word of apology.

DOBBITT: I'm sorry.

HANRAHAN: For what?

DOBBITT: I'm not entirely sure. But I feel it's necessary to clear the air.

HANRAHAN: Unless your apology is false, in which case it only muddies the waters. Is this contrition or cowardice, Dobbitt?

DOBBITT: I'm not a coward.

HANRAHAN: Or maybe you're too scared to admit it. Are you brave enough to admit you're a coward?

DOBBITT: Yes!

HANRAHAN: Aha!

DOBBITT: But that makes me strong!

HANRAHAN: It also makes you a coward.

DOBBITT: Why can't I be brave enough to admit I'm a coward without actually being a coward?

HANRAHAN: Because then you'd be boasting about something that isn't true, which would make you a liar.

DOBBITT: I'm certainly not a liar!

HANRAHAN: But we've already established you're a coward, and cowards will lie when they don't have the courage to tell the truth. By insisting on your bravery, you have admitted you're a coward and a liar. Maybe you weren't entirely honest about your so-called bravery. That would let you off the hook.

DOBBITT: I might have stretched it a bit.

HANRAHAN: Which means you know you're a liar and a coward but you aren't brave enough to come out and admit it. You're living in a sad little dream world, Dobbitt.

DOBBITT: What about you, Hanrahan? Are you so perfect?

HANRAHAN: Of course not. But I'm an honest man and precious few can say that.

DOBBITT: I can say that. Usually.

HANRAHAN: And I don't go boasting about all my wonderful qualities.

DOBBITT: I wasn't boasting!

HANRAHAN: Chatter chatter chatter chatter chatter, for God sakes, Dobbitt, this is why I enjoy the river alone!
       (They watch in silence.)
       Merkin's light just went off. He has to throw it in my face every time he works late.

DOBBITT: Will he be joining us at the river?

HANRAHAN: Hah! Merkin wouldn't know how to look at a river.

DOBBITT: He has a great deal of authority here, doesn't he?

HANRAHAN: Is that what he told you?

DOBBITT: He said he makes decisions for the entire department.

HANRAHAN: You and I are the entire department. We're his fiefdom.

DOBBITT: He said the two of you were great friends.

HANRAHAN: What a grotesque parody of friendship *that* would be!

DOBBITT: Then you . . . dislike him?

HANRAHAN: Oh, I can see there's a fox in the henhouse, a snake in the grass, a monkey on my back, a wolf in sheep's clothing—

DOBBITT: I just thought—

HANRAHAN: You just thought you'd put words in my mouth! Well I choke on your words and I spit them out because I won't be stained by your calumny! If you ever try to put another word in my mouth I'll bite your fingers off.

DOBBITT: I'm sorry, Hanrahan. It won't happen again.
(Dobbitt is staring off in the distance. We can just make out several pairs of dim yellow eyes in the darkness.)
Hanrahan, look! What are those eyes out by the fence?
HANRAHAN: *(Not turning around.)* Animals.
DOBBITT: Yes, I know they're animals.
(Looks over his shoulder at Hanrahan not looking.)
You're not even looking!
HANRAHAN: I've seen them before.
DOBBITT: What species do they belong to?
HANRAHAN: I believe they're free agents. It's nothing to worry about, Dobbitt, they're outside the fence.
DOBBITT: What do they do?
HANRAHAN: They huddle in the dark and they stare at us. *(Hanrahan starts off.)*
DOBBITT: Hanrahan? Are you going to the room?
HANRAHAN: I was going to.
DOBBITT: I could walk with you.
HANRAHAN: That's not necessary. If you'd like to go to the room, go now.
DOBBITT: If you'd like to go first, that would be fine—
HANRAHAN: Go, Dobbitt! Go and be done with it!

Dobbitt leaves. Hanrahan is alone on the bridge as lights fade.
Lights up on the room. Dobbitt is in his pajamas kneeling by the bed praying. Hanrahan enters.

HANRAHAN: Ah, the evening prayer. What an oddly touching sight. And what are you praying for, Dobbitt?
DOBBITT: It's personal.
HANRAHAN: Of course. Between you and your deity. So sorry to overstep my bounds with this small gesture of friendship.
DOBBITT: If you must know, I was praying for the happiness of my wife.
HANRAHAN: And you think kneeling on the floor of a hut in the desert will in some way contribute to her happiness?
DOBBITT: Yes, I do.
HANRAHAN: What would make your wife happy?
DOBBITT: My safe return home.
HANRAHAN: So you're really praying for yourself.

DOBBITT: I'm praying for what would make my wife happy.

HANRAHAN: Do you know what *I* think would make your wife happy? If her car started making an odd knocking sound and she pulled into a gas station and the mechanic put the car up on the lift and then led her into the back room and unbuttoned her blouse and caressed her milky-white breasts with his rough, blistered hands until her nipples stood at attention like recent graduates of the Military Academy.

DOBBITT: You don't know my wife well enough to talk about her that way.

HANRAHAN: Don't I?

DOBBITT: I won't have you make a mockery of her happiness!

HANRAHAN: Let's just assume for a moment that the sudden, savage groping of an auto mechanic *would* make her happy. Would you still pray for her happiness?

(Dobbitt starts praying to obliterate what Hanrahan is saying.)

DOBBITT: Our father, who art in heaven, hallowed be thy name . . .

HANRAHAN: Would you pray that the auto mechanic tears off her dress and throws her down on a dirty pile of blankets underneath an outdated pornographic calendar and has his mechanic's way with her while her car is perched high on the lift for a close inspection by the other auto mechanic who hears the faint sounds of lust emanating from the back room and thinks maybe he'd like to have a little visit with your nude, flushed, panting, all-too-compliant wife as well? Would you pray for that, Dobbitt? Or are you just one more goddam hypocrite? *(Dobbitt stops praying, stands, and faces Hanrahan.)*

DOBBITT: Alright, Hanrahan. What have you got against me?

HANRAHAN: You're alive on this planet at the same time I am.

DOBBITT: People have always liked me.

HANRAHAN: People also like chocolate bunnies and Hallmark cards and warm baths. Being liked is no great achievement.

DOBBITT: I treat people fairly and I expect the same in return. Haven't I been fair with you, Hanrahan?

HANRAHAN: You've been a perfect little gentleman.

DOBBITT: Then why don't you like me?

HANRAHAN: Why does it matter?

DOBBITT: Because . . . I don't want to be alone.

HANRAHAN: We're all of us alone, from our first hopeful breath to the last horrible death rattle rising in our parched throats. We're alone, Dobbitt, regardless of how I treat you!

DOBBITT: Why can't you just meet me halfway?

HANRAHAN: *(Sizing him up.)* I'll meet you a third of the way.

DOBBITT: Alright. That's a start. My only request is, no more gutter talk about my wife.

(Hanrahan goes into the bathroom and is heard gargling.)

No matter how far apart we are, she makes me feel I'm not alone.

HANRAHAN: *(Offstage.)* She's made many a man feel he's not alone.

DOBBITT: What?

HANRAHAN: *(Offstage.)* Nothing.

(Hanrahan comes back.)

DOBBITT: I thought you said something about my wife.

HANRAHAN: Catherine?

DOBBITT: Oh, Lord.

(Hanrahan casually prepares for bed as Dobbitt watches him.)

That was a lucky guess. You've never seen my Catherine.

HANRAHAN: Tell me, does she still wear her hair long, so it cascades in all its coal-black glory over her alabaster shoulders? Or perhaps she's cut it to look more businesslike and severe.

DOBBITT: Stop it.

HANRAHAN: I hope she didn't cap her tooth. I always felt that little chip gave her a rather wild and eccentric kind of beauty.

DOBBITT: I demand to know how you know this.

HANRAHAN: I once had a brief stopover at the Tampa plant, doing mop-up work with the Elite Checkers—

DOBBITT: That's where I met her. During a routine audit.

HANRAHAN: And there was lovely, lonely Catherine, getting her feet wet in the typing pool.

DOBBITT: You could have gotten all this from looking at my file.

HANRAHAN: Quite possible.

DOBBITT: Hanrahan, you must be honest with me. Did you know my Catherine?

HANRAHAN: *Know* her?

DOBBITT: Please.

HANRAHAN: Relax. I know for a fact she honored you completely from the moment she accepted your marriage proposal.

DOBBITT: Oh, excellent. Excellent. I've never had reason to doubt her virtue, but, well, thank you.

(The men get in their respective beds. Hanrahan turns off his light. Dobbitt is about to.)

Hanrahan? What about *before* she accepted my proposal? When I was courting her?

HANRAHAN: She didn't do anything a healthy, spirited young woman on her own in the city for the first time wouldn't do.

DOBBITT: Thank you. *(Dobbitt turns out his light.)*

HANRAHAN: Yes, she got it all out of her system so she could be true to you. You can rest easy, Dobbitt, she won't feel the need to go off and try something she's never done. You're a very lucky man. *(They lie there in the darkness.)*

DOBBITT: Hanrahan? *You* never—I mean your relationship with my Catherine was—

HANRAHAN: My relationship with your wife was no different from the relationship she enjoyed with many young men. Now let's get some sleep, Dobbitt, tomorrow's a big day.

In darkness we hear the radiator clanging and the wind whistling through the window which won't close.

Lights up on the room. Hanrahan, in the bed next to the window, is shivering, wrapped up in several blankets. Dobbitt, in the bed by the radiator, has kicked off all his blankets and is lying there sweating. They slowly get out of bed and start to get dressed. A single beep from the intercom. They both glare at it. Lights fade.

Lights up on Merkin's office. Merkin is peering out through the blinds and eating dry cereal from a bowl. He returns to his desk. Dobbitt and Hanrahan enter. Hanrahan quickly slides into the chair. Dobbitt stands.

MERKIN: So. You're both here.

DOBBITT: Would you prefer just one of us?

MERKIN: This time I want both of you. But there will be times when I want one of you, or perhaps, the other.

HANRAHAN: How are we supposed to know which one you want?

MERKIN: This is why I wanted to see you both. This affects everyone in the Checking Department. When I want to see Dobbitt, there will be a single beep. Like this. Beep. When I want to see Hanrahan, there will be two beeps. Like this. Beep beep. Is that understood by all parties?

HANRAHAN: Is there a God above us!

MERKIN: What is it, Hanrahan?

HANRAHAN: Why don't you just lop off my arms and be done with it?

MERKIN: That's a separate discussion.

HANRAHAN: I've had that one beep for nearly a year! I as much as own one beep and you simply give it to him!

DOBBITT: I don't mind. I'll happily be two beeps.

HANRAHAN: Your happiness is of no consequence in this matter. *(To Merkin.)* I don't believe you, Merkin. How can you look at yourself or anyone else in the mirror?

MERKIN: What if I were to give Dobbitt two beeps? Mightn't you feel a bit slighted? This Dobbitt fellow blows in from the country and all of a sudden he has twice as many beeps as you.

HANRAHAN: I could accept that. I'm not a crybaby.

MERKIN: You're certainly acting like one.

HANRAHAN: I am not!

MERKIN: You are too!

HANRAHAN: Let's ask Dobbitt.

MERKIN: Dobbitt, Hanrahan's acting like a little crybaby, isn't he? *(Merkin and Hanrahan glare at Dobbitt.)*

DOBBITT: Well . . . I think he feels misunderstood—

MERKIN: See? Crybaby!

HANRAHAN: What an equivocating ball of putty.

MERKIN: What about it, Hanrahan? If Dobbitt is acquiescent, would you like your one beep back?

DOBBITT: "Acquiescent" is my middle name.

HANRAHAN: It's too late. My beep has been tainted. I know in your mind's eye it belonged to Dobbitt, however briefly. I couldn't hear my own beep without thinking maybe it was Dobbitt you wanted.

MERKIN: Well, this is a fine pickle. While we stand here bellyaching about our beeps, the work isn't getting checked.

(Merkin and Dobbitt watch Hanrahan pout.)

HANRAHAN: Oh, give Dobbitt my beep. I'll settle for the two.

MERKIN: That's the spirit!

DOBBITT: I know how much that beep meant to you, Hanrahan. I'll honor it as best I can.

MERKIN: Dobbitt, you've been allocated your beep and it's put the entire department in a tizzy. I suggest you go on your merry way.

(Dobbitt leaves.)

I'm a little wary of Dobbitt. He doesn't say enough.

HANRAHAN: Urge him to say more.

MERKIN: I couldn't do that. Often when he does say something I don't like it.

HANRAHAN: Are you sorry he's here?

MERKIN: Dobbitt does fine checking. I just wish he wouldn't sit in judgment. I wish he could loosen up and be more like us.

HANRAHAN: Do you think we're alike?

MERKIN: We have our differences. But I'd say we're more alike than we are different.

HANRAHAN: And Dobbitt?

MERKIN: He's more different than alike. I think being Dobbitt would be a terrible thing.

(Pause.)

Do you agree?

HANRAHAN: He seems happy.

MERKIN: Are you siding with him?

HANRAHAN: I side with no one.

MERKIN: But you don't seem to think it would be terrible to be Dobbitt and that saddens me.

HANRAHAN: I think it would be terrible to be anyone but me.

MERKIN: It's not terrible being me, I can assure you.

HANRAHAN: Not for you. For me it would be ghastly.

MERKIN: Ghastly? Why?

HANRAHAN: If I found myself you, I'd only remain you for the time it took to jam a loaded pistol in my mouth.

MERKIN: But if you were me then it wouldn't be you being me it would be me being me, which, as I've said, is far from ghastly. And I am a greater authority on being me than you could ever hope to be.

HANRAHAN: I'll have to take your word for it, not being you.

MERKIN: I'm disappointed in you, Hanrahan. I thought if we both felt contempt for Dobbitt it could bring us closer together.

Lights fade on Hanrahan and Merkin.
Lights up on the room. Dobbitt is reading a letter. Hanrahan comes in whistling with a sheaf of notes and sits down at the typewriter. The whistling stops. Hanrahan sees a scone next to the typewriter.

HANRAHAN: What the devil is this?

DOBBITT: A scone.

HANRAHAN: What is it doing here? This is my time to typewrite.

DOBBITT: I put it there. For you.

HANRAHAN: Get it away. Remove the scone.

DOBBITT: I've seen you eat scones, Hanrahan.

HANRAHAN: My scone consumption has nothing to do with you, Dobbitt. It's a personal matter.

DOBBITT: I thought it would make you happy.

HANRAHAN: No, it was to make *you* happy. To buy me, body and soul, with a pitiful scone so I'd be one more dreary hopeless cipher who "likes" you. What rubbish.

DOBBITT: It was a small act of kindness, which you don't understand.

HANRAHAN: It was a hideous, craven attempt to purchase me like a bolt of chintz or patio furniture for the niggardly price of a wretched little scone. Is that all you think I'm worth? A scone? A scone? A scone?

DOBBITT: I never thought that, Hanrahan.

HANRAHAN: Then tell me, oh great and godlike Dobbitt, what am I worth?

DOBBITT: In scones?

HANRAHAN: Since that is your currency, yes. In scones.

DOBBITT: I don't know you well enough to give an exact figure. I'm sure you're worth many many scones.

HANRAHAN: Thousands?

DOBBITT: Yes, thousands!

HANRAHAN: Not millions?

DOBBITT: Millions! Millions of scones!

HANRAHAN: Do you know why Merkin gave us separate beeps? Because you make him uncomfortable.

DOBBITT: No! It's because there's only one chair and you always take it!

HANRAHAN: I knew you were storing it up, all the venom, all the hate. Well let me tell you, I've earned the right to sit in that chair and if you ever sit there while I'm in the room I'll bloody your face.

DOBBITT: He wanted to give me a chance to sit down. That's why I have my own beep.

HANRAHAN: You don't have your own beep. You have *my* beep which is on loan out of the goodness in my heart until you're gone.

DOBBITT: You can't drive me away. You drove the last one away but I'll outlast you. I'm a survivor.

HANRAHAN: Survivors are the first ones to go.

DOBBITT: Not me! I've moved steadily up through this company.

HANRAHAN: Until now. He's not happy with you.

DOBBITT: What did he say?

HANRAHAN: It's the way you just stand there, Dobbitt.

DOBBITT: I stand there because there's only one chair!

HANRAHAN: It's the things you say, not to be overshadowed by the things you don't say. You might reverse the two. Say the things you wouldn't say and hold back on the things you would say.

DOBBITT: And you think that might help?

HANRAHAN: I'm just reporting what was said. It seems Merkin would prefer that you be a slightly different person than you are.

DOBBITT: I see. Thank you. I'll do what I can.

HANRAHAN: Look, Dobbitt, you can use the typewriter for a while if you like.

DOBBITT: Where will you be?

HANRAHAN: Out here. I'll show you.

(They go out into the sunshine. Hanrahan sits down in a tire from a tractor. He pulls a letter from his pocket.)

I'll just sit here and read this letter from my wife.

DOBBITT: And she writes you, I had no idea!

HANRAHAN: Every week, like clockwork. If she ever missed a

week I'd assume she was dead in a pool of blood at the bottom of the cellar stairs.

(Leans back.)

Ahhh, this is all it takes, a ray of sunshine, a letter from my one true love, a stolen hour that's all mine—

DOBBITT: Unless Merkin beeps.

HANRAHAN: That's the beauty of it, Dobbitt. I'm just far enough away so I can't hear the beep. This spot is perfectly safe.

DOBBITT: So if you don't hear your beep—

HANRAHAN: I can't be expected to go, can I? I've got that bastard by the balls! This is where his system breaks down. A man has to have a little freedom, doesn't he? Go on, Dobbitt, go peck away at your silly reports. Peck peck peck, Dobbitt, peck peck peck! *(Dobbitt starts off, then stops.)*

DOBBITT: What should I do if I hear your two beeps?

HANRAHAN: It's only important that *I* don't hear.

DOBBITT: But then I'm enmeshed in your conspiracy. You sit out here, innocent, while I'm sullied by your chicanery. I won't have it, Hanrahan. You must sit close enough to hear your beeps.

HANRAHAN: That defeats the whole purpose! As an honest man, if I hear my beeps I have to go!

DOBBITT: And if *I* hear your beeps I have to tell you. Why don't you be honest about your deceit and ignore the beeps?

HANRAHAN: The day is ruined.

(Hanrahan and Dobbitt go back inside. They look at the intercom.)

He'd better not beep unless he's got a damn good reason.

DOBBITT: It's been a while since he beeped.

HANRAHAN: So?

DOBBITT: Shouldn't we be concerned?

HANRAHAN: Fat lot of good that will do us.

DOBBITT: I think he's punishing us. Why would he punish us?

HANRAHAN: He's a malignant, two-faced bottom-feeder! He's out to get me.

DOBBITT: For what?

HANRAHAN: I need a perfect recommendation from Merkin. My life is in his hands. My temper has ruined me in this company, Dobbitt. One more bad report and I'll be through—

DOBBITT: And then what?

HANRAHAN: Exactly. These days a man without a company is a corpse. But you, Dobbitt, you have no excuse for being such a toady.

DOBBITT: I'm no toady!

HANRAHAN: Toady, toady, toady!

DOBBITT: Stop that! I wish he'd beep.

HANRAHAN: He will. He has to. Sometime.

DOBBITT: Our checking has been acceptable.

HANRAHAN: Our checking has been excellent! This isn't about checking. This is about the criminal abuse of authority. Our only defense is to stop caring.

(Hanrahan tries to busy himself, although his attention is on the intercom. Dobbitt follows suit.)

Look at you, Dobbitt. If you're so anxious, why don't you just scamper over and see your master?

DOBBITT: I've drawn the line with Merkin. If he wants to see me then he has to beep.

HANRAHAN: So you're *demanding* to be treated like a dog.

DOBBITT: Yes, but everything after that is gravy.

(They wait. A muffled beep. They both spring to attention.)

Wait! Did you hear . . .

(Another muffled beep.)

HANRAHAN: One or two?

DOBBITT: One.

HANRAHAN: I could have sworn there were two, Dobbitt.

DOBBITT: One and then one again. That doesn't equal two.

HANRAHAN: I'm not sure about the first one.

DOBBITT: It was there. And unconnected to the second.

HANRAHAN: Then it's you.

DOBBITT: How do you think he sounds today?

HANRAHAN: Not unhappy. But certainly not happy, either. I'm sure you have nothing to worry about.

(Calls after him.)

Just don't be yourself!

(Dobbitt heads off as lights fade.)

Lights up on Merkin's office. He's wielding the "void" stamp, slamming it down on one document after another. Dobbitt comes in trying to be more the way Merkin would like him to be.

MERKIN: Happy, Dobbitt?

DOBBITT: For the most part. Although I miss my wife and—

MERKIN: Is this small talk?

DOBBITT: I suppose it is. Yes.

MERKIN: Let's have none of that. Make yourself comfortable.

   (Dobbitt starts to sit.)

   No need to sit. This won't take but a minute.

   (Dobbitt stands.)

   Do you like parties?

DOBBITT: Pardon me?

MERKIN: Surely you've been to a party.

DOBBITT: Yes. I quite enjoy parties.

MERKIN: On Friday there will be a holiday gala for the entire compound to celebrate Economic Recovery and Realignment Day. I trust you'll attend?

DOBBITT: I'd be thrilled! I'll finally get a chance to meet some of the workers.

MERKIN: Will you be seeing Hanrahan?

DOBBITT: We live in the same room. We work the same job.

MERKIN: Will you be talking to him?

DOBBITT: Of course.

MERKIN: So you two talk, you and Hanrahan?

DOBBITT: Well . . . yes.

MERKIN: And what do you talk about?

DOBBITT: Different things. Day-to-day things.

MERKIN: It sounds like the kinds of things that friends talk about. Are you two friends?

DOBBITT: In a manner of speaking.

MERKIN: Is he the best friend you ever had?

DOBBITT: No.

MERKIN: So you find him a hard man to get along with? A bit on the nasty side?

DOBBITT: I suppose there's some of that.

MERKIN: A vitriolic, contentious son of a bitch? A scurrilous pus-muncher?

DOBBITT: Well . . .

MERKIN: I hear what you're saying. It's a wonder you've stood it so long. He drove the last one mad. Haney.

DOBBITT: What happened?

MERKIN: Day after day with Hanrahan, the poor fellow had enough. One lunch hour he found a tub of glue in the supply shed.

DOBBITT: What did he do?

MERKIN: Drank it down. Glued all his innards together. They needed a hammer and chisel to complete the autopsy. Quite a testimony to the glue but a dark day on the compound. Pity it wasn't Hanrahan. I'm not sure I'll put him on our guest list. *(Dobbitt leaves as lights fade.)*

Lights up on Hanrahan on the bridge at dusk, smoking his cigar. Dobbitt joins him, taking his customary position looking upstream, his back to Hanrahan. A few more pairs of yellow eyes in the distance.

DOBBITT: Hanrahan? I feel that we may be in prison.

HANRAHAN: Why would we be in prison?

DOBBITT: Perhaps we're guilty.

HANRAHAN: Of what?

DOBBITT: It's just a feeling I have.

HANRAHAN: You think perhaps we've done something?

DOBBITT: Sometimes things happen and you hardly even know it. You rush out of a store forgetting something's in your pocket. You add the numbers wrong on your taxes. You're coming home on a foggy night and there's a sudden thumping sound and the next morning you notice what might be blood on the fender so you wash the car and play eighteen holes and fall asleep in front of the TV with a mug of beer—I mean these are things we've all done but how many of us ever get caught?

HANRAHAN: If we were in prison, wouldn't there be walls all around us?

DOBBITT: There *are* walls all around us. With barbed wire on top and patrolled by armed guards.

HANRAHAN: If we were in prison we wouldn't be free to leave.

DOBBITT: Do you know anyone who has left this compound?

HANRAHAN: That's by choice.

DOBBITT: Then you think we *could* leave?

HANRAHAN: If we got by the guards.

DOBBITT: Why are they there if not to keep us inside?

HANRAHAN: Maybe to protect us from what's outside.

DOBBITT: And what's outside?

HANRAHAN: It must be much worse than what's in here to justify all the guards. Let's say this *is* a jail, Dobbitt. How are the conditions?

DOBBITT: If it's a jail, I have to admit it's not bad. It's really pretty decent.

HANRAHAN: And what if it's a workplace?

DOBBITT: Then it's entirely unacceptable.

HANRAHAN: And being a rational man, you'd rather be in a place that's pretty decent rather than one that's unacceptable, true?

DOBBITT: But that makes me a prisoner.

HANRAHAN: Exactly! Because you believe you're better off as a prisoner. Face it, Dobbitt, you've made yourself a prisoner in what is quite clearly not a jail—

DOBBITT: How can you be so sure?

HANRAHAN: For one thing, you wouldn't survive in a real jail.

DOBBITT: Yes I would! I'd be a model prisoner!

HANRAHAN: But you'd never figure out what was really going on.

DOBBITT: I'd obey all the rules. I'd keep my nose clean—

HANRAHAN: Whereas I would understand the Byzantine system of power and intimidation and I would thrive—

DOBBITT: Why must you always be the best, Hanrahan? Why can't I be the better prisoner?

HANRAHAN: Actually, Dobbitt, you'd do fine. You'd be a much-desired jailhouse wife. Especially among the older convicts who'd sown their wild oats and just wanted a clean cell and a little cuddling at day's end—

DOBBITT: Hanrahan! Stop!

(Hanrahan turns and sees Merkin approaching with a memo.)

Good evening, Merkin.

MERKIN: Is it? I can't tell with all these damn bugs. *(He swats and scratches.)*

How can you stand it? *(Accusingly.)*

Or don't they bother you?

HANRAHAN: They're quite an annoyance, right, Dobbitt?

DOBBITT: A damn nuisance alright.

(Dobbitt and Hanrahan swat and scratch like Merkin.)

MERKIN: Did you tell Hanrahan about the Economic Recovery and Realignment Day Party?

DOBBITT: I thought you might want to tell him yourself.

HANRAHAN: A party? And I wasn't told?

MERKIN: Dobbitt kept it to himself.

HANRAHAN: Didn't want to invite me, Dobbitt?

DOBBITT: I thought Merkin would do the inviting.

MERKIN: Are you saying I have nothing to do but ruminate on galas!

HANRAHAN: That's a cheap shot at Merkin, Dobbitt.

DOBBITT: I didn't mean that!

MERKIN: He was supposed to tell you.

HANRAHAN: I think Dobbitt's a little gadfly.

DOBBITT: I'm not a little gadfly!

HANRAHAN: Buzz buzz buzz, up the social ladder. Didn't want me at his party.

DOBBITT: I want you at my party.

MERKIN: Now he thinks it's *his* party.

HANRAHAN: It's not *your* party, Dobbitt!

MERKIN: You're a slippery snake, Dobbitt. A short-timer with a long reach.

DOBBITT: I hope you'll come to the party, Hanrahan.

HANRAHAN: The party's been tarnished for me.

MERKIN: I'm sorry to report it's been tarnished for our entire department. Read this. From our Regional Director. *(Merkin hands them the memo.)*

DOBBITT: This sounds spectacular! Skits, fireworks, games of chance—

MERKIN: Read the bottom.

HANRAHAN: "Checkers welcome from 5:30 to 6:15."

DOBBITT: That's an outrage! They're making us leave before the buffet dinner with sing-a-long to follow!

HANRAHAN: I won't be a part of it.

MERKIN: I'm not going. *(They both turn on Dobbitt.)*

DOBBITT: Well *I'm* not going!

MERKIN: Then we'll stand together as a department. There will be no Checkers at the party this year.

DOBBITT: That'll show the bastards!

MERKIN: We'll have our own party!

HANRAHAN: Do you mean it, Merkin?

MERKIN: Of course I mean it! A giant gala for Checkers only! Get out your party clothes, men!

(Starts off, then turns.)

Don't worry, Hanrahan, there won't be any dancing.

(Merkin hurries away. Dobbitt and Hanrahan stop swatting and scratching.)

DOBBITT: Don't like to dance, Hanrahan?

HANRAHAN: There's a lot you don't understand, Dobbitt. I'd like to keep it that way.

(Lights fade on Dobbitt and Hanrahan on the bridge.)

Lights up on Merkin. He's standing on a chair in his office putting up crepe paper. Lights fade.

Lights up on the room. Hanrahan is getting ready for the party in front of a tiny mirror. The sound of a shower. A yell from the bathroom, where the door is partly open.

DOBBITT: *(Offstage.)* What the devil is wrong with this shower!

HANRAHAN: What happened?

DOBBITT: *(Offstage.)* I just got a blast of cold water!

HANRAHAN: That's not as bad as what happened to me.

DOBBITT: *(Offstage.)* What happened to you?

HANRAHAN: I was in the shower when the water suddenly turned ice-cold.

DOBBITT: *(Offstage.)* That's exactly what happened to me!

HANRAHAN: No, Dobbitt, this was far worse because it happened to *me*. *(Hanrahan is pleased with himself as he gets ready to go.)*

DOBBITT: *(Offstage.)* I suppose you're going to rush over and get the only chair.

HANRAHAN: You'll be on your feet for hours! I can hardly wait.

DOBBITT: *(Offstage.)* It's a party, Hanrahan. You'll look like a fool, planted in your chair while the rest of us are mingling and carrying on.

(Two beeps from the intercom.)

HANRAHAN: Well, there's *my* invitation.

(Pause.)

Don't hear any invitation for *you*. Looks like you won't be going to the party after all, Dobbitt.

(Hanrahan makes loud footsteps toward the door to sound as if he's leaving.)

Still no beep for you, little man. Don't wait up!

(Dobbitt comes out, shirtless, his face covered with shaving cream, brandishing a straight razor.)

The typewriter's all yours tonight.

DOBBITT: You bastard. You're behind this, Hanrahan, you've poisoned Merkin against me. Well I won't have it. You're a pathetic, lonely, friendless malcontent but you won't find me glued together like Haney. I'm going to fight you to the death.

HANRAHAN: Stop it, Dobbitt, stop it.

DOBBITT: You've taken everything else but you can't take this party away from me!

(Dobbitt chases Hanrahan, taking a wild swipe with the razor, which Hanrahan eludes. Then, as Dobbitt prepares for another assault, Hanrahan trips while moving away. He's helpless on the floor. Dobbitt is about to cut his throat with the razor when there's a single beep from the intercom. They both stop and look at it.)

HANRAHAN: There's your invitation, Dobbitt. Better get dressed.

DOBBITT: My God, Hanrahan, my God. I tried to kill you.

HANRAHAN: It's the first honest emotion you've expressed since you got here. I'd say you're making excellent progress.

DOBBITT: What if I'd cut your throat?

HANRAHAN: You'd have gotten the chair. *(Dobbitt slumps on the bed.)*

DOBBITT: We have to do something, Hanrahan. Or we won't make it out of here.

HANRAHAN: What do you suggest we do?

DOBBITT: It's Merkin. He's playing us off each other.

HANRAHAN: Merkin is Merkin. And never the twain shall meet.

DOBBITT: But we must do something about him!

HANRAHAN: Perhaps we'll outlast him. He's angling to get out.

DOBBITT: Where to?

HANRAHAN: Anywhere but here. It's the company motto, no matter where you're stationed.

DOBBITT: He always calls us over separately. What if we tell each other the truth of whatever is said in his office?

HANRAHAN: The truth?

DOBBITT: Yes. The truth.

HANRAHAN: I don't think you're up to the truth, Dobbitt. The truth doesn't come in a little gift box with a colorful bow.

DOBBITT: I can handle the truth.

HANRAHAN: The truth is a wound in your heart that won't heal. The truth is the last nail in the coffin. The truth is a cold hand reaching up and turning out the light forever. That's the truth.

DOBBITT: The truth is he didn't want to invite you to the party.

HANRAHAN: No?

DOBBITT: The truth is, he thinks you're a nasty, contentious son of a bitch.

HANRAHAN: I see.

DOBBITT: The truth is, he thinks you poison every room you walk into.

HANRAHAN: Go on.

DOBBITT: The truth is, he wishes *you* had drunk the glue, Hanrahan. He wishes you were dead.

HANRAHAN: Beautiful. I'm proud of you, Dobbitt.

DOBBITT: *(Extending his hand.)* You and me, Hanrahan?

(They shake hands.)

BLACKOUT

ACT TWO

In darkness we hear the sounds of a boisterous party with laughter, songs, and music. Then lights up on Merkin's office. Merkin, Hanrahan, and Dobbitt are looking out the window at the party. They're in their party clothes and sipping punch. There's a plate of cookies on Merkin's desk and a few tired party decorations.

MERKIN: I wouldn't set foot in that party for all the money in the world.

DOBBITT: It looks a bit desperate, don't you think?

HANRAHAN: It makes a mockery of merrymaking.

MERKIN: As if something's missing. Like the heart and soul of this compound.

HANRAHAN: *(Raising his glass.)* Long live the Checkers!

DOBBITT: Why don't they like us?

MERKIN: The high moral ground we walk makes them dizzy. They think we'd judge them.

HANRAHAN: We would! We'd check their party the way we check their work. Anyway, it's best not to fraternize. Our judgments must be cold and impartial.

DOBBITT: But must we always be outside, our noses pressed to the window?

HANRAHAN: They're the ones outside, Dobbitt.

DOBBITT: But we're always here and everyone else is always there. I never knew how lonely it would be when I chose to be a Checker.

MERKIN: You don't choose checking, checking chooses you. My daddy was a Checker and his daddy checked before him. He'd say, "Any man can work, it takes an extraordinary man to check work."

HANRAHAN: My daddy was a worker. Loathed Checkers, thought they were maggots, bloated with the blood of honest workers. I only became a Checker to cause him pain and disappointment. Then it grew inside me until that's who I am. A Checker.

DOBBITT: Here here!

(They raise their glasses.)

I may be a neophyte, but there isn't a man alive who loves checking as I do.

HANRAHAN: I love it more than you, easy. It's my whole life.

DOBBITT: It's *my* whole life. It's who I am.

MERKIN: We all love checking. But none has given up more for the calling than me.

DOBBITT: I've only seen my wife eleven weeks in the three years of our marriage.

HANRAHAN: Good God, what a holiday you've had! I love my wife more than life itself, but I wouldn't even recognize her if she walked in that door.

MERKIN: Don't talk about sacrifices. I was a continent away when my daughter was born. And it was a damn difficult delivery, let me tell you.

HANRAHAN: With all due respect, Merkin, I believe the birth of my son was worse than anything your wife might have gone through—

DOBBITT: When *my* son was born the umbilical cord was tight around his neck—

HANRAHAN: Piece of cake, Dobbitt. When *my* son was born it was a breach delivery and my wife was in horrible screaming agony for weeks—

DOBBITT: Maybe *my* wife simply handled it better—

MERKIN: When *my* wife gave birth she died. Beat that, boys, death! *(Dobbitt and Hanrahan are stopped in their tracks.)*

HANRAHAN: Merkin, I'm sorry, I had no idea . . .

MERKIN: Oh, yes. I had an off-country assignment, Thailand. I get the telegram that she died in childbirth. The company gave me Domestic Tragedy Leave for the funeral.

DOBBITT: Three days per death per family member?

MERKIN: I'm talking *paid* Domestic Tragedy Leave, if you can believe that!

HANRAHAN: Beautiful!

MERKIN: I walk up the little path to my house feeling like a slug for missing her death like I missed everything else in her life and who should greet me at the door but my wife. Damndest thing. They managed to bring her back, she hadn't been dead long—

HANRAHAN: Long enough for them to write a telegram—

MERKIN: Which they forgot about when the next shift came in. Human error. So we had a high old time that night, let me tell you, I mean my God, what a gift.

DOBBITT: What was she like after she died?

MERKIN: Quite similar. Except she sang differently. I'd hear her doing the dishes, puttering around the house, and she'd start to sing. But it was possessed, not like any human voice you ever heard. Like someone else was singing through my wife. It gave me the chills. I'd go outside, rake leaves, wherever I was I'd hear that voice, moving through the house like a ghost. She knew something I didn't know and she couldn't tell me. That's when I took the assignment down here. There wasn't room in that house for both of us. *(The phone on Merkin's desk rings.)*

HANRAHAN: They're probably wondering if we'll come to their party.

DOBBITT: Tell 'em we can't tear ourselves away from our own party!

MERKIN: *(On phone.)* Hello? Yes, yes. I see.

(Hanrahan and Dobbitt move together to talk. Merkin covers the phone.)

Don't talk among yourselves, I'll only be a minute.

(Back on phone.)

I'll attend to it immediately.

(Merkin hangs up. Outside, the festive sounds of the celebration continue.)

The river is on fire.

DOBBITT: *Our* river?

MERKIN: With everything we've poured into it, all it took was an errant firecracker and it burst into flames. I don't quite know what to do.

HANRAHAN: Isn't that up to the Regional Director?

MERKIN: The Regional Director is temporarily incapacitated by the soiree. I'm the ranking officer and I don't know what to do.

DOBBITT: Convention would seem to call for putting out the fire.

MERKIN: I wish it were that simple. Drinking water on the compound is in short supply. The only water I'm authorized to use is from the river.

HANRAHAN: Which would quite literally add fuel to the fire.

MERKIN: Exactly. It could turn an accident into an incident. Or an incident into a disaster. Or a disaster into a tragedy.

DOBBITT: Then we can rule that out.

MERKIN: Except the alternative is to do nothing. Which will be perceived as weakness and could cripple me in the company. Crisis management is quite a stepping-stone around here. This is my hour to shine.

DOBBITT: Is there some middle ground?

HANRAHAN: Between doing nothing and doing something that makes the situation infinitely worse?

DOBBITT: Some decisive action that is without consequence. Can't you issue a strong statement condemning the fire?

HANRAHAN: It's best to do nothing, Merkin. Let it burn itself out.

MERKIN: But this is my fire and I must put my stamp on it. Fire units are awaiting orders, I have to tell them *something!*

(The phone rings. Merkin stares at it, paralyzed.)

HANRAHAN: Do nothing, Merkin, nothing at all.

MERKIN: But they're all in a dither! Something must be done!

DOBBITT: Hanrahan's right. Do nothing.

(Merkin looks from the ringing phone to Dobbitt and Hanrahan.)

MERKIN: Look at you, the innocent bystanders, trying to ruin me with your help.

(Picks up phone.)

This is Merkin. I want all nonburning water from the river pumped onto the fire. Now!

(Merkin hangs up the phone. Dobbitt and Hanrahan look out the window.)

DOBBITT: It's cast quite a pall on the other party.

HANRAHAN: That's the good news.

MERKIN: What's the bad news?

HANRAHAN: Now the river is burning out of control.

MERKIN: Without leadership skills I'll be stuck in this compound forever. I've got my eyes on Spain, boys, and this could be my ticket out. *(Dobbitt and Hanrahan stare out the window as lights fade.)*

Lights up on the bridge. Dusk. Dobbitt enters carrying a guidebook. He stares off in the distance. More pairs of yellow eyes peer out of the darkness. Hanrahan takes his customary position looking off the other side of the bridge.

DOBBITT: There's more of them, you know. By the fence. I saw them up close. They have sharp little teeth and insolent yellow eyes. They're not in my guidebook to local flora and fauna, Hanrahan.

HANRAHAN: You won't find them in any book.

DOBBITT: For God sakes, what are they?

HANRAHAN: Would you feel better if they had a name? Would that make them go away?

DOBBITT: If they had a name I'd know who was staring at me, watching every move I make, waiting . . .

HANRAHAN: What do you imagine they're waiting for?

DOBBITT: I don't know! I'm not inside their horrid little heads. But I know what waiting looks like and they are waiting!

HANRAHAN: They're on the other side of the fence.

DOBBITT: No, they've burrowed under the fence. I've been watching them, Hanrahan, every night they're a few inches closer. Something must be done!

HANRAHAN: What would you do?

DOBBITT: Someone should set a trap. Catch one and study it in a laboratory and find out what it is, for God sakes!

HANRAHAN: How would we lure it into a trap? If we don't know what they are how can we be expected to know what they like? Perhaps they're workers who took a plunge in the river.

DOBBITT: Merkin must take it up with the Regional Director. I look into their eyes and I am very concerned.

HANRAHAN: Merkin can't even requisition another typewriter. What do you think he'd do with a real problem? *(They stand in silence.)*

DOBBITT: Hanrahan? I miss the river.

HANRAHAN: I miss it too.

DOBBITT: All I see is the blistered bank where it used to be.

HANRAHAN: *(Looking more intently.)* It looks as if something has started to grow.

DOBBITT: Already?

HANRAHAN: Look for yourself.

DOBBITT: Do you mean that, Hanrahan?

HANRAHAN: Turn around. Have a look. *(Dobbitt turns around and the two men look in the same direction.)*

DOBBITT: Flowers are starting to bloom. I always admired your view.

HANRAHAN: It's something, isn't it? Look wherever you like.

DOBBITT: Thank you.

   (Nighttime sounds. Dobbitt shivers.)

This reminds me of home. The terror I can't quite see.

HANRAHAN: Do you miss Catherine?

DOBBITT: I miss the idea of Catherine. I miss the future I used to dream about with Catherine. I miss missing Catherine.

HANRAHAN: I've had a mistaken impression of your marriage.

DOBBITT: The company values a solid family life and I'm lucky enough to have one. We both love to be at home. Just not at the same time.

HANRAHAN: Ah.

DOBBITT: Too much time together, well, if things get out of whack, that hurts me in the company. Don't get me wrong, in every other way we're perfect. It's just this one issue of proximity. It's quite a risk.

HANRAHAN: It's not that way with my wife and me, Dobbitt. For us the risk is being apart. I sense it in her letters, she's slipping away, like a ship easing silently off into the fog. I can just make out the dim outline of what was there, but soon that will be gone, too.

DOBBITT: I'm sure it will all work out when you see her—

HANRAHAN: *(Strange intensity.)* I would like to be needed, Dobbitt. I would like my existence to truly matter to someone else in the world.

(Lights fade on Dobbitt and Hanrahan.)

Lights up on Merkin at his desk. A trophy—a silver fireman's helmet—is on his desk. Dobbitt enters.

MERKIN: Ah, Dobbitt. Make yourself comfortable.

(Dobbitt starts to sit.)

No need for that! I don't imagine this will be a long meeting. If it is, well, feel free to sit down.

DOBBITT: How will I know the length of the meeting until it's over?

MERKIN: I suppose you won't.

DOBBITT: And then it will be too late.

MERKIN: Quite right. Human error. If you feel the meeting starting to elongate, well, the chair will be waiting.

DOBBITT: Perhaps I should just sit now. To be on the safe side.

MERKIN: No need to jump the gun. I'll have you out of here in a jiffy, if all goes well. I'm expecting a call from the Regional Director, maybe even a personal visitation, for God sakes! There's an open assignment in Spain.

DOBBITT: Excellent!

MERKIN: So to have you sitting here, well, it wouldn't do.

(Briskly gets out memo.)

I received your memo concerning unidentified animals outside the fence.

DOBBITT: Inside the fence! That's my point! They're in the compound with us and we don't have a clue as to what they are.

MERKIN: They're outside the fence until someone at the appropriate level says they're inside the fence. I've memoed the Regional Director. I'll expect a prompt memo back, at which point you will be the first to be memoed.

DOBBITT: I could ask for nothing more.

MERKIN: Well, I'd say we made the right call on the chair.

(Dobbitt starts for the door.)

Oh, Dobbitt? There's one more matter of a rather unfortunate nature. Hanrahan's wife has left him, poor bastard.

DOBBITT: My God! I'm—

MERKIN: Yes, you're shocked, of course. I know exactly how you feel. No need to drag us both through it.

DOBBITT: Why did she leave him?

MERKIN: All that time alone, seems she got a little too close to the Lord. Joined an order, now she's off to a convent. Took an oath of celibacy. Solitude. Silence. Eventually she hopes to give up breathing.

DOBBITT: He never mentioned it.

MERKIN: He doesn't know.

(Holds up letter.)

He received—or will receive—a Dear Hanrahan letter. You can imagine my discomfort when I read it.

DOBBITT: How can you read his mail, Merkin?

MERKIN: I make time for it, Dobbitt, just as I make time for yours. No one's getting slighted here.

DOBBITT: And you've kept it to yourself?

MERKIN: With regards to his marriage, Hanrahan is out of the loop.

DOBBITT: Doesn't he belong in that loop?

MERKIN: Do you know what he'd do if he knew? He'd go roaring back to the country, and all he's worked for would be out the window. With his history of malfeasance, bad temper, and petty chicanery the company would have no choice but to freeze him out. There he'd be with no wife and no company to boot.

DOBBITT: You're not even going to show him this letter?

MERKIN: I'll show him the letter next week when the work is done and I've written him a glowing report.

DOBBITT: If he doesn't hear from her this week he'll assume she's dead, he told me himself.

MERKIN: He'll receive a letter this week. It just won't be this one.

DOBBITT: What will it be?

MERKIN: Whatever you choose to write.

DOBBITT: Me?

MERKIN: As unfair as it may be, you know him far better than I do.

(Gets out copies of letters.)

These copies of past letters from the esteemed Mrs. Hanrahan will serve as an excellent guide I'm sure. Your nom de plume will be Jacqueline Hanrahan.

DOBBITT: You're asking me to lie to Hanrahan?

MERKIN: I'm asking you to lie *for* Hanrahan. He'll survive losing his wife, but once the company cuts bait it's a fast drop to the bottom of the ocean, isn't it?

DOBBITT: But Hanrahan treasures honesty more than anything.

MERKIN: More than his own survival?

DOBBITT: I don't know. I'm just . . . nonplussed.

MERKIN: Well I suggest you get yourself plussed and give me your answer right now.

DOBBITT: If I have to answer right now my answer is no.

MERKIN: Well, there it is, a swift dagger to the heart.

DOBBITT: I've struggled with my decision—

MERKIN: For several seconds.

DOBBITT: You wanted an immediate answer.

MERKIN: You didn't even sit down.

DOBBITT: You told me not to sit down!

MERKIN: I thought you'd want to go off and think about it some more.

DOBBITT: Could I go off and think about it some more?

MERKIN: Alright. But don't go off and think about it some more and then come back here with the same answer.

DOBBITT: You mean if I go off and think about it some more I have to agree to write the letter?

MERKIN: Why else would you go off and think about it some more?

DOBBITT: I might go off and think about it some more and come to the same conclusion that I can't do it.

MERKIN: Then tell me now and save us both the tedium of your going off and thinking about it some more.

DOBBITT: But how can I know the result of going off and thinking about it some more without going off and thinking about it some more?

MERKIN: How will I know you really did go off and think about it some more if you come back in here and still say no? Can you give me the assurance you'll come back in here and say yes?

DOBBITT: I can't assure you I'll come back in here and say yes unless I go off and think about it some more.

MERKIN: Very well then, a simple no would suffice.

DOBBITT: No.

MERKIN: By God, you're something of a sadist, aren't you? Shooting that word at me over and over as if you had a crossbow.

DOBBITT: I'm trying to do what's right. I'd do anything for Hanrahan except lie.

MERKIN: But lying is the one thing that can save him. So you really are saying you'll do nothing for him. Which surprises me.

DOBBITT: Why?

MERKIN: Oh, let's not be coy, Dobbitt. I know what you and Hanrahan are.

DOBBITT: What?

MERKIN: Don't make me say it.

DOBBITT: Say it, Merkin. What are we?

(Advancing on Merkin.)

I demand that you say it! What are we?

MERKIN: Alright, I'll tell you. You're . . . palsy-walsy.

(Pause.)

There, I've said it.

DOBBITT: Careful, Merkin. That kind of talk hardly dignifies your station.

MERKIN: If Hanrahan leaves his post early, my reference letter will doom him for the remainder of his time on this planet. I need to know what you intend to do.

DOBBITT: In that case . . . I will try to save him.

MERKIN: That's the spirit!
(Hands Dobbitt the letter.)
With her oath of silence, Dobbitt, these are her last words
on this earth. Except for whatever you choose to write.
DOBBITT: I hope I'm doing what's right.
MERKIN: It's you and me, Dobbitt!
(They shake hands as lights fade.)

*Dobbitt crosses to the tractor tire, sits down, sets out the letters, and
begins to write as lights fade.*
*Lights up on Merkin in his office. He's carefully folding the letter
and putting it in an envelope, which he seals as lights fade.*
*Lights up on Hanrahan on the bridge. He tears open the envelope
and begins to read. He does a small, solitary dance of joy. Dobbitt
approaches the bridge, and Hanrahan pockets the letter.*

HANRAHAN: What news from Merkin? What malicious little jewel
was cast at your feet? What petty slur, what glittering gob of
transparent puffery landed in your vicinity?
DOBBITT: He's taking up the animal issue with the powers that
be.
HANRAHAN: You've been gone for hours.
DOBBITT: I've been checking the plants. One week to go and
we're completely caught up to manufacturing.
HANRAHAN: He said nothing about me?
DOBBITT: No. Nothing.
HANRAHAN: Aha!
DOBBITT: What?
HANRAHAN: I knew the truth would be too much for you to bear.
Look at you, eyes averted—
DOBBITT: I tell you, he said nothing!
HANRAHAN: Do you honestly believe you can fool me for an
instant?
DOBBITT: Alright! You've got me.
HANRAHAN: I knew it! Tell me everything!
DOBBITT: *(Pause as he considers.)* He said your venomous nature
is the reason you excel at checking. Your only joy is belittling
others—
HANRAHAN: Yes?

DOBBITT: And the very thing that makes you good at your job makes you unfit for human life as we know it—
HANRAHAN: Hallelujah!
(Laughing, he embraces Dobbitt.)
A compliment! I knew you were holding out on me. Now Merkin will have to give me a good report. And with a good report I'll get an in-country assignment and can live with my wife. At long last, my life is beginning!
(Looking at the somber Dobbitt.)
Why can't you share in my happiness, Dobbitt? Must everything be about you?

Lights fade on Dobbitt and Hanrahan on the bridge.
Lights up on Merkin's office. Hanrahan enters.

MERKIN: Were you and Dobbitt laughing?
HANRAHAN: When?
MERKIN: Yesterday.
HANRAHAN: I don't remember.
MERKIN: Let me help you. I saw the two of you on the bridge. Laughing.
HANRAHAN: Then yes. We laughed.
MERKIN: There you were, outside my window laughing, throwing it in my face like scalding water.
HANRAHAN: We meant no harm.
MERKIN: What were you laughing about?
HANRAHAN: I can't say.
MERKIN: You two must laugh a lot if you can't remember what you were laughing at. Do you know how many times you and I have laughed together, Hanrahan? Do you?
HANRAHAN: No.
MERKIN: Twice. And one of those times you weren't even laughing. I was all alone out there in midlaugh when I realized you were merely coughing, so it has been just once for us. In a year. And yet you and Dobbitt stand out there on the bridge, flaunting your mirth.
HANRAHAN: I'm sorry if it caused you pain.
MERKIN: I still remember what we laughed at. We were standing over there by the window, looking out at the parking lot. And

there was a hard wind coming off the desert which swept the cap off one of the engineers taking his break. He chased after it but as soon as he got near it the wind would dance the little cap away from him again. He kept rushing after it but he was always a step too late, until he lost sight of where he was and with a final burst of speed he smashed face-first into a utility pole. Knocked the poor bastard cold. Do you remember how we laughed, Hanrahan? Tears were streaming down our faces and our insides ached. I'll bet we laughed a damn sight harder than you laugh with Dobbitt.

(Pause.)

You two were laughing at me, weren't you?

HANRAHAN: No, Merkin.

MERKIN: If you know you *weren't* laughing at me then you must know what you *were* laughing at.

HANRAHAN: No, Merkin, it only means we *never* laugh at you!

MERKIN: Listen to you. You speak as though all you and Dobbitt ever do is laugh. Ha, ha, ha, ha, ha. How many times would you say you and Dobbitt laugh in a week?

HANRAHAN: I don't have any idea.

MERKIN: You're such a wizard with figures, come on, over fifteen?

HANRAHAN: I don't know, Merkin.

MERKIN: Then it's over fifteen. More than twice a day. I suggest you put some of that time you spend laughing into your checking.

HANRAHAN: Is our checking suffering?

MERKIN: *Our* checking? Your checking is acceptable. I won't discuss Dobbitt's checking with you.

HANRAHAN: Fair enough.

MERKIN: We're near the end of the order, Hanrahan. It would be a shame to blunder now.

HANRAHAN: Yes. Thank you. *(Hanrahan goes to the door.)*

MERKIN: Hanrahan? Why don't you ever laugh in here? With me?

HANRAHAN: Alright. I will. That would be nice. Thank you.

MERKIN: No need to stand on ceremony. We could laugh together.

HANRAHAN: Now?

MERKIN: Yes, now.

HANRAHAN: Alright. What would you like to laugh at?

MERKIN: I don't know. Dobbitt?

HANRAHAN: Yes. Dobbitt.

(They laugh without conviction.)

The truth is, my happiness has nothing to do with Dobbitt. I received a letter from my wife. Do you have any idea what it's like to be truly loved and accepted?

MERKIN: No, of course not.

HANRAHAN: I didn't either. Until I received this.

(Hanrahan gets out his wife's letter. Merkin turns away as lights fade.)

Lights up on Dobbitt typing a report. Hanrahan enters.

HANRAHAN: My happiness is a problem for Merkin. It's like a terrible rock about to fall on his head and smash him to pieces. He wants it to be gone.

DOBBITT: Perhaps you should temper it in his presence. That's what I do.

HANRAHAN: But my happiness is different from yours, Dobbitt. It can't be tempered. You know I've felt my wife drifting away from me in recent letters, hence my anxiety to go home. Then I received this.

(Reading.)

"When everything else is stripped away, the pain, the hurt, the endless aching years of doubt, the rainy afternoons when the whole world closes in, the desolate lonely nights without comfort, the sudden torturous intoxications of what might have been, the relentless impossible hope that can't be squelched—when all of that falls away, what remains is you and I, the two of us, together, today, tomorrow, and forever, because without you—"

(Stops, pockets the letter.)

Dobbitt, this letter has given me a joy I didn't think possible. Never has she spoken so eloquently to the yearning in my heart. Never before have I felt so needed.

DOBBITT: I'm glad you have this moment of happiness, Hanrahan.

HANRAHAN: It's not a "moment of happiness." It's a lifetime of happiness, it's an eternity of happiness, it's a happiness that won't stop at the grave—

DOBBITT: But things change so quickly. Maybe all we can really trust is what we see before us—

HANRAHAN: See here, Dobbitt, it's a pity you don't have what I have, but I won't let you trample on my happiness.

DOBBITT: I only wish to point out how fleeting one's joy can be. To protect you from whatever hurt is waiting—

HANRAHAN: I won't live my life in fear of what might happen. Do you know what this means? It means I'm not alone.

DOBBITT: No, you're not alone, Hanrahan.

HANRAHAN: And now that my wife has assured me I'm not alone, we're free to be apart.

DOBBITT: What do you mean?

HANRAHAN: With Merkin leaving, you and I could stay on. One tour of duty running the department and we'll go back to the country at the highest level. We'll be set, Dobbitt, we'll be *them*.

DOBBITT: You'd really stay on?

HANRAHAN: It can all be ours! I can step out of the purgatory I've inhabited since my damnable night of dancing. Oh, I've been haunted, Dobbitt. There I was, a young jackal on his way up the vine, my first company party, sweating through my suit, and you have to understand, this was during my drinking days. My wife and I ended up on the dance floor, a terrifying place for a man who can't dance. And even at the time I knew they were watching, a little cabal of them, laughing, pointing, carrying on. So I didn't disappoint them, I danced as no man has ever danced, flinging my limbs in a multitude of directions, 'til I was the only one out there and the entire party was just a sorry blur around me. And my poor wife, watching me with an awful, stricken smile. It followed me through the company, all these years like a monomaniacal ferret, my dancing was the first sign they had that old Hanrahan wasn't like the rest. Not quite right for the key post. The off-country assignments followed. The lackluster recommendations. I did everything I could think of to lift this curse. I even learned to dance. Not that it ever erased the memory of that grisly night.

(He turns on the radio.)

Come here. I'll prove they were wrong, all of them!
(As the music builds Hanrahan leads Dobbitt in a dance.)
I'm not bad, am I?

DOBBITT: You're quite good.

HANRAHAN: Don't patronize me!

DOBBITT: I mean it, you're very good! Not that I'm an expert—

HANRAHAN: Obviously. You're not nearly as good as my wife.

DOBBITT: Sorry.

HANRAHAN: I can stop the whispering forever if I run this department. And I want you to run it with me, Dobbitt. We'd be a wonderful team, wouldn't we?
(They dance to the music. It's a moment of perfect happiness.)

DOBBITT: Yes. If we could accept each other's shortcomings.

HANRAHAN: Relax, Dobbitt, I can accept your shortcomings and I'm sure you'd do the same if I had any.

DOBBITT: And we can forgive each other's mistakes, however great they may seem?

HANRAHAN: You're forgiven your many mistakes, Dobbitt.

DOBBITT: I must admit, you've taught me a great deal. I'll stay on with you, Hanrahan.

HANRAHAN: Excellent!

DOBBITT: I think your wife is right. Without you I'll never be the person I want to be. I'll stay on with you, Hanrahan.

HANRAHAN: *(Stops dancing.)* I never read you that part of my wife's letter.
(Lights fade on the two men looking at each other.)

Lights up on Merkin's office. Dobbitt enters.

MERKIN: Do you know how close I am to the Regional Director? *(Waves a memo.)*
He memoed me right back on the animals. Most memos get backed up for *weeks* in that office. You're looking at a 72 hour turnaround. Any closer we'd be tongue-kissing.

DOBBITT: What did he say?

MERKIN: Nothing to worry about. The authorities have ruled that the animals are on this side of the fence. Therefore, they have, in effect, been captured.

DOBBITT: But if they're on this side of the fence then they're in here with us. To do whatever it is they intend to do.

MERKIN: We can't even identify them so I don't think there's any sense speculating about their intentions.

DOBBITT: But if we can't identify them then how can we have captured them?

MERKIN: You're not going to rock the boat are you? Because I'll push you overboard before I let you rock the boat.

DOBBITT: Then you agree with the Regional Director's logic?

MERKIN: He's my closest friend and most trusted ally. I defer to his judgement and I suggest you do the same.

DOBBITT: Merkin, I feel we're in trouble.

MERKIN: See here, Dobbitt, you've just started to make a name for yourself in this company. Don't go out on a limb with this animal issue. What are your plans, anyway?

DOBBITT: I'd like to stay on the compound for the next order.

MERKIN: Well, well, well! This is good news indeed. You've certainly grown as a Checker and as a man under my tutelage, and I'll be sure to note that in your report. With my transfer to Spain, I'll recommend that you run the department yourselves, if we can talk old Hanrahan into staying around.

DOBBITT: Oh, I think he'll stay.

MERKIN: Ah, yes, I sometimes forget how close you two are. Let's get your paperwork in order.
(Getting out papers.)
Your new contract . . . and your release papers, soon to be moot.
(Dobbitt signs the new contract.)

DOBBITT: You'll tell Hanrahan about his wife?

MERKIN: Right away. Now that the work is done.

DOBBITT: Because this deception has eaten me up inside. It's very important that he think of me as an honest man.

MERKIN: You wouldn't want him to know who you really are.

DOBBITT: I *am* an honest man. I deceived him for a reason.

MERKIN: There's always a reason for deception, Dobbitt.

DOBBITT: You were the one who talked me into it!

MERKIN: And it was about as difficult as tying my shoe. Now that we'll never see each other again, I can tell you I never much liked you. You've never been comfortable in my presence.

DOBBITT: In that spirit of honesty, I wonder if it's because you have tyrannized me and sought to make every moment of my life a bitter taste of hell.

MERKIN: I'm your boss. It's expected.

DOBBITT: It will be a pleasure to run this department the right way, with you gone, Merkin.

MERKIN: You've become quite a brave soul, haven't you?

DOBBITT: I learned from Hanrahan the value of honesty and speaking one's mind.

MERKIN: I don't think you were a very bright pupil. Goodbye, Dobbitt. May we go to our graves without ever seeing each other again.

DOBBITT: Likewise, Merkin.

(Merkin slams the "void" stamp on Dobbitt's release papers. It echoes in the silence as lights fade.)

Lights up on Hanrahan in the room locking up his wife's letters. Two beeps from the intercom. Lights fade.
Lights up on Merkin's office. Merkin is on the phone.

MERKIN: Yes . . . yes . . . yes . . . yes . . . yes . . . yes . . .

(Hanrahan appears in the doorway. Merkin makes a wild waving motion at him. Hanrahan starts to back out. Merkin waves more desperately and Hanrahan comes back in. Merkin hangs up the phone.)

Sit down, Hanrahan.

HANRAHAN: I'd rather stand.

MERKIN: Sit! Please!

HANRAHAN: No, I won't! Dobbitt is conversant with my personal correspondence.

MERKIN: So?

HANRAHAN: I want to know how this is possible.

MERKIN: What happens between you and Dobbitt is outside my bailiwick.

HANRAHAN: He read and memorized what is most precious to me in the whole world.

MERKIN: It's nothing a double lock can't fix.

HANRAHAN: I'm afraid this is beyond fixing.

MERKIN: If it's beyond fixing then it must be a fixation. Have you a fixation on Dobbitt?

HANRAHAN: I have a fixation on honesty.

MERKIN: Which is putting me in quite a fix. But I'll take care of it. I'll bust him down to trainee. Cut off his benefits. Place him on long-term probationary status. I can tie him up in paper so tight he'll never get out. *(Merkin slams his void stamp down ominously.)*

HANRAHAN: I've come for my release papers, Merkin.

MERKIN: I was told you were staying on.

HANRAHAN: My tour of duty is over. I'm leaving.

MERKIN: Where to?

HANRAHAN: I know where I'd like to go. But it's up to you.

MERKIN: Hanrahan, you can't leave. I won't let this happen.

HANRAHAN: Why would it possibly matter to you? You'll be in Spain.

MERKIN: They wouldn't have me.

HANRAHAN: They singled you out. You were a shoe-in.

MERKIN: *(Tosses the award in the trash.)* The Regional Director said my crisis management skills are too valuable to lose. Damn that fire! I almost wish it never happened. He said it would be an insult to send a man of my caliber to Spain. If only I'd acted with cowardice!

HANRAHAN: You certainly seemed frightened and unhinged to me.

MERKIN: I'm afraid it's too late for that.
(Pause.)
Hanrahan. If you go I'll have no one to talk to.

HANRAHAN: You haven't talked to me the entire time I've been here.

MERKIN: I wanted to. I tried to. We just never hit on a topic of mutual interest. Human error.

HANRAHAN: And now it's too late.

MERKIN: Give me a chance, Hanrahan. We'll laugh together, like you and Dobbitt. I'll do whatever it takes to be your friend.

HANRAHAN: Will you?

MERKIN: Yes! I promise.

HANRAHAN: Alright. Then it's you and me, Merkin. *(They shake hands.)*

MERKIN: Anything you want, Hanrahan, come to me. My door is frequently open.

HANRAHAN: I want an in-country assignment so I can spend time with my wife. *(Merkin looks helplessly at Hanrahan as lights fade.)*

Lights up on the bridge. Dusk. Dobbitt appears with a bouquet of stunning wildflowers. Hanrahan approaches from the other direction, carrying a suitcase.

DOBBITT: Hanrahan! Look what's growing in our bog! We've improved on nature.

HANRAHAN: Very nice.

DOBBITT: Where are you going?

HANRAHAN: Home. The helicopter's waiting.

DOBBITT: And you'll return in three days? That's what they give us for Domestic Tragedies, isn't it?

HANRAHAN: My life is hardly a Domestic Tragedy.

DOBBITT: I was under the impression there was no hope.

HANRAHAN: Of what?

DOBBITT: I understood her vows prohibit her from even being in the presence of a man.

HANRAHAN: Whose vows? What the devil are you talking about?

DOBBITT: Your wife joining an order, the convent—my God, Hanrahan, I thought you knew!

HANRAHAN: I know nothing. Except that you have violated my trust.

DOBBITT: Yes, to save you—

HANRAHAN: From what? My wife has left me and joined an order?

DOBBITT: The time apart, the endless waiting, the years drifting by, it all became too much—

HANRAHAN: How is it you know all this, Dobbitt?

DOBBITT: I wrote the last letter. So you'd stay 'til the work was done.

HANRAHAN: You wrote the last letter? All those words were yours?

DOBBITT: Merkin was ready to snuff you in the company if you left early. I wrote the letter to keep you here the last week. So all your years of work would pay off. So you'd have what you wanted for so long.

HANRAHAN: Yes. An in-country assignment with my wife. Which Merkin has finally given me.

DOBBITT: My God. Then you really are gone. I'm all alone in this Godforsaken desert.

HANRAHAN: And I'll be all alone in that house. How could you do this to me, Dobbitt?

DOBBITT: It was the hardest thing I've ever done. I gave up my honesty for you.

HANRAHAN: But that was the one thing we pledged each other—

DOBBITT: Which is why it was such a hellish ordeal to lie. It took every fiber of my being. I wonder if you'd have done the same for me.

HANRAHAN: Lied? Of course not!

DOBBITT: Then you'd have sunk me like a stone so you could call yourself an honest man. Tell me you'd lie to me, Hanrahan.

HANRAHAN: Alright, I'd lie to you. I'm lying right now.

DOBBITT: Thank you. That means a lot.

(Pause.)

Hanrahan? These were the most wonderful days of my life.

HANRAHAN: Yes. They became wonderful as soon as they were over.

DOBBITT: Is there a chance our paths will cross again? Perhaps at some other far-flung site?

HANRAHAN: I'm afraid the company doesn't work that way. A brief encounter with a kindred spirit is the most one can hope for. We're the lucky ones, it never happens to most people.

DOBBITT: But we could have stayed on here together! It all could have been ours! This could have been the beginning—

HANRAHAN: Yes. It was ours for the taking. What a pity we didn't take it.

DOBBITT: Running the department won't be half so much fun without you.

HANRAHAN: I'm afraid you won't be running it. Merkin didn't get the post. His bravery has made him indispensable.

DOBBITT: Merkin is staying on? Then I'm truly alone. What can I do, Hanrahan?

HANRAHAN: What we all learn to do. Drift silently through the void from one assignment to the next, 'til our time is up.

DOBBITT: I don't think I can bear it.

HANRAHAN: You'll be amazed at how fast the years hurtle by. It's the days that last an eternity.

(The sound of a helicopter.)

Well.

DOBBITT: Yes. Of course.

HANRAHAN: *(Starts off, then stops.)* Dobbitt? If this helicopter leaves the compound, at least you'll know this is no prison. You'll be free.

DOBBITT: I still have to stay here.

HANRAHAN: But you'll know in your heart you can go.

DOBBITT: Goodbye, Hanrahan.

HANRAHAN: Goodbye, Dobbitt.

(Hanrahan leaves. Dobbitt is alone on the bridge clutching the flowers. The sound of the helicopter lifting off. Dobbitt watches and waves.)

DOBBITT: Hanrahan! I'm free! I'm free!

(The helicopter fades. Dobbitt sees the yellow eyes of the mysterious animals glowing in the gathering darkness. There are more of them and they're much closer. He shivers.)

BLACKOUT

END

Marsha Norman

Trudy Blue

Trudy Blue was directed in 1995 by George de la Peña with the following cast:

GINGER .... Joanne Camp
DON .... Leo Burmester
MARIA, ADMIRER .... Karenjune Sánchez
SUE .... Karen Grassle
CONNIE, SALES PERSON, WAITRESS .... Ann Bean
ANNIE .... Anne Pitoniak
VOICE OF SWAMI, SALES PERSON, PUBLISHER ..... Larry Larson
JAMES .... Tony Coleman
BETH .... Jennifer Carpenter
CHARLIE .... Larry Barnett
WAITER .... James McDaniel*

Scene Design .... Paul Owen
Costume Design .... Laura Patterson
Lighting Design .... Mimi Jordan Sherin
Sound Design .... Martin R. Desjardins
Property Master .... Mark J. Bissonnette
Stage Manager .... Julie A. Richardson
Assistant Stage Manager .... Susan M. McCarthy
Dramaturg .... Julie Crutcher
Casting arranged by Laura Richin Casting

---

*Member of the ATL Apprentice/Intern Company

Trudy Blue

PROLOGUE

Ginger and Don are in bed, propped up on their respective pillows. Reading.

GINGER: How's your mother feeling? Did you talk to her today?
(Don doesn't answer. She closes her book.)
I'm going downstairs. Do you want anything?
(She sits up.)
Like a glass of water or anything?
(She looks over at him.)
Don?

DON: I said "no."

GINGER: You did?

DON: There's something the matter with your hearing, have you noticed? Especially on the phone.
(Imitating her.)
What? What?

GINGER: My hearing?

DON: Your hearing. Don't stay up too late. How late were you up last night?

GINGER: I don't know. Three.

DON: Oh. If you'll give me the registration for the Volvo, I'll take it out with me tomorrow and put it on.

GINGER: You're going to the country tomorrow?

DON: I told you that. Jesus, Ginger. Just for the day, though. I'll be back by eight.

GINGER: You told me you were going to the country? What is tomorrow?

DON: Tuesday. Yes. I told you. I rented a workshop.

GINGER: A workshop?

DON: Yes. If you will remember our discussion last weekend, I can either stop making tables altogether, or just stop making them in the house. So I rented a workshop.

GINGER: It wasn't about the tables. It was about the time you spend making the tables. It was about how I don't see you.

About how the first thing you do when we get out to the house is leave.

DON: I'm not leaving, Ginger. I'm getting the mail.

GINGER: Checking on the boat. Going to the hardware store. The liquor store. The bait store. Buying magazines. Getting the cars washed, the oil changed, the tanks filled, the mats cleaned. Buying trash bags. Lightbulbs. Tape. Dog food. Bird food. Fish food.

DON: Do you think I like doing those things?

GINGER: I don't know, Don.

DON: If you didn't want any animals, you should've told the kids no.

GINGER: That would have been popular.

DON: Since when did you worry about being popular?

GINGER: What are you going to do in your shop?

DON: Make tables.

GINGER: To sell?

DON: No, not to sell. It would be really stupid to take the one thing I really enjoy doing, and turn it into work.

GINGER: But your tables are beautiful. People love them. You should take one out to Ralph Lauren and—

DON: Just stop it, Ginger. O.K.? I'm never going to make any more money than I do right now. And I'm never going to like what I do. And if that means I'm never going to be good enough for you, then that's just too bad. This is who I am. And this is who you married.

GINGER: I'm sorry. It's just I keep thinking—

DON: Stop thinking. Stop thinking about what would make *my* life more interesting to you. I am not a character in your new novel. I'm your husband. Cut me some slack.

She gets out of the bed, puts on her slippers and robe. Don looks up.

DON: Would you bring me a glass of water when you come up?

GINGER: I could be a while. Do you want me to bring it up right now?

DON: That would be great. Thanks.

GINGER: You're going to move all your equipment into this shop?

DON: I have to have a place to go, Ginger. What do you want me to do, hang around the house all weekend and watch you read?

GINGER: Do you want ice in your water?

DON: That would be great. Thanks. I love you.

GINGER: I love you too. Goodnight.

(She goes out the door.)

SCENE 1
LUNCH WITH GINGER

Ginger sits at a table for two in a popular lunch spot.
This is actually a series of lunches, in which her conversation remains continuous, but three of her friends rotate into the lunch one at a time, somehow. This change of companions may occur while Ginger looks at the menu, unfolds her napkin, talks to the waiter, or it may be handled with lighting. What is important is that while Ginger does notice that her friends come and go, she seems to accept that this is how things are.

Maria approaches. She is a real estate broker.

MARIA: Ginger, hi. Sorry I'm late. The traffic is terrible.

GINGER: It's O.K. I just got here. You look terrific.

MARIA: What a great little place. How did you know about it?

GINGER: I'm going to an ear doctor in this neighborhood.

MARIA: *(Looking at the menu.)* Nothing serious, I hope.

GINGER: Well. We still don't quite know what it is. My left ear keeps plugging up, like I have water in it from swimming. It doesn't actually hurt, it just makes me feel a little further away. Not that I need to feel any further away. If I get any further away, sooner or later, someone will realize I'm actually gone.

Lights go out on Maria and come up on Ginger's best friend, Sue.

SUE: This day. Lord. Oh well. What's good?

GINGER: I like the omelets. You know, eggs in time of stress.

SUE: *(Reaching in her bag.)* Oh, here. I brought you the new Anna Quindlen. How's *your* book coming?

GINGER: Good. God knows who's going to read it, but hey.

SUE: What do you mean? Everyone who reads will read it. How close are you?

GINGER: Actually, I'm stuck. I can't seem to figure out . . . whether . . . what she should . . .

SUE: *(Seeing the waiter.)* Know what you want?

GINGER: *(Looking up as if at the waiter.)* Swiss and bacon, I think. And a small salad. And some juice. Can you make a mix of orange and pineapple?

Lights go out on Sue, and come up on Ginger's friend, Connie, a nurse.

CONNIE: Everything O.K. at home?

GINGER: The kids are good. Don's good. Except he thinks he's too fat.
(She has to laugh.)
I had this weird thought the other day about how different the world would have been if Darwin had called it, "The Survival of the Fattest."

CONNIE: You're so funny.

GINGER: But then I thought, maybe that's why diets don't work.

CONNIE: None of them work.

GINGER: Well, what if the reason they don't work is that diets are about individuals, you know, what individuals want. Whereas what the *species* wants is for people to have enough fat on them to survive. And the more fat you have, the better your chances are of survival. So even though *you* want to be thin, your body takes its direction from the species, and the species says eat. You know?

CONNIE: The bread looks great. Want some?

GINGER: Thanks. I mean, what if the species is really in charge of everything? What if the things we *think* we need, love and children and a place to live, are really just things the species needs, to keep itself going? But the only way the species can *get* these things is to trick us, with hormones mainly, into thinking *we* need them.

MARIA: Well, I know what I need. A new coat. I've looked all over town, and I can't find what I want.

Ginger knows she's said too much, and tries to take a lighter approach.

GINGER: Well, the species would certainly like for you to be warm. What are you looking for?

MARIA: Oh, you know, black, soft, something I can wear everywhere.

GINGER: Like something a species would put on a big black Lab.

MARIA: Exactly.

GINGER: Or a lot of little rabbits.

MARIA: You're so funny.

GINGER: You'll find it. Did you try Bergdorf's?

MARIA: I'm waiting for the sale. You should try this dill butter. Now tell me. What's the new book about? Anybody I know?

GINGER: No, no. It's just about some people who can't figure out why they have the lives they have. Not that they don't like their lives, just that the thrill that made them choose this particular man, or this particular kind of work, they don't feel that thrill any more. All they feel is guilt that they're not taking good enough care of them.

MARIA: Oh good. The food is here. Yours looks wonderful.

GINGER: Want to trade?

MARIA: No, no.

GINGER: I mean, maybe the reason people don't change more than they do, is the species likes for you to stay put. So. After it gets your children out of you, the species just cuts you loose. And without the species to tell you what you want, you really don't want anything.

MARIA: *(To the waiter.)* Could I have some ketchup please?

GINGER: I'm sorry. I should know not to talk about something before it's finished. It's just . . . well, did you ever look at your family and think, "Who are these people?"

SUE: But you love your family.

GINGER: I know. My work too. I don't know what it is.

SUE: Do you believe this Michael Jackson thing?

GINGER: I know. It's crazy. But obviously, the species doesn't want us to know it controls us like this. Because nobody will talk about this with me. Nobody.

SUE: How's your ear doing?

GINGER: About the same. Thanks for asking, though. I'm seeing this new doctor Mary told me about tomorrow. Are you reading anything?

SUE: Just *Anna Karenina*. Again.

GINGER: Well. We all know what that means.

A moment.

SUE: You?

GINGER: The new Marquez is good. The last story is unbelievable. About three pages in, I got this incredible sense of dread about what was going to happen. Worse than any horror story I ever read. And all I wanted to do was turn to the last page to see if I was right. My hand actually went up to turn to the end, and I literally had to put my hand under the covers to keep reading the page I was on. You have to get it.

CONNIE: And what happened? You can tell me. You know I won't read it.

GINGER: Oh nothing. Just this amazing girl died, and this boy she was so in love with didn't know about it til after she was buried.

CONNIE: How are the kids?

GINGER: They're good.

CONNIE: Want any dessert?

GINGER: Does anybody ever ask you a personal question?

SUE: What do you mean, personal?

GINGER: Something they're not supposed to ask. Something you'd tell them if they asked, but they don't ask.

SUE: I don't think so.

GINGER: But why is that? Does the species not want us to get personal, so we won't realize how bad we feel and won't go around tearing things up?

SUE: You don't think people know how they feel?

GINGER: I don't. I think after a certain point, people put these huge sections of their lives on auto, you know. Like there's this big switchboard and people go through and . . .

(Mimes flipping switches.)
this is my family, and this is where I live, and this is what I do, and this is what I eat, and these are the people I have lunch with, and these are the books I read, and this is my radio station, and here's what I think about this and this and this. And they don't think about it any more. So they never try anything else.

SUE: But if you know you like something, why should you try something else?

GINGER: Because if you don't, then all you are is comfortable. Is that what we're doing here, trying to get comfortable? Do you think it's even possible? O.K. Say you actually *got* comfortable. *Then* what would you do? Go to sleep? Die? What?

SUE: Would you like to come to the gym with me some day?

GINGER: You don't feel silly exercising with all those young people?

SUE: I think they're cute, actually.

GINGER: Anyone in particular?

SUE: I wish. It's really been a long time since I've been attracted to anybody. It used to happen all the time.

GINGER: I know.

CONNIE: Like in college.

GINGER: It's not us, I can tell you that.

MARIA: Oh good.

GINGER: It's the species. It doesn't need us to find mates any more, so it just doesn't turn us on to anybody. Or them to us.

MARIA: I can't believe how cold it is out there. I don't know what I would've done if I hadn't found my coat. I love my new coat. So what are you up to?

GINGER: I'm taking a painting class.

MARIA: I didn't know you were interested in painting.

GINGER: Maybe I'm not. Maybe the species just needs me to find some little hobby so I'll stay out of the way til I die. You know, so it can save all the jobs for the people who are having babies.

SUE: How's Don?

GINGER: He's good. He's rented a little woodworking shop in the country.

SUE: Is he any good at it?

GINGER: No. He says it soothes him.

SUE: How's your ear?

GINGER: It's O.K. I can hear enough.

SUE: You seem a little down.

GINGER: Put your money away. I've got it.

SUE: *(Getting up.)* Did you tell me what your new book is about?

GINGER: Yes, but I gave up on it. Just . . . threw it away. I've never done that before.

SUE: You're not working on anything?

GINGER: No, I am. It's an old idea, actually. But I'm thinking I might know how to do it now. It's about . . . well, it's about pleasure.

SUE: *(Stricken.)* Pleasure? What's that?

CONNIE: Do you mean erotic pleasure, or like cooking?

MARIA: Well. I can't wait to read it. Thanks for lunch.

SUE: Pleasure? Really? Are you serious?

GINGER: *(With a smile.)* I could be.

> *(A moment.)*
>
> I know.
>
> *(A smile.)*
>
> How odd.

BLACKOUT

SCENE 2
TRANSITION
GINGER'S MOTHER AND HUSBAND

Lights come up on a peaceful woman sitting in a chair. This woman need not leave the stage as the piece continues. Lights can simply go out on her.

ANNIE: Ginger was a happy child. So happy. Happy all the time. Singing and dancing and playing by herself. I kept telling her how nice it was outside, but I have to admit it was sweet that she wanted to stay down in the basement with me. None of the other neighborhood children were well . . . good enough to play with her, really, so I would iron and she would play school, making little books, writing things. Even before she knew how, she was writing, scribbling on the paper and then hiding her little messages behind the runner on the stairs. She didn't know I knew, but I did. But I didn't read them.

(A moment.)

If she had wanted me to know what she thought, she would've just told me.

A moment. Don enters the area defined by Annie. He is reading a magazine.

ANNIE: Her husband, Don, is . . . it's hard to say. I didn't know him very well.

Don is not talking to Annie, but he is not unaware of her presence.

DON: I met Ginger's father a few times. I liked him. She always called him the original unknowable man, but hey. What's to know? He was friendly.

ANNIE: Don designed their house. I don't know why he doesn't get more work as an architect. He's a very smart man.

DON: The house doesn't work. Not for me, it doesn't. I tried to tell Ginger it wouldn't, but she kept having all these ideas. And the thing ended up so personal that we'll never be able to sell it. The kids like the fireman's pole, though. I'll give her credit for that. So, fine. We'll just plug it up when they leave.

SCENE 3
DAWN WITH GINGER

Curtain rises on a beautiful outdoor deck, furnished comfortably, but exquisitely. Hanging baskets of fuschia and ivy are everywhere. It is just dawn. And it looks like it's going to be a stunning day. The air will be cool and clear, and the sun will be warm. A eucalyptus-scented

candle is burning. It is a safe world.
Ginger enters from the house, closing the glass door behind her. She
is brushing her hair. She wears a loose pair of white silk pajamas,
over which she wears an unbelted kimono. On her feet are Chanel-type
bedroom slippers.
She puts down her hairbrush, takes her yoga mat from the baker's
rack in the corner, unfolds it and places it on the deck. She takes off
her kimono and slippers, then walks to the tape player in the corner,
inserts a tape and pushes Play.
As the New Age music of the tape begins, Ginger stands on the mat,
relaxed and serene, and rolls her head slowly from side to side.

VOICE OF THE SWAMI: The chariot of the mind is drawn by wild
horses. These horses have to be tamed.

She brings her hands into the prayer pose.

VOICE OF THE SWAMI: Standing erect, feet together, bring your
hands in front of your chest in the prayer pose. Keeping your
body completely still, breathe slowly through the nostrils.
Bring your mind into a state of quiet awareness, concentrat-
ing only on your breathing. In. Out. In. Out.
(A moment.)
And now, when you next exhale, join me in the Salutation
to the Sun.

Ginger now performs the Salutation to the Sun chanting with the
Swami.

GINGER AND THE SWAMI'S VOICE:

Om Namo Suryaya
Om Namo Bhaskraya
Om Namo Divaya

James, a lean, handsome, mysterious man comes up the steps, wear-
ing loose pants, but no shirt. Ginger bows to him, and he to her. He
might be a wizard.

GINGER AND JAMES: Namaste.
GINGER AND THE SWAMI'S VOICE:

Om Namo Tejaya
Om Namo Prkashaya

James does a few stretches, then joins Ginger for the second repetition of the Salutation to the Sun, chanting with her. She is happy to see him, but not surprised.

GINGER, JAMES, AND SWAMI'S VOICE:

Om Namo Suryaya
Om Namo Bhaskraya
Om Namo Divaya
Om Namo Tejaya
Om Namo Prkashaya

Ginger and James smile comfortably as the Swami's voice on tape begins again. Something about the voice sounds slightly different.

VOICE OF THE SWAMI: The goal of tantric yoga is to transform your lovemaking from a brief and entirely genital encounter, to a transcendent sensual meditation, leading to a union that transcends the boundaries of everyday experience.

The glass door slides opens and Ginger's daughter, Beth, sticks her head out. She doesn't seem to see James.

BETH: Mom?
GINGER: Right here.
BETH: O.K.

The girl, apparently happy just to know where Ginger is, closes the door and the voice on the tape comes back up.

VOICE OF THE SWAMI: You begin by sitting quietly together,
  (Ginger and the man sit.)
meditating or praying or simply opening to the sounds around you.

Ginger and James follow the Swami's instructions.

VOICE OF THE SWAMI: As you embrace and kiss, align your throats, hearts and bodies, and breathe as one. In and out.

Easily. Freely. Now, begin to touch one another with utmost sensitivity. Reveal to each other those places where you feel fear or shame.

The door opens and Ginger's son sticks his head out. He doesn't seem to see the man.

CHARLIE: Mom?
GINGER: Hi.
CHARLIE: What's today?
GINGER: Thursday.
CHARLIE: Damn.

He leaves quickly, as though it being Thursday means he has to do something right away. The Swami's voice continues on the tape.

VOICE OF THE SWAMI: Return to the butterfly pose and sit calmly for a moment, feeling centered and at peace.

Ginger and James sit up now, facing each other in the butterfly pose.

VOICE OF THE SWAMI: Today you will learn the Set of Nines. In which you will discover a powerful current of energy connecting you at the genitals, rising up to the heart, bridging the space between you, and dropping back to the genitals again.

They are amused.

GINGER AND JAMES: O.K.
VOICE OF THE SWAMI: As you listen to the instructions, place your hands on your breasts in order to feel the heat from your hands entering the skin.

The door opens again and Ginger's husband, Don, comes out. He doesn't seem to see the man lying next to her.

DON: Honey?
GINGER: Hi, Don.
DON: It's almost seven.
GINGER: Thanks.

Don goes back inside as the Swami's voice begins again. James may reach across to Ginger and take her hands in his.

VOICE OF THE SWAMI: To begin the Set of Nines, the man enters the woman with nine shallow thrusts. He withdraws and pauses before entering again, this time for eight shallow thrusts followed by one deep thrust.
JAMES: I think I know where this is going.

But it sounds so good to Ginger that she can't really respond.

VOICE OF THE SWAMI: Again he withdraws, pulling back briefly from the edge of orgasm.
BETH'S VOICE O.S.: *(Calling out.)* Mom?
VOICE OF THE SWAMI: Now the man takes seven shallow thrusts and two deep thrusts, and withdraws.

James nods and begins to speak with the Swami.

JAMES AND SWAMI'S VOICE: Six shallow, three deep, withdraw; five shallow, four deep, withdraw; four shallow, five deep, withdraw; three shallow, six deep, withdraw . . .
CHARLIE'S VOICE O.S.: *(Calling out.)* Mom!
JAMES: *(To Ginger.)* Do you want to stop?
GINGER: No.
JAMES AND SWAMI'S VOICE: Two shallow, seven deep, withdraw. One shallow, eight deep, . . . withdraw . . .
DON'S VOICE O.S.: *(Calling out.)* Ginger!
VOICE OF THE SWAMI: Until . . .
GINGER: *(Calling to them.)* Just a minute!
SWAMI'S VOICE: Until the man brings his lover to orgasm with nine deep thrusting strokes.

There is a silence.

GINGER: Probably worth a try.
JAMES: I'm in.

And after a moment, James helps Ginger stand up, and facing each other once again, they assume the prayer pose as the Swami signs off.

VOICE OF THE SWAMI: O Life-giving Sun, offspring of the Lord of Creation,

Don enters, but waits through the Swami's blessing. Ginger joins in with the Swami.

GINGER AND THE SWAMI'S VOICE: —let me behold thy radiant form, that I may realize that the Spirit far away within thee, is my Spirit, my own inmost Spirit.

Ginger and James bow to each other as before.

GINGER AND JAMES: Namaste.

James leaves and Don starts talking as Ginger folds up her mat and blows out the candle.

DON: Are we still on with Jerry and Sue tonight?
GINGER: Yes, but I haven't talked to her yet, so I don't know what we're doing.
DON: Just so it's not Mexican.
GINGER: O.K.
DON: And for God's sake, not at *their* house.
GINGER: Are you going to be this way tonight?
DON: What way?
GINGER: If you don't like them, why don't you just say you never want to see them again?
DON: Because it wouldn't do any good.
GINGER: Don. They're the only friends we have.
DON: They're not my friends.
GINGER: They could be.
DON: Oh sure. If I liked them they could. If I were somebody else who liked them. Well, believe me, if I could be somebody else, I would.
GINGER: You would? Who would you be?
DON: I don't know. What difference does it make? I can't be anybody else, can I? So why should we talk about who, exactly, I could never be?
GINGER: Because I want to know. Who is it?
DON: I don't know.

(A wild idea.)
Mohammed Ali.

GINGER: Please.

DON: Or you.

GINGER: Me?

DON: Of course you. Isn't it everybody's dream, to make a living by not going to work?

GINGER: Writing is work.

DON: Come on. You don't work the hours lawyers work. Or sales girls even. You talk on the phone, and have lunch with your friends.

GINGER: That's not all I do.

DON: Are we still on with Jerry and Sue tonight?

This seems familiar to Ginger, like maybe she's had this conversation before, but maybe not, so she continues bravely on.

GINGER: Yes, but I forget what we're doing.

DON: Just so it's not Mexican.

GINGER: I remember now. She's cooking.

DON: Oh for Christ's sake. You can't even sit down in their house without some bird flying over your head, or some handicapped cat jumping in your lap.

GINGER: Why do you have to be this way? They have pets because they can't have children. She's my oldest friend.

DON: She's not older than I am. Nobody is older than I am. I've asked you not to say "old."

GINGER: Don, please.

DON: I'm sorry, honey. I'll see you tonight. Are we still on with Jerry and Sue?

GINGER: We're going to that Chinese place you like.

DON: Does *Jerry* have to come?

GINGER: He's Sue's husband!

DON: But they're so terrible to each other. If I'm going to watch a fight, I'd rather see one on TV. Why don't you girls just go out by yourselves?

GINGER: Could you pick up the dry cleaning?

DON: No problem. What are we doing tonight?

GINGER: I'm having supper with Sue.

DON: Great. There's a fight on TV I want to watch.
GINGER: Bye, hon.

He kisses her on the cheek and leaves. The son comes by and kisses her.

CHARLIE: Mom!
GINGER: Charlie!
CHARLIE: Your hair looks funny.

The daughter runs to catch up to him. She poses for Ginger.

BETH: Mom?
GINGER: *(Still thinking there's hope.)* Beth!
BETH: How do I look?
GINGER: Great. You look great.

Ginger remains on the stage.

BLACKOUT

SCENE 4
TRANSITION: GINGER, HER MOTHER, AND JAMES

Lights come back up on Annie still sitting in her chair.

ANNIE: I don't know why these girls today wait so long to have their children. Why if Ginger had had hers when I told her to, they'd be so much older by now. They'd be in college. They might even have jobs. At the very least they wouldn't still be children. But she said no. She had plenty of time to have children. Girls that age think they have their whole lives in front of them. But . . . at least she had her children. A girl and a boy. And I have to say, in spite of everything, she was a perfect mother.

Ginger approaches Annie and responds.

GINGER: That's not true.

ANNIE: She was a perfect daughter.

GINGER: There's no such thing as perfect.

ANNIE: Everything you *do* is perfect!

GINGER: It is not! I don't even *want* it to be. I'm not trying to live a perfect life.

ANNIE: You could.

GINGER: Stop it. Just stop it.

ANNIE: What do you want, my permission not to live a perfect life? My congratulations on not living a perfect life? Well, listen here, young lady. If you're not living a perfect life, I don't want to hear about it.

GINGER: What *do* you want to hear about? How I'm planning the perfect Christmas? Perfect for whom? The whole purpose of perfect is to make us feel bad. Like we don't measure up. Well I'm sorry, but could we go find whoever this is who's measuring us all the time, and take away their goddamn stick?

ANNIE: Their stick?

GINGER: *(Really irritated now.)* Their measuring stick. You know, the one that's marked . . . Really Bad, Bad. Not Good, Not Good Enough, Perfect. It's killing us.
(A small smile.)
I found that once I quit trying to put on the perfect outfit,
(A moment.)
. . . I could actually get dressed.

ANNIE: The last Christmas I spent with you was perfect.

GINGER: I'm glad you thought so.

ANNIE: You didn't.

GINGER: Christmas to me feels like a happiness test. One I have failed for years now.

ANNIE: What is the matter with you today?

GINGER: You think it's just today?

ANNIE: Are you sick? You seem a little flushed.

Ginger suddenly wishes her mother would understand, is suddenly willing to try.

GINGER: I can't seem to fit in anywhere. I don't know the rules.

ANNIE: You know the rules because I told them to you. You just broke the rules.

GINGER: No, I didn't.

ANNIE: You talked to strangers. Didn't you?

James appears on the other side of the stage, cleaning his sax.

GINGER: That was a real rule?

ANNIE: Very.

Annie exits. Sue appears.

SUE: Are you seeing someone? I think you're seeing someone.

GINGER: No. I'm not.

SUE: Then why do you look so happy?

GINGER: I'm flirting with someone. But he started it.

SUE: Is he married?

GINGER: No.

SUE: How long has he not been married?

GINGER: Stop it.

SUE: How long has he not been married?

GINGER: Two years.

SUE: O.K. That's long enough. Does he have children?

GINGER: They live with their mother.

SUE: What does he do?

GINGER: He plays the sax.

SUE: *(Suddenly very sober.)* How well does he play the sax?

GINGER: Like a dream.

SUE: I see.

GINGER: It's not just that.

SUE: Oh, sure.

GINGER: Sue. I told you. We're flirting. Oh, I don't know. What do I do?

SUE: Well. I don't think you have to stop flirting.

Sue exits. Ginger picks up the phone on her desk, and hears the message on James's machine.

JAMES ON TAPE: Hi. This is James. You can leave me a message at the tone, or you can come to Mabel's and buy me a drink between sets. Up to you. Bye.

GINGER: *(Leaving him a message.)* James. My name is Ginger Andrews. My agent said you would be willing to talk to me about Morocco. About oases, actually, for a book I'm thinking about. Well, it's about pleasure in general, but he seemed to think you were my best bet. So. My number is—
(A moment.)
Why do I think you don't return calls? O.K. I'll come find you at Mabel's on Thursday night. I'll be wearing . . . I have red hair and a notebook. Bye.

James begins to play the saxophone. Lights down on Annie's area.

SCENE 5
GINGER AT WORK

Ginger is working at her computer. Don appears.

GINGER: Hi.

She continues to type.

DON: Hi.

Ginger looks up while typing a sentence.

GINGER: Yes?
DON: If you'd had an affair, would you have told me?
GINGER: You think I'm having an affair?
DON: That's not what I asked. I asked . . .
GINGER: . . . if I had had an affair, would I have told you.
DON: Yes.
GINGER: I don't think so, Don. No. Probably not.
DON: Right.
GINGER: Why would I?

DON: No. That seems right to me too. I was just checking. I'll see you later.

He starts to leave.

GINGER: You don't want to know?

DON: I don't want to look stupid.

GINGER: Why would my having an affair make you look stupid?

DON: Because it would mean I couldn't keep you from having them.

GINGER: My affairs would have nothing to do with you.

DON: That can't be true.

GINGER: It's not.

DON: Would they have anything to do with the fact that we don't have sex?

GINGER: No.

DON: Really?

GINGER: No.

DON: So they do.

GINGER: They could.

DON: That can't be all of it though. Don't tell me. You're afraid of getting old.

GINGER: I'm not getting old.

DON: I didn't say you were.

GINGER: No. I'm not. I'm not getting old. I thought I would by now. But I'm not.

DON: You don't think you're immortal.

GINGER: No. Thanks, though.

DON: But wouldn't having affairs make you feel bad?

GINGER: I wouldn't have them if they made me feel bad.

DON: O.K. They'd make you feel great. Then what?

GINGER: Then I would come home, I guess.

DON: But what if I found out? What if I saw you going into whatever it is you'd go with them?

GINGER: I would try to explain, I guess.

DON: And what if I left you because of it?

GINGER: Then you would be gone.

DON: But I could take the children way. Accuse you of being an unfit mother—

GINGER: I'm a great mother.

DON: —and take the children away.

GINGER: A lot of things could take my children away, Don. Drugs, or TV, or a terrible disease, or bad luck with a car or, God, what if they grew up?

DON: Would you talk to your lovers?

GINGER: Yes, Don. Lovers like to be talked to.

(A moment.)

Some more than others, of course.

DON: And what would you talk about?

GINGER: About ourselves, mainly. About when we first knew we were going to make love, and how long we waited, and how it wasn't fair that we couldn't see each other whenever we wanted.

DON: And what would they say? Would they ask about me?

GINGER: No, Don. They would say that I was beautiful.

The phone rings.

GINGER: *(Picks it up.)* Hello?

Don walks out of the room, as Ginger erases something on the computer.

GINGER: Hi Sue.

(Listens.)

I'm just working. No. It's O.K.

(Listens.)

I don't know *what* it is. Maybe it's not even a book. Maybe it's a nervous breakdown.

(Then quickly.)

It's a joke, Sue. I'm fine. I'm obsessed. I don't want to be here.

(Changing the subject.)

So. Where shall we eat tonight? Is Jerry coming?

(Listens.)

No, no. Don's still in Chicago. Yeah. So first we'll go look for your coat and then we'll decide where to eat. If we find something at Barney's we can just eat there. O.K. Say six-thirty?

(Listens.)
Very funny. See you then, honey bun.

Ginger hangs up the phone, opens a soda and studies the computer screen.

GINGER: About when we first knew we were going to make love, and how long we
(Changes a word.)
resisted, and how it wasn't fair we couldn't see each other whenever we wanted.

Don walks back in.

DON: And what would they say? Would they ask about me?
GINGER: No, Don. They would say that I was beautiful.

The phone rings.

GINGER: Hello.

Ginger practically swears into the phone hearing who it is.

GINGER: I'm sorry. Was I supposed to call *you?*
(Listens.)
Oh good. O.K. No. I haven't thought about it. I agree to phone interviews and then I forget to write them down, so . . . Yes. I remember that it was just one question. I just don't remember what that question was, exactly.
(Listens.)
Oh that's right. Of course.
(Stating her answer.)
What is most helpful for writers to hear, is . . . how fabulous they look and how everybody wants to go to bed with them.
(She laughs.)
No. That's the real answer.
(A moment.)
You're welcome. Yes, please. Send me a copy.

Ginger hangs up the phone.

GINGER: *(Quickly.)* Bullshit, bullshit, bullshit.

Ginger unwraps a stick of gum. She looks up and sees Don standing there.

DON: Surprise!

GINGER: Don!

DON: I'm early.

GINGER: Why didn't you call?

DON: This is my home. Do I have to call before I come over?

GINGER: What's up?

DON: I read this new . . . whatever this thing is that you're writing. About having these affairs. Is this me, this Ron character?

GINGER: Where did you find it?

DON: On your desk.

GINGER: I didn't leave it on my desk.

DON: O.K. It was under a big stack of papers on the floor. But I found it. So you must have meant for me to find it.

GINGER: Maybe I did.

DON: Are you telling me you've had affairs?

GINGER: It's not about me. It's about—

DON: Don't insult me, Ginger.

GINGER: It doesn't say she's had affairs. Just that she's—

DON: Thinking about it?

GINGER: Yes. She, the main character, Trudy, is thinking about it.

DON: And you're not.

GINGER: Are you asking me if I'm having an affair?

DON: *(After a moment.)* No.

GINGER: *(After a moment.)* Is there anything else you don't want to know?

DON: Not that I can think of. No.

GINGER: I'm going to keep working a little longer, I think.

DON: I'm going to bed.

GINGER: All right.

DON: Goodnight, hon.

GINGER: Goodnight.

Don turns to leave, then turns back.

DON: I just want you to know that if anything ever happens to you, if you die . . . the first thing I'm going to do, after I stop crying, is go into your study and read everything you've ever written. Not just your short stories and books, but your notes, your journals, your letters . . . everything you've ever written.

Ginger nods and Don leaves. She waits a moment, then turns back to the computer and types.

GINGER: "Ron turned away."

She looks up at the door, as though waiting for him to come back in.

GINGER: "Ron turned away, took one step, and fell into the bottomless pit."

Then going on, apparently unable to stop herself, speaking as though reading to a child.

GINGER: "Poor Ron. Didn't he see the pit? Hadn't she *told* him there was a pit? Hadn't she told him how every day she had to work so hard not to fall into that pit? Well, he should've listened to her. The pit is there, all right. Only now, it has a man in it. And he is really pissed off."
(*A smile.*)
Will Ron get out of the hole? Will Ginger get out of her study? Tune in tomorrow for another episode of . . .
(*Her anger coming through.*)
"*Trudy Blue, girl in love.*"

SCENE 6
TRANSITION

The phone rings again.

GINGER: Hello.

She hears the voice, recognizes who it is, is thrilled to hear it's him, but lowers her voice.

GINGER: Oh hi! Where are you, are you here? I was afraid you
wouldn't get in.
(Listens.)
You do?
(Listens in rapture.)
I'm sorry. Maybe I didn't hear that right.
(Having heard it perfectly.)
Would you say that again?
(Listens.)
I have missed you so much. I've never missed anybody like
this. It's getting to where seeing you is just some kind of break
between these bouts of missing you. So? Where shall we
meet?

She listens. Trying not to convey her disappointment.

GINGER: Oh. All right. No, no. You sound exhausted. It would
be a little tricky to get out of here anyway. O.K. Good.
(Listens.)
I love you too. Goodnight, sweetie.

She hangs up the phone.

SCENE 7
GINGER IN THE SPY SHOP

Ginger walks into a Spy Shop. There are several other shoppers.
A clerk comes up to her. He is dressed very neatly, and though he is
probably a neo-Nazi, he tries to conceal that.

CLERK: May I help you?
GINGER: Yes.
(She is very nervous.)
I was just walking by, and saw the lie detection phone in the
window and I—
CLERK: Certainly.
(Getting it out of the case.)
What kind of business are you in?
GINGER: It's . . . very small. We—

CLERK: You'll be pleased with this. It's the top of the line in vocal stress measurement devices. Someone is lying to you?

He looks up, as though he must maintain a constant surveillance over the front door.

GINGER: I don't know.

CLERK: What security measures do you currently employ?

GINGER: *(A moment.)* None.

He shakes his head reprovingly, looking around the store again.

CLERK: Well, then. The first thing you have to know is that there's no such thing as perfect security.

GINGER: I wondered.

CLERK: There is only effective security.

GINGER: That might be enough.

CLERK: We'll talk about that later. Now.
(Showing her the phone.)
When a subject is under emotional stress, his vocal chords will, as you have no doubt noticed, tremble.

GINGER: *(After a moment.)* Quiver. Yes.

CLERK: *(A moment.)* The Model 862 gives you a baseline readout here . . . for the subject's normal voice, usually somewhere around 20.

GINGER: And I establish this baseline by—

CLERK: By first asking questions the subject would have no reason to lie about, such as . . .

GINGER: What day is this, what year is this . . .

CLERK: Exactly. Then once you have a baseline, any response which produces a reading significantly higher than the baseline, is clearly a lie. I didn't get your name.

GINGER: Trudy. Trudy Blue.

CLERK: Bill Evans. Now. It usually takes about five responses to establish the baseline. After that, you simply ask what it is you really want to know. What kind of business did you say you were in?

GINGER: I didn't.

CLERK: Please. Trudy. Come with me. I have something I want to show you.

Ginger follows him to another room.

CLERK: This is better. In this area, nothing we say can be heard by anyone else in the store.
GINGER: Really?
CLERK: Try it. Scream if you want.

Ginger looks around, then screams . . .

GINGER: Help!!!!!!!!!

No one turns around. She smiles.

GINGER: That's good. And we can't hear them either. That's really good. How do you do it?
CLERK: It's our business, Trudy. Now. Let's talk about the chances of your private information falling into the wrong hands.
GINGER: All right.
CLERK: Do you conduct sensitive discussions in your office?
GINGER: I do. Yes.

That's what he was afraid of.

CLERK: But not on the telephone, I trust.
    (She indicates yes.)
    Not in your car too.
    (She indicates yes.)
    In public?
GINGER: I'm sorry.
CLERK: *(Stunned.)* Trudy, if this information were used to your disadvantage, wouldn't the consequences be inconvenient?
GINGER: I'm sorry.
CLERK: Don't apologize. Just take care of it. I'm sorry.
    (Realizing he went too far.)
    That's why you're here, isn't it?
GINGER: Can I try the phone?
CLERK: *(He begins to plug things in.)* Of course. What makes you think they're lying to you?
GINGER: There's nothing in particular. It's just—

CLERK: They usually are. Go ahead. Dial the number.

The phone rings. Ginger picks it up. But instead of the clerk on the phone, we hear James's voice. The clerk is monitoring over a set of earphones, as if from a surveillance van. James picks up the phone.

JAMES'S VOICE: Ginger!

GINGER: James.

JAMES'S VOICE: What's up? You don't sound like yourself.

GINGER: I don't feel like myself either.

The clerk signals to begin the baseline check. Ginger remembers what she's doing. James enters, taking his saxophone out of its case.

GINGER: What day is this?

JAMES: Thursday.

The clerk nods. James wipes off the sax.

GINGER: The tenth, the eleventh?

JAMES: The tenth. This is a terrible connection. Why don't I call you back on—

GINGER: No. You can't. I'm trying out phones. Only I realized I couldn't know what they sounded like unless I called somebody. I hope I'm not interrupting anything.

JAMES: No, no.

The clerk indicates this may be a lie.

GINGER: Well, I'll let you go then—

The clerk indicates she must keep talking.

JAMES: Any chance we can get together later?

GINGER: About five I could.

JAMES: Is six too late? There's something I have to take care of.

The clerk indicates this is a lie. Suddenly, Ginger is nervous.

JAMES: I miss you, Ginny.

The clerk indicates this is the truth. She is very relieved.

GINGER: I miss you too. I'll see you at six.
JAMES: Six it is. Same place. I love you.
GINGER: I love you too.
JAMES: Bye.

Ginger hears the click then looks at the phone. The clerk unplugs the telephone and looks at her. She did not look at the clerk for affirmation that James loves her.

CLERK: So it's personal.
GINGER: *(Watching James.)* Deeply.
CLERK: Why don't I come to your office tomorrow and do a silent sweep, just so we know what we're up against? Or if you can't wait that long, I could lease you a jammer to take home with you right now.
GINGER: No, I think I know what to do.
CLERK: No. You don't. You're an amateur. I like you, Trudy. I don't want to read your name in the paper one of these days.
GINGER: No. Neither do I. Thank you very much.

Ginger sees James waiting for her at a table. She moves toward him and starts to speak, but lights come up on Annie first and she speaks.

SCENE 8
GINGER, HER MOM, AND CONTROL

ANNIE: What did you want, Ginger?
GINGER: I wanted to be taken away.
ANNIE: Any place in particular?
GINGER: Just away. I wanted someone to know where I was, come find me and take me away.
ANNIE: And bring you back later?
GINGER: No. I wanted to live my other life.
ANNIE: Somewhere else.
GINGER: I know how it sounds.
ANNIE: And so do I. It sounds like something you said as a ten-year-old when you didn't want to take out the garbage.

"Oh, I can't take out the garbage, Mother, there are kidnappers in the alley and they'll come and take me away."
(Pretending to be scared.)
Ooh—kidnappers.
(Shaking her head.)
You weren't afraid of those men. You were *hoping* there was somebody out there, weren't you? You *wanted* to be taken away.

GINGER: Well. I guess I did.

ANNIE: Ginger. I told you this when you were a girl and I'm telling you again now. These fantasies are *not* the answer.

GINGER: What fantasies? What answer? There isn't any answer. Not to these questions there isn't.
(Listing them.)
If I have never been happy, is there any reason to think I ever could be? If I have never felt safe, is there any reason to keep longing for a place where I will feel that way?
(James appears.)

JAMES: Yes.

GINGER: *(Softly, to him.)* What did you say?

JAMES: I said yes.

GINGER: Is that the answer? Yes?

JAMES: Is that so hard?

GINGER: Yes!

JAMES: All right, it's hard.
(A moment.)
It's still the answer.
(A moment.)
Yes. Yes, ma'am. Yes, sir. Yes.

Lights down on Annie. Ginger walks over to James.

SCENE 9
DRINKS WITH GINGER AND JAMES

James is seated by himself, perhaps cleaning his saxophone. Ginger enters the bar, sees him, pauses a moment, as if gathering her courage, then walks toward him. He looks up and, seeing her coming, smiles and motions her over.

JAMES: Ginger. Is that you?
GINGER: Ginger Andrews, yes. Did you get my message?
JAMES: It made me laugh.
GINGER: I'm sorry.
JAMES: But I like to laugh.
GINGER: Thank you for meeting me.
JAMES: The pleasure's mine. Sit down.
GINGER: I won't take long.
JAMES: Take as long as you want.
GINGER: Well, I'm a writer, and—
JAMES: I know.
GINGER: —a novelist, mainly, but I've been thinking about doing a book about pleasure.
JAMES: Ginger. I can see who you are.

Ginger hears more in his response than he meant. Or exactly what he meant. She drops her pen. Or in some way betrays herself.

GINGER: You can?
JAMES: Sure I can. What does your hat say?
GINGER: It doesn't say anything. That's why I . . . My hat says I hate my hair.
JAMES: Could I see it?
GINGER: You want to see my hair?
JAMES: I do. But if it makes you uncomfortable, please. Go on. If I've upset you I'm sorry. I tend to do that.
GINGER: On purpose?
JAMES: It's beautiful hair.
GINGER: Do you upset people on purpose?
JAMES: Well, I don't stop myself, if that's what you mean.
GINGER: *(Beginning to relax.)* And do you have this effect on everybody?
JAMES: People should affect each other. Now.
   (A moment.)
   I'm hungry. Are you hungry?
GINGER: I am, actually.

JAMES: Then let's go eat. What are you hungry for?

A waiter appears.

WAITER: What would you like?
GINGER: Just a Chardonnay, I think.
JAMES: What kind of beer do you have?
WAITER: Bud. Bud light. Bud dry. Bud wet.

> *Ginger laughs. They are better acquainted now. More playful. It is another day. But the passage of time is indicated more by their attitude than by any change in lighting or staging.*

GINGER: How could you ask me that?
JAMES: *(As if innocent.)* Ask you what?
GINGER: If I was hungry. What was I hungry for. You know what I was hungry for from the moment you saw me.
JAMES: *(Remembering the subject.)* Actually. I wanted to say angry. Were you angry. But that didn't seem like a good way to start so I decided to try something harmless like . . . feeding you.
GINGER: Harmless.
JAMES: But now I have to know.
GINGER: All right.
JAMES: What do you do with your rage?

A moment.

GINGER: I sell it.
JAMES: Ah.
GINGER: I do. I sell it. I make things out of hurt and loss and I sell them. Books and things.
(She laughs.)
Isn't that what everybody does? Isn't that what you do with yours?
JAMES: No. I let mine eat me up.
(He has to laugh.)
Keeps the weight down.
GINGER: I thought the music just washed yours away.
JAMES: Washed what away?
GINGER: I don't know. I don't know what we're talking about.

JAMES: Your mouth. Does everybody tell you about your mouth?
GINGER: No.
JAMES: Are they blind?
GINGER: Maybe they are. That would . . .
JAMES: Explain a lot.

The waiter appears.

GINGER: Do you know what you'd like?
JAMES: What would I like?
GINGER: We could do that.
JAMES: God, you're beautiful. I'm away from you all week, and I
  think of you as smart and sexy, and I forget how beautiful
  you are.
GINGER: James. James. Tell all these people to go away.
JAMES: Do you think they can see us?
GINGER: I believe they can. Yes.
JAMES: Well, then.
  (Turning to talk to them.)
  Excuse me, ladies and gentlemen, but my Ginny here wants
  to be kissed, and if I'm going to kiss her the way she wants
  to be kissed, you're just going to have to look the other way
  a moment.
  (A thought.)
  Or if you wanted to leave, that would be even better.
GINGER: *(Looking away.)* How do you know how I want to be
  kissed?
JAMES: Are you saying I don't?
GINGER: *(Quietly.)* No. I'm asking you how you know.
JAMES: I need more time with you. This once a week thing is no
  good. Want to join the band?
GINGER: I do actually. What can I play?
JAMES: Whatever you'd like.

The waiter appears.

WAITER: Anybody know what they want?
GINGER: I lied to you, James.
JAMES: You don't love me?
GINGER: No. I do. I lied to you about what I do with my rage.

JAMES: Well.

GINGER: I think it's the best question anybody ever asked me. I just didn't know the answer so I made one up.

JAMES: That's all right. I'll ask you again. What have you done with your rage?

GINGER: I buried it.

JAMES: Where?

GINGER: I forgot.

(Amused in spite of herself.)

Right?

JAMES: *(Like in a horror movie.)* But will it stay dead? No! Here it comes. The Rage of the Living Dead.

And suddenly, they are like two children, playing monsters.

GINGER: *(Running away.)* Help! Help!

He chases her.

JAMES: *(In another accent.)* Every day I will eat a little part of you . . .

GINGER: Mother!!!!!

As they fall to the floor wrestling.
A waiter appears. Ginger and James stop and look up at him. James is supremely annoyed.

JAMES: You want to know what we want.

WAITER: I do.

JAMES: *(Getting up.)* Can't you tell? Jesus Christ.

The waiter leaves, and James pulls some folded pages from inside his jacket pocket.

JAMES: This is wonderful, Ginny.

He hands her the pages. She makes her way back to the table.

GINGER: How much did you read?

JAMES: Everything you gave me. I love it. I love your Trudy Blue. She's a lot like you.

GINGER: She's me off the leash. A girl I'd like to play with.

JAMES: Me too.

GINGER: Somebody I'd like to know.

JAMES: I liked her joke about the hundred-year-old couple.

GINGER: It was Beth's joke actually. But you know writers. If you don't want us to take it, you better not say it in front of us.

JAMES: What's she going to do?

GINGER: Beth?

JAMES: Trudy.

GINGER: Solve the mystery, I guess. Isn't that what detectives usually do?

A waiter walks through. For once she is glad to see him. She flags him down.

GINGER: I'll have a kir on the rocks.

JAMES: Answer my question, Ginger. What is Trudy going to do with this man, this lover? I forget his name. Jason, is it?

GINGER: She doesn't know yet.

JAMES: Then can you tell me what you're doing next week?

GINGER: Next week?

JAMES: Yeah. We're playing in New Orleans again all next week. Why don't you come down with me?

GINGER: Why don't I come to New Orleans with you next week?

JAMES: It's a great city.

GINGER: It certainly is. Dear Don. I have gone to New Orleans with James. You don't know him. It's a great city.

JAMES: No?

GINGER: I can't.

JAMES: That's too bad. All right, then. Drink up, Ginny my girl. Your Cousin James is going to play for you. What would you like to hear?

GINGER: Please. Just sit with me.

She takes the conversation into what might be safer territory.

GINGER: Why do you call yourself Cousin James? You're not my cousin.

JAMES: No. But if I were, that would be even more reason not to do what we do. Does it bother you?

GINGER: I like it.

JAMES: I could be your Uncle James, if you like, or your Brother James. Just so we're related somehow.

GINGER: All right, cousin . . .

A woman comes up to the table now. She is wearing a silky short black trenchcoat.

FAN: I hate to interrupt you, but I heard you play last week at Mabel's. You made me cry.

JAMES: Thanks.

FAN: *(To Ginger.)* I'm sorry.

GINGER: That's all right.

FAN: I don't have any paper for an autograph. Would you . . .

GINGER: *(Offers her a matchbook.)* Here.

But that isn't what the fan wants.

FAN: Would you sign my hand?
(She unbuttons her cuff.)
Or maybe my arm?

Ginger is embarrassed. James laughs.

JAMES: Sure.

Ginger watches as the fan pushes her sleeve up further and James signs her arm.

JAMES: What's your name?

FAN: Trudy.
(A moment.)
Trudy Blue.

JAMES: Sit down, Trudy.

Ginger is upset. Her imagination has led her someplace she doesn't exactly want to go.
Suddenly, Don enters. He is surprised to see Ginger.

DON: Ginger.

GINGER: Don.

DON: What are you doing here?

GINGER: What do you mean?

DON: I thought you had a meeting with your editor.

GINGER: We finished early, so I came—

Beth appears, laughing. Her nose in a book.

GINGER: —home.

And we realize we are not in the restaurant. We are in their house.

DON: What's so funny?

GINGER: We don't allow laughing in this house?

DON: I thought she forgot how.

GINGER: Don.

BETH: *(Very silly.)* O.K. Tell me if you've heard it. It's the Divorce Court, and there's this hundred-year-old couple standing in front of the judge, and they've been married for eighty years and they are really miserable. And from the looks of them, they have been this miserable for the whole eighty years, and the judge leans over and says, "You poor old people. Why in God's name, did you take so long to get a divorce?"

DON: I've heard this one.

GINGER: Don . . .

DON: I have.

GINGER: Well, I haven't. Beth. Why did the poor old people take so long to get a divorce?

BETH: They wanted to wait til the kids died.

Don grabs the book away from her.

DON: I don't want you reading this stuff.

GINGER: Don. It's a joke book.

DON: Divorce is not a joke. Kids dying is not a joke.

BETH: Don't fight. I hate it when you fight.

DON AND GINGER: We're not fighting.

BETH: You are too. The only time you're not fighting is when one of you isn't home.

DON: I give up.

GINGER: Where are you going?

DON: To the basement.
BETH: I hate this.
GINGER: Where are you going?
BETH: Girl Scouts.
GINGER: You're not a Girl Scout.
BETH: Mom. It was a joke.

Beth and Don exit, and Ginger turns back to James and Trudy.

GINGER: I better go. I'm meeting Sue at Barney's and then we're
   having supper.
TRUDY: Bye.
JAMES: Do you have to leave?
GINGER: Do you want to meet at Sam's later?
JAMES: I want to. But I don't know if I can. I have to make a call.

*Ginger doesn't want to leave at all now. This Trudy person seems to
be staying here with James.*

GINGER: All right, then.
JAMES: Good-bye, gorgeous.
GINGER: Bye, sweetie.

*Ginger kisses him, then takes a few steps backward, then stops to
watch. Trudy looks at him.*

TRUDY: She's not happy.
JAMES: She could be.
TRUDY: *(A little giddy.)* In this lifetime?

James looks at her a moment.

JAMES: How old are you, Trudy?
TRUDY: We can talk on the way, James. Are you ready?
JAMES: Where are we going?
TRUDY: Someplace warm, that's all I care about. If we leave right
   now, we can wake up on the beach.

She pulls a tiny bathing suit out of her pocket.

TRUDY: Yes no?

Ginger can't watch any more. She leaves.
A waiter appears. He speaks to Trudy and James.

WAITER: Anybody know what they want?
TRUDY: I do.
JAMES: *(Standing up.)* Me too.

James leaves. Trudy looks up at the waiter.

TRUDY: What kind of beer do you have?

SCENE 10
TRANSITION

JAMES: You're absolutely right, Ginny. Humans are always going to feel incomplete, always going to be looking for our other half. It's who we are. We have to mate. And we're not amoebas or something that can mate by themselves, so we have to find somebody that fits with us. Only if we don't know too much about ourselves, how can we know what we're looking for? We shake hands, "Is it you?" We kiss, "Is it you?" We try. But it's so hard, that sometimes you tell yourself you don't need anybody else. But it's no use. All you do then is just end up filling your empty half with something else, like work, or your children, or you know, chocolate bars . . .

SCENE 11
SHOPPING WITH SUE

Ginger and Sue walk through a very chic department store.

GINGER: What are you looking for?
SUE: Something to make me feel good.
GINGER: This is nice.
SUE: God. What would I do if for some reason I couldn't shop?
SALES PERSON: Hi.

SUE: Hi.

SALES PERSON: *(Very friendly.)* Would you like to be helped or ignored?

SUE: I don't know yet.

GINGER: *(To the sales person.)* Just let us wander a little.

SUE: Oh. I almost forgot.

She reaches in her purse. And something makes us think she hasn't "almost forgotten" at all. In fact, this letter might be the point of this whole trip.

SUE: Look what came to my house today.
(She produces an envelope.)
Mail for you.

GINGER: What is it?

SUE: How should I know? It's from a real estate agent in Montana. What are you doing, Ginger?

Sue hands Ginger the letter.

GINGER: I don't know anything about this. They must have gotten my name from a—

SUE: Ginger, when they send you junk mail, they send it to *your* house. Not mine. Now what is this? And don't tell me it's research. I want the truth here.

GINGER: I was feeling sorry for myself.

SUE: Yeah, yeah.

GINGER: And thinking about the last time I was deeply happy.

SUE: Why the hell would you want to do that?

GINGER: It was at Lolo Hot Springs.

The sales person comes out with a stack of beautiful scarves.

SALES PERSON: Look what just came in.

SUE: Wasn't that the hot springs in that Redford movie, what was the name of it, *A River Runs Through It*?

GINGER: Yes. It's in Montana. My friend Stu took me there one winter. With a couple of his friends.

SUE: This almost looks like a Fendi.

GINGER: Why don't we go to Fendi?

SUE: No, no. I'm not dressed.

GINGER: They don't care.

SUE: I do.

> *(Putting on a coat.)*
> So that last time you were happy you were in a hot tub in Montana?
> *(Picking one for Ginger.)*
> This one looks like you.

> *Ginger takes the scarf, but just holds it. Sue tries on several as Ginger talks. The scarves are all very amusing. Some fluffy, some brightly colored, but all very tempting one-of-a-kind creations. Nothing ordinary in sight.*

GINGER: Not a hot tub. A hot springs. A geothermal . . . never mind. We drove down this incredibly dark mountain from skiing. And there was snow up to here on both sides of the road and a fair amount of snow actually *in* the road, and the sound of the tires was really loud, you know that squishy sound of tires driving over snow, and my knee really hurt where I fell, but the supper Stu packed was good. Cold beer, and roast beef on dark rye bread with sweet butter, and for dessert these huge brownies—

SUE: You were stoned.

GINGER: We were stoned. And there were these slippery sweet plums somebody's aunt put in a jar at the end of summer, and finally I wondered more or less out loud where we were going, and Stu said Lolo Hot Springs.

SUE: The plums were slippery? What were you eating them with, your fingers?

> *(To the sales person.)*
> They're not quite right. Thank you.
> *(To Ginger.)*
> Shall we try jewelry? The buyer finds wonderful gold here. Please. Go on.

> *They walk toward another department, as Ginger continues her story. . .*

GINGER: Well finally, we pulled off the road but there were still

no lights. Lights hadn't really caught on yet in Montana. And
then I saw it.

SUE: Maybe a charm bracelet. Remember charms? Remember
charm?

GINGER: The building looked like a bar, like a roadhouse. But
we went in anyway. And it *was* a bar. An old bar. With old
wood and old signs, and pictures of miners and moose heads
and some stuffed fish . . .

The sales person comes up to them with a tray of jewelry.

SALES PERSON: Hello, Mrs. Parker. What are we looking for today?

SUE: I wish I knew. Is that a Piaget? I love old Piagets.

*Ginger drifts further into her memory. As Sue and the sales person
look at watches.*

GINGER: And we went up to the bar and got our margaritas. Big
margaritas in big paper cups. And Stu opened the back door
and there it was. Like a great big swimming pool, only with
steam rising up from it, and snow sprinkling down on it, and
right in back of it, a sheer wall of solid rock like a mountain
rising straight up into the night. Black sky. Billions of stars.
The smell of juniper and wood fires . . .

SUE: *(Putting a watch on Ginger's wrist.)* Please try this on. I want
to see how it looks on somebody else.

*Ginger tries on the watch, but in an absent sort of way. She is only
aware of the weight of it. As though she must remember to take it off
before she gets in the water.*

GINGER: And nobody had to tell me what to do next. I just
seemed to know. Went right into the dressing room and put
on my bathing suit, and came back out with my clothes in a
little wire basket, and put the basket in the rack, and it was
cold, maybe twenty degrees, maybe not, and we took our
margaritas and stepped into the pool.
(A moment.)
And it was so hot. And it felt so good.

Sue takes the watch off Ginger's wrist.

SUE: *(To the sales person.)* It's stunning. Where did it come from, do you know?

GINGER: And then we just paddled around, swimming away from our margaritas and then swimming back to them. Thinking how happy we were. Not thinking. Just happy.
(A moment.)
And we forgot about everything except the water and the air and just floated around, and drank our drinks, and talked about nothing, and kissed each other, and came out later after everyone left and made love, and what I have wondered ever since that night, was why none of those vocational counselors in high school ever told me I could grow up to run a hot springs.

SUE: *(To the sales person.)* Well. Good. Have it cleaned and I'll come back and try it again on Friday.

Ginger and Sue wander off into another area.

GINGER: That was a beautiful watch, Sue.

SUE: Let's look at cashmere. You like cashmere, I know. Maybe they've got some cashmere longjohns for when you move to Montana.

GINGER: Did I say I was moving to Montana?

SUE: You didn't have to.
(To the sales person.)
I'd like to try a wrap, I think. Or a stole, maybe. Am I old enough for a stole?

SALES PERSON: Certainly.

Sue wants to know the truth now.

SUE: No, no. The black.
(Then to Ginger.)
You get a letter from a real estate agent and you obviously know it's coming because—

Ginger opens her letter but doesn't read it yet.

GINGER: All right. Yes. I found a real estate agent and called to
see if there was a cabin or something I could rent for a . . .
month. And I gave the agent your address so I didn't have
to talk with Don about it before I knew what I wanted to do.

Ginger reads the letter. Sue puts on a cashmere wrap.

SUE: And?

Ginger scans the letter looking for the answer. Sue waits eagerly.

GINGER: They say they have a few things I might be interested in.
SUE: Ginger. It's Montana.

Sue drapes a wrap around Ginger.

GINGER: What's wrong with Montana?
SUE: You hate the cold.
GINGER: Maybe I've changed.
SUE: What do you mean, you've changed? Does Don want to go
to Montana? Do the kids want to go to Montana?
GINGER: I didn't say maybe *they'd* changed. I said maybe—
SUE: Do they want to go to Montana?
GINGER: No. They don't. I tried it out on them the other day. I
said, "I'm going to run a hot springs in Montana." And Don
said "Well I'm going to run a dive shop in Key West."
SUE: Oh great. And the kids?
GINGER: Charlie said he was going to run Disneyland, and Beth
said she was too.
SUE: So.
GINGER: So at least the kids can live together.
SUE: I'm sorry. I didn't realize it had gotten that bad.

Sue turns to the sales person.

SUE: Can you hold this for me til tomorrow?
GINGER: It's beautiful, Sue.
SUE: I don't know. Let's look at coats. Do you mind?
GINGER: What do you mean, do I mind? I'll go wherever you
want.

Ginger realizes how upset Sue is.

GINGER: What?

SUE: I don't want you to leave me.

(Trying to lighten up.)

Who would I talk to? Do you have a lover?

GINGER: No . . .

SUE: Because if this is about a man, if this is just about running away with some man and living happily ever after, I am really going to be pissed off. Who do you think you are, goddamn Snow White?

GINGER: Jesus, Sue.

SUE: I'm sorry. I don't know what I'm so upset about.

GINGER: Yes, you do. It's becoming very clear why women used to die in their forties.

SUE: Don't tell me.

GINGER: Because it was easier. Now, please . . .

A sales person appears.

SALES PERSON: Mrs. Parker. Did you decide on that coat? Would you like to try it on again?

SUE: Yes, please.

(Then to Ginger.)

Why can't you just be happy with Don? You have nice kids, and a great job, and a house that you like, and terrific friends, and you have spent a lot of time and energy getting all that stuff together. And now you want to be happy too? O.K., O.K. Maybe I do too. But how happy do you have to be?

GINGER: *(Stunned by this.)* You're *afraid* I'll be happy.

SUE: I am not.

GINGER: You are.

(Her anger growing.)

You're afraid I will find something that will actually make me happy, while you, who have given up on happiness, will be miserable for another forty-five years.

SUE: I will not be miserable for another forty-five years! Jesus, I hope I don't live another forty-five years. But I promise you, a new man will not make you happy. A new job, a new house, a new car, a new hair color, or running a goddamn hot springs will not make you happy.

GINGER: You don't know that. *I* don't know that.

The sales person appears with a beautiful short white fur coat.

SALES PERSON: Here we are.

Sue puts it on. It is stunning. She wraps herself up in it.

SUE: Don't do this to me, Ginger. Please don't do this.

GINGER: I thought you were my friend.

SUE: It's a man. It has to be. You wouldn't be ready to leave everything if there weren't somebody waiting for you. Is it Stu? Who is it? Tell me his name.

GINGER: How do you know I'm ready to leave?

SUE: This is a big mistake, Ginger.

GINGER: I've made them before.

SUE: Why won't you tell me his name?

GINGER: I can't just leave on my own? I have to have a man waiting for me?

SUE: What is his name?

GINGER: I don't like this. I don't like this one bit.

SUE: You don't care about anybody in your life except you. Why did you even come here tonight? Why aren't you gone already?

GINGER: I have to go. I can't go to dinner. I'll call you tomorrow.

SUE: I've seen you do some selfish things in your life, Ginger, but this is the worst.

GINGER: How do you know what I'm going to do?

SUE: You'll do whatever you feel like doing. Do you have any idea the pain you're about to cause? No. You don't, do you? And you don't care.

Ginger cannot answer her. She leaves. The clerk comes out with Sue's coat in a bag.

SALES PERSON: If you'll just sign here, Mrs. Parker.

Sue takes the coat, signs the bill, nods to the woman and leaves.

SCENE 12
HER CHILDREN'S BEDTIME

IN ANNIE'S AREA
Beth and Charlie, Ginger's children, appear in their nightclothes. It
may seem as if they are lying in their beds.

CHARLIE: I don't know where she went, and I don't know why
she went there, and I don't care.
BETH: Charlie . . .
CHARLIE: And I hope she stays there and never comes back. I
hope she gets hit by a truck.
BETH: That could happen.
CHARLIE: She didn't even say good-bye.
BETH: She said good-bye to me.
CHARLIE: Did not.
BETH: Did too.
CHARLIE: What do I care? Half the time she was here she wasn't
here, so what else is new?
BETH: She's gone, Charlie. Get over it.
CHARLIE: Leave me alone.
BETH: Leave you here by yourself and go out with my boyfriend?
O.K. Bye.

Lights come up on Annie. We were not aware she was here.

ANNIE: Does Charlie talk in his sleep?
BETH: Every night of my life.
CHARLIE: She wouldn't have left me if she liked me.
BETH: That's right.
ANNIE: Who is he talking about?
BETH: His teacher.
(A moment.)
His teacher moved away.
ANNIE: Why are you so mean to him?
BETH: He's my brother.
ANNIE: And why are you so angry?
BETH: What do you care?
ANNIE: I'm your grandmother. You're supposed to tell me things.

BETH: Yeah, and you're supposed to make me cookies and send me money. Where's Mother? Do you know?

ANNIE: No, I don't. Did she say where she was going?

BETH: Sure she did. That doesn't mean that's where she went.

ANNIE: All right. Where did she *say* she was going?

BETH: She said she was having supper with Sue.

ANNIE: If you don't think she's having supper with Sue, what *do* you think she's doing? Do you think she's out having fun?

BETH: Is there life after death?

ANNIE: No, dear.

BETH: Then how am I talking to you?

ANNIE: Well, you do notice I mainly say things you've already thought of.

BETH: You're in my mind?

ANNIE: I'll leave if you want me to.

BETH: That's all right. I like talking to you.

ANNIE: You're not talking to me, dear.

BETH: Right. If I was talking to the real you, when I asked if there was life after death, you'd have said "Yes, dear." Right? You'd have lied.

ANNIE: That's right.

BETH: So I'm talking to myself here?

ANNIE: It runs in the family.

BETH: Do people like me?

ANNIE: They love you. Your father loves you. Your mother loves you.

BETH: Then where is she?

ANNIE: Beth, your mother is just having dinner with her friend.

BETH: Why?

ANNIE: She'll be back soon.

BETH: When?

Lights go down on them and come up on

SCENE 13
DINNER WITH A FRIEND

Ginger sits on the bed in a hotel room. She picks up the phone, dials, then listens as the concierge answers.

GINGER: *(Listens.)*
   Oh. I'm sorry. I wanted room service.
   (Listens.)
   Thank you.
   (Waits to be connected.)
   Yes. Hi. Could I get some coffee and juice? Yes. For two.
   Orange. And some kind of water, what kind do you have?
   O.K. One fizzy, one non. And I want a smoothie, too. Banana.
   No. Yes, all right. I'll take two. And I'm sure there's a wine
   list here somewhere, but what's the best chardonnay you
   have? No, I like the New Zealands, actually. Is there a Cloudy
   Bay? There is? Amazing. All right. No. No food. I'm just
   thirsty. Thank you.

*James comes out of one of the other doors wearing a thick white terry
bathrobe.*

JAMES: The jacuzzi is great. You should try it.
GINGER: I don't want to get my hair wet.
JAMES: They have a dryer.
GINGER: I don't want to dry my hair. I want to not get it wet.
   (Then recovering.)
   Maybe this wasn't a good idea.
JAMES: You look sad.

*James opens his arms and she walks into them. He begins to rub her
back.*

GINGER: My friends hate me.
JAMES: How could they?
GINGER: Because I don't want what they want.
   (A moment.)
   But *they* don't want it either. They just don't want me to *say*
   I don't want it.
JAMES: I think they're envious of you.
GINGER: Why?
JAMES: Because you're not afraid to know what you know.
GINGER: What do I know, James? Is there something I know that
   I'm not telling myself?
   (A moment.)

And if I'm so brave about the truth, how come I'm afraid of the jacuzzi?

JAMES: You're avoiding me.

GINGER: *(A little irritated.)* I'm avoiding a bath.

JAMES: Why?

GINGER: Because it will make me want you.

JAMES: And you don't want me?

GINGER: No. I do. Want you.

There is a knock at the door.

WAITER: Room service.

JAMES: Saved by the bell.

The waiter enters, carrying the tray of liquids. He has been wondering about all these liquids all the way up to the room. And indeed, the tray does look strange. It looks like a bar set up.

WAITER: Don't tell me. Did you guys just get back from the desert?

After a moment, James answers. Looking at Ginger. None of this is directed at the waiter.

JAMES: Actually, no. We just stopped in here on our way *across* the desert.

GINGER: We still have the last half to go.

James signs the check, and the waiter leaves. James is very careful with her now.

JAMES: What would you like?

GINGER: A glass of wine.

He pours them each a glass of wine, takes hers to her, then offers a toast.

JAMES: To us. To happiness.

GINGER: To happily ever after?

JAMES: Why not? Wait right here, Princess. I'll go put on my doublet and tights.

GINGER: Nobody has ever lived happily ever after.

(Walking away from him.)

If we had a shred of courage, we'd tell our kids the truth. "And after they married, the prince and princess lived for fifty years, and some days were better than others, and for the most part, they could stand it."

JAMES: What's going on, Ginger?

GINGER: *(Not answering.)* No. I get it. Maybe there wasn't any prince. Maybe the poisoned apple actually killed Snow White. And the prince was just some happy little druggy little hallucination she had right before she died.

JAMES: What do you want, Ginger?

GINGER: I don't want to want *anything.*

JAMES: I see.

GINGER: I want to be a Buddhist.

JAMES: It's a peaceful life they say.

GINGER: You're no help.

JAMES: Don't be mad at me. You're the one saying it's all so impossible.

GINGER: Is that what I'm saying?

JAMES: Yes. Well, maybe it's not impossible. But the odds on true love are very long.

GINGER: Even with you? Is that what I feel about you? That's not what I feel about you, is it?

JAMES: Well of course not. But that's because I'm perfect.

GINGER: *(Laughs, teasing him.)* You're not perfect.

JAMES: I'm not? Then tell me something that's not perfect about me.

GINGER: *(Giving in, flirting.)* All right. You're perfect. You're the man of my dreams.

JAMES: That's right. I am. But that doesn't mean there isn't someone out there who—

GINGER: What do you mean, someone out there?

JAMES: A real man who could—

GINGER: A real man? What are *you,* a ghost?

JAMES: More like a wish.

GINGER: *(Quietly.)* Oh no.

JAMES: A longing. A need.

GINGER: You're in my mind.

(He doesn't answer.)
Please don't let this be true. You're not real.
JAMES: Ginny, Ginny, the things in your mind are as real as can be.

Ginger is stricken almost dumb with sadness and despair.

GINGER: I can't live with you? I can't wake up next to you?
JAMES: You always have. I thought you knew.
GINGER: You're a part of me.
JAMES: A part of you that adores you.
GINGER: What are you telling me? That I've given up? That I've fallen in love with myself?
JAMES: Ginny. That's not giving up.
GINGER: *(Her fury beginning to burn.)* I was so stupid. I was so lonely.
JAMES: I'm never leaving you, Ginny.
GINGER: *(Pulling away from him.)*
Get away from me. You're not enough. If I'm going to have a lover, I at least want one I can see.
(Not looking at him.)
I can't believe this. I see you in the bar, I hear you play, something happens between us, and yes, I'm attracted to you, but then. Then you say something wonderful, something I'd always wanted to hear someone say, something I thought nobody thought but me, and before I know it, I'm saying all kinds of things to myself. You know who I am. You know when I'm lying. You know why I'm sad. You know what I want. You know what I really want. What I don't even *know* I want. You know what I need.
(A moment.)
The only problem is—
(Throws something.)
I'm not talking to you any more. I'm standing there talking to my idea of what would make me happy.
JAMES: Don't do this.
GINGER: This will teach me, all right. It's good to know what you want, Ginger. And very brave to ask for it.
(Her fury peaking.)

But next time, why don't you try asking it of someone who actually has it to give?

(A cry of grief.)

Oh James. . . .

JAMES: Don't be so—

GINGER: Don't tell me what to do.

(He moves in front of her.)

Get out of here. And don't even think about telling me I might never find you again, because right at this moment, that is my fondest dream. I hope to God I never see you again.

He doesn't move.

GINGER: Leave me alone!

JAMES: Whatever you say.

He takes off his white robe, hands it to her and walks through the door to the jacuzzi. Holding the robe to her face, Ginger slowly sinks to the floor.

SCENE 14
AFTER DINNER

Ginger walks into the children's bedroom to say goodnight. She kisses Charlie, then Beth.

GINGER: Goodnight, sweetheart. I love you so much.

BETH: Where were you?

GINGER: I had supper with Sue.

BETH: Then how come Sue called here looking for you?

GINGER: When was this?

BETH: She wanted to say how sorry she was you had a fight, and see if you would come back to the restaurant and have supper with her.

GINGER: All right. I'll call her.

BETH: That was five hours ago, Mom. Where were you?

GINGER: I was so mad at Sue. I walked around. I stopped in a bar. I met a man. We went dancing. I left the country with him and now I'm living in Madagascar making necklaces to sell to the tourists.

BETH: Where were you, Mom?

GINGER: I was walking around thinking. I know it sounds weird, but that's where I was. Where's Daddy?

BETH: Your daddy or mine?

GINGER: Why are you so mean to me? What did I do?

BETH: You gave me a home, in which I am now trapped.

GINGER: You'll be leaving soon enough.

BETH: Yeah, but you can leave whenever you want.

GINGER: Can I get that in writing?

BETH: *(Very angry.)* So go if you want to go. I don't see anybody trying to stop you.

GINGER: *(Very quickly, very irritated.)* Fine. I'm leaving. Do you want to come with me, or stay here?

Beth sits up in the bed and grabs Ginger.

BETH: No! You can't leave! Where are you going? Mom! You can't go.

GINGER: Beth, Beth. It's all right. I'm not going anywhere. I'm right here.

As Ginger holds Beth, lights come up on Annie.

ANNIE: She's a very disturbed child.

GINGER: She's fourteen.

ANNIE: You've told her too much.

GINGER: Could you just shut up?

ANNIE: *(Answering honestly.)* I don't know.

Ginger puts Beth back in her bed and pulls the covers back up over her.

GINGER: Good night, sweetheart. I love you to the end of the earth.
(A moment.)
Did you brush your teeth?

BETH: Yes, Mom.

GINGER: Good. Now tell me good night.

BETH: Good night, Mom.

Ginger kisses Beth, then they repeat a poem they wrote together when Beth was little.

GINGER AND BETH:

Good night to all the birds above
And all the fish below.
Goodnight to all the ones we love,
And all the rest, Yo-ho.

SCENE 15
BEDTIME WITH GINGER

Ginger enters the bedroom. Don is sitting in bed, balancing the checkbook.

GINGER: You're awake.

DON: You noticed.

GINGER: What are you doing?

DON: Balancing the checkbook. When I do it in the morning, I stay mad all day. So I thought I'd try it at night.

GINGER: Isn't that what we pay Michael for?

DON: I'm supposed to take his word for how much money we have? It's not his money. What does he care? How was dinner?

GINGER: You didn't miss anything.

DON: Where did you go?

GINGER: O'Neals.

DON: I know where you were, Ginger.

GINGER: Where was I, Don?

DON: You got in a fight with Sue and you walked out on her.

GINGER: She said some terrible things to me. I don't want to talk about it. I went to the movies.

DON: I don't believe you.

GINGER: Don't believe me, then. What I really did was meet my lover in a hotel and make mad passionate love. I'm going to bed.

DON: Did you know you went to see seventeen doctors last month?

GINGER: Yes, I did, Don. Good night.

DON: All right, but the hypnosis isn't deductible unless it's both prescribed and administered by a real doctor.

GINGER: You mean an M.D.

DON: By an M.D., yes. So maybe you could get Bruce to prescribe it for you the next time. Assuming there is a next time. I didn't know hypnosis was so expensive.

Ginger doesn't answer, but begins to change into her pajamas.

DON: How is your hearing?

GINGER: It depends on which doctor you believe. The first one said there was nothing wrong, the second one said there was nothing wrong, and—

DON: Does your therapist know about this?

GINGER: And the third one said I just didn't want to listen to my husband and kids screaming all the time.

DON: We don't scream all the time.

GINGER: I'm just telling you what he said.
(Notices the list.)
You made a list? Fine. Who's next?

DON: The gynecologist.

GINGER: She said I looked great. But it seemed like I had lost faith in you. And maybe I should get more exercise, or maybe meditate. She said basically I had to decide what I wanted out of life.

DON: And the herbalist?

GINGER: He said my body wasn't producing enough heat.

DON: No kidding.

GINGER: What does that mean?

DON: Well, let's see. How do we put this in laymen's terms? Someone whose body is not producing enough heat is . . . oh, I know, cold. But how could we tell if she was cold? Well, feeling the temperature of her skin would be a good way, but she doesn't want to be touched, so that's a problem. But it's common knowledge that cold people don't want to be touched. Yes. Cold fish, they're often called. So that's it. You should've come to see me sooner. The problem with you, Ginger, is that you are a cold fish.

GINGER: I'm definitely out of my element. I'll give you that much.

DON: *(Finding another check.)* Now what the hell is soul retrieval?

GINGER: You think I don't want to be touched?

DON: Not by me, you don't.

GINGER: Not the way you touch me, no. You're right.

DON: I wasn't asking for a lesson.

GINGER: You weren't going to get one.

A moment.

DON: I'm worried about you, Ginger.

GINGER: Don't be.

DON: You're sick.

GINGER: I'm not.

DON: You're not sleeping, you don't care what you say, you're not yourself. I think you should check yourself into someplace for a few weeks and go get some help. Don't worry about the kids. We'll be fine.

GINGER: I'm not sick. I'm angry.

DON: You've always been angry.

GINGER: Maybe so. But now, I'm angry at you.

DON: No. You're not mad at me. You're mad at men. But I shouldn't have to take the blame for all the bad men you've known. Why don't you call Dr. Sterling and ask her for the name of a treatment center? Maybe there's a new medication you could take that—

GINGER: *(Stunned.)* Maybe there's a medicine that would make me love you?

DON: Are you telling me you wouldn't take it?

GINGER: I think we're about through here, Don. I think it's getting real clear that nobody loves anybody. Except the kids. The kids love us and we love them. We just don't love each other. And sooner or later the kids will see that we don't love each other, and I really don't want them thinking that it's O.K. to sleep and eat and celebrate Christmas with someone you don't love. So.

DON: I love you, Ginger. And I want nothing more than to spend the rest of my life with you.

GINGER: No you don't.

DON: How do you know whether I love you or not? Isn't that something *I* know, not you? We all know you're a very smart woman, but couldn't there be one tiny little thing that had escaped you?

Ginger is suddenly released. Suddenly very calm.

GINGER: Actually, Don. If it doesn't feel like you love me, then you don't.

Don realizes something has happened, but instead of regrouping, he goes more on the attack. Ginger gets out of her pajamas and puts her clothes back on.

DON: I don't love you unless you *believe* I love you? I have to convince you I love you? Come on.

GINGER: Good-bye, Don.

DON: What are you doing?
  (No answer.)
  Ginger.
  (No answer.)
  What the hell are you doing?
  (No answer.)
  Talk to me.

She goes to his wallet. Takes out all the cash and puts it in her purse.

DON: That's *my* wallet.
  (He grabs her as she walks past.)
  Ginger!

She breaks away from him.

DON: What are you doing?

GINGER: I'm leaving.
DON: Where are you going?

She doesn't answer.

DON: You're not going to say good-bye?
GINGER: I already did. You weren't listening.

And she walks out the door. Don sits up straighter in the bed.

DON: Ginger!

He hears the door slam downstairs.
He waits a moment, then picks up the phone, dials, and leaves a
message on the machine. For all that has gone on, he seems quite
calm. Even a little irritated.

DON: Hi, Dr. Sterling, this is Don Wilson, Ginger Andrews's
husband. She's just left the house very disturbed, and she
didn't take any of her medication with her. I'm afraid she
might be . . . well, suicidal. I've never seen her this way.
Would you call me if she calls you?
(A moment.)
Sorry to bother you about this. It's probably nothing. If she
shows back up here, I'll let you know.

Don hangs up the phone.

SCENE 16
THE BOOK PARTY

This feels like a combination book party and memorial service. Her
new book is out. But Ginger is gone. Don, her three friends, Annie,
and her publisher are here. A waiter circulates as if among a crowd.

EDITOR: *(As to a larger group.)*
Ladies and Gentlemen. I know you want to say hello to
Ginger's husband and friends, so I won't take long. I'm Kate
Morgan. I was Ginger's editor here at Herald Books. I know

she would be pleased that so many of you could be here today.

(Holding up the book.)

I want to personally thank all those who helped bring her wonderful book to life. I feel her presence with us here, I do. So if you will, please join me in raising a glass to the publication of . . . *Trudy Blue, girl in love.*

There is applause and we find Sue talking to Don.

SUE: *(Holding a copy of the book.)* Did you read it?

DON: Yes, I did.

SUE: What did you think?

DON: What do you think I think? Ginger took my life and made it into a goddamn novel.

SUE: It was her life too, Don. I think she had the right to do that.

DON: It wasn't the truth.

SUE: It wasn't you?

DON: Of course it was me. But she didn't have to tell everybody. O.K. Sure. I said that stupid thing about running the dive shop, but I was kidding. Besides, what she was really mad about was about how much money I spent on dive gear and dive trips, but do you know how much money she spent on doctors? I got a lot more good out of diving than she ever did out of those doctors. I'm not the one who ended up in therapy.

SUE: She thought her therapist was very good.

DON: She was all right. I mean, I never met Dr. Sterling, but since Ginger started seeing her, she actually seemed to be, you know, present, about half the time.

SUE: Excuse me, Don. I have to—

DON: You know what I think? I think Ginger was still pissed off about that time she had pneumonia and I went on a dive trip the day of her CAT scan. But I knew she didn't have cancer. She knew she didn't have cancer. And anyway, I asked her if she wanted me to stay home and she said no.

SUE: You did?

DON: I'm sure I did.

SUE: Well.

(Looking around.)
I'm sorry she's gone, Don.

DON: I know. Thanks.

The other two friends from the lunch scene appear.

MARIA: Isn't it Ginger's birthday tomorrow?

CONNIE: No, it's the sixteenth.

SUE: It's the eighteenth.

MARIA: What's Don going to do now?

SUE: I don't think he's decided yet.

CONNIE: How could she do this to us?

A light comes up on Annie.

ANNIE: I'm not surprised, actually. It was just like Ginger to do something like this. I suppose I could tell her friends that they would get over losing her, but I don't think they will. I certainly haven't. And I lost her a long time ago.
(A moment.)
I could also tell them she might come back. But I don't think she will. I just hope that wherever she is, she can find some way to be happy there.

The editor comes up to Don.

EDITOR: Don, the publicity department was wondering if you would like to do some interviews for us.

DON: Interviews about what?

EDITOR: If you're uncomfortable talking about your relationship, we understand, of course. I didn't think you would go for it, but I promised I would ask. So don't worry about it. I'll just tell them you were unavailable.

Don has no idea how to respond to this.

DON: Thanks.

Lights fade out on the party and come up on:

SCENE 17
LOLO HOT SPRINGS

*Steam rises from the magnificent hot pool at the base of the mountain.
The night is clear and cold, four zillion stars glitter in the dark sky.
It smells like eucalyptus and rosemary. A single large paper cup sits
on the rocky edge of the pool.*
*Suddenly, Ginger bursts out of the water in the center of the pool, as
though she swam the length of the pool underwater and her lungs
are now desperate for air.*

GINGER: Ah!

*We notice, however fleetingly, that Ginger is not wearing the top of
her bikini. She sinks back into the water in complete surrender to the
hot water and cold air and then paddles over to her margarita at
the side of the pool.*
*She takes a sip. She rests her head on the edge of the pool. She sees
the moon.*

GINGER: Dear Sue,
My happiness is in orbit around me like the moon. Not really
mine, but rather like something I glimpse on many nights in
various forms. Full. Half. Waning. Waxing. Usually seeming
quite familiar, but sometimes so startling, I can't remember
ever seeing it before. Because it circles me, if I don't see it
tonight, that will only mean it's on its way back. I'll call you
one of these days. But it could be a while. As to the questions
in your letter, no, my ear hasn't bothered me at all since I've
been here. And yes, the kids are fine. I'm glad you liked
Trudy Blue. She likes you too.

*She looks at her margarita. She smiles. She raises her glass in a toast.
To herself. To the night. To the mountain.*

GINGER: Love, Ginger.

END